VB = mc2™

The Art of Visual Basic™ Programming™

J. D. Evans, Jr.

ETN Corporation™
Software Development Library Series™
U.S.A.

VB = mc²™: : The Art Of Visual Basic™ Programming™
A Thinking Hat™ Book
Second Edition / April 1992

Designed by J. D. Evans, Jr.
Produced and Published by ETN Corporation
Edited by Harriet Yoder and Richardine Acton Evans
Cover Art by J. D. Evans, Jr.
Typesetting by ETN Corporation

All rights reserved.
Copyright (c) 1991, 1992 by J. D. Evans, Jr.

No part of this book may be reproduced or transmitted in any form or by any means, electronic or mechanical, including photocopying, recording, or by any information storage and retrieval system, without prior permission in writing from the publisher.
For information, contact: ETN Corporation

The information in this book is provided on an "As Is" basis, without warranty. Neither the author nor ETN Corporation shall have any liability to any person or entity with respect to any liability, loss, or damage caused or alleged to be caused directly or indirectly by the instructions contained herein or by the computer software and techniques described herein or supplied on diskette in electromagnetic format.

Registered and unregistered trademarks used herein are the properties of their owners. Use of such trademarks in this book is not intended to convey endorsement of or other affiliations by the owners of such trademarks with the book.

Thinking Hat Books are published by ETN Corporation. ETN Corporation, VB = mc²: The Art of Visual Basic(TM) Programming, PowerLibW, PowerShoW, A Thinking Hat Book, Thinking Hat, and The ETN Corporation Software Development Library Series are trademarks of ETN Corporation, RD4 Box 659, Montoursville, PA 17754-9433 USA. Visual Basic is a trademark of Microsoft Corporation.

PRINTED IN THE UNITED STATES OF AMERICA

10 9 8 7 6 5 4 3 2 1 A

Acknowledgments

The author wishes to acknowledge the assistance of Harriet Yoder and Richardine Acton Evans for editing the book, the assistance of Wynne Yoder for managing the business and production, and the guidance and encouragement of his mother and father in their efforts to teach him to read, write, and think.

This book was typeset with Microsoft Word For Windows Version 2.0 running in Microsoft Windows Version 3.1. The original copies of the book were printed on a Hewlett Packard LaserJet III. Cover art was created with CorelDraw Version 2.0. Screen captures were done with Tiffany Plus Version 2.50U.

The author also wishes to express his appreciation for the help, encouragement, and technical advice of his friends, Bob Besaha, Gregg Morris, Thu-Thuy Nguyen, Quang T. Ton, and Heng Tan. Special thanks go to Pat O'Keefe for his sense of humor and for the phrase, *born knowing*.

Thanks also go to Bob Dombroski, Edward J. Ellerbeck, George Porter, Raymond W. Six, and Jonathan Zuck for identifying technical errors in the first edition and for comments, suggestions, and technical advice used in editing the second edition.

Preface to the Second Edition

When I started beta testing *Thunder* (a.k.a., Visual Basic) back in May 1991, I began keeping a mental list of things that were important but difficult to discover and hard to understand about this remarkable new language. In September 1991, I decided to write this book and, in November 1991, I completed it.

Knowing that my writing style is somewhat unusual for technical books and wanting to avoid the bureaucracy and editorial influence often associated with using an established publisher, I decided to publish and market the book myself. Being cautious in business matters led me to choose to print the first edition of the book on a Sharp SF9400 copier.

It takes approximately eight hours to print 40 copies of the book, and (even though the copier does its job with near flawless consistency) book sales have now exceeded the capacity of the machine (and the endurance of the people who operate it). It is time to print the book on a printing press! I marvel at the facts that (1) it is possible to write and typeset a book entirely within Windows on a single PC, (2) it is possible to print the book on a xerographic copier, and (3) it is possible (albeit *tedious*) to publish a book with no more equipment than a 386-33MHz PC, an HP LaserJet III, and a Sharp SF9400 copier (presuming you have access to a good bookbindery).

I love books and am especially happy when I find a book that tells me things that *someone* has arbitrarily decided I do not need to know. It was not so very long ago that it was both illegal and punishable by death to print and read books. While this book is not, in Herman Hesse's words, *"For Madmen Only,"* it does contain allegories inspired by his works as well as the works of Lewis Carroll and (with a little help from *Puck* regarding the behavior of push buttons) William Shakespeare.

In the past few months, I have learned from its readers that **VB = mc^2: *The Art of Visual Basic Programming*** has a life of its own that continues to be a source of amazement to me. Based entirely on reader response, I now believe that this book will eventually become a *classic*. For that reason, I made very few changes in the second edition: (1) grammatical errors have been corrected, (2) technical errors have been corrected, and (3) one anecdote has been added. (I could not resist adding it!) The first edition of the book is now well on its way to becoming a collector's item (a phenomenon that can be *subtly* enhanced by an astute publisher).

I hope you enjoy reading the book as much as I have enjoyed writing it and that it enables you to look at Windows and Visual Basic application designing and programming from an enlightened and unique perspective.

J. D. Evans, Jr.

Table of Contents

Introduction	1
The Basics	23
More Basics: Windows	37
Events, Properties, and Methods	55
Forms, Modules, and Controls	91
Hocus Pocus: Who's Got Focus?	123
Strings, Structures, and Other Strange Things	139
Smart Objects	157
Generic Form Design: The Calculator	181
Code Examples	205
The Generic Calculator	206
The Text Viewer	243
The SQL Select Generator	277
Appendix A: VB Tables and Comments	443
Visual Basic Events	451
Visual Basic Functions [and Statements]	453
Visual Basic Methods	457
Visual Basic Objects	459
Visual Basic Properties	460
Visual Basic Statements	464
Index:	467

Introduction

In the early summer of 1991 the universe of Windows programming changed in a rather dramatic--but subtle--way. An event occurred which in hindsight appears to be obviously predictable but was nevertheless quite unexpected: Microsoft announced and delivered a revolutionary, new programming language called Visual Basic.

Prior to Visual Basic, if you wanted to build a Windows application, you used the Windows SDK/C or some derivative thereof and were faced with two almost overwhelming obstacles: (1) you had to learn an enormous amount of new information and (2) you could not get more than 24 hours out of a day. It was not, however, all that bad because if you made the effort then you were rewarded with guaranteed work at top rates. This is still the case today: if you want to do contract programming, then learn Windows SDK/C programming. It will take you anywhere from six months to several years to become proficient in Windows SDK/C. Since I began Windows SDK/C programming, I have had no problems getting contract work and getting paid what I think my time is worth.

If you are new to Windows programming, then learn how to program with Visual Basic. I can tell you from personal experience that there is nothing better than Visual Basic for quickly and productively programming Windows applications. There are many very good Windows languages, and if you learn one or more of them you are not wasting your time in the long run; but there is simply nothing that compares to Visual Basic at this time. Please note that you are being told this by an experienced Windows SDK/C programmer.

Now, of course, there is no language so powerful as C; there is no language better than C; and the Windows SDK is really an operating system extension to C (and is therefore perfect); but who cares? If you already know how to program with Windows SDK/C, Visual Basic will be trivial for you to learn. If you do not know Windows SDK/C programming, you have to start somewhere, and Visual Basic is the easiest and most productive place to start.

On first inspection, you can easily get the impression that Visual Basic is a toy because there are not very many functions and it just appears to be such a simple language. But that is precisely what is both revolutionary and subtly amazing about Visual Basic. There are things which you can do with Windows SDK/C that you cannot do with Visual Basic, but these things are not required for the vast majority of practical Windows applications. As you learn more about Visual Basic, you will naturally begin learning about Windows SDK/C and then suddenly find that you know all three. Even then, you will do the majority of your programming in Visual Basic and use Windows SDK/C only for the weird stuff.

I know enough about Windows SDK/C programming and have sufficient practical experience to do anything that can be done in Windows, but I prefer to use Visual Basic because it is so fast and so easy to use that my time---which I greatly value---is used efficiently and productively. I can have an idea for a screen and be testing the screen in the same day with Visual Basic. That is simply amazing when compared to Windows SDK/C.

With Visual Basic I can translate my ideas into working code almost as quickly as they occur, and the process becomes even quicker as I learn more about the fine art of Visual Basic programming. It does help considerably to understand Windows SDK/C programming when using Visual Basic, but it is not a requirement. One purpose of this book is to give you some insights into why things work the way they do and why you can do nearly everything you need to do with nothing more than Visual Basic and a few Visual Basic tool kits.

Visual Basic Tool Kits sounds like an interesting concept and it is. One of the fundamental keys to successful Windows programming is to not reinvent the wheel. Because Hewlett-Packard writes a device driver for my HP LaserJet III and because that driver is automatically included in Windows, I do not have to know a single thing about operating the printer other than to turn it on and put paper in it--in my Windows applications, it is just there. I rely on Hewlett-Packard for my printer driver, and they do a very good job. Similarly, you will find that there are quite a few software development tools for Visual Basic--available in tool kits--that will make your programming more efficient and much easier. There will be more and more tool kits as time goes by (and time is of the essence in Windows).

There are so many opportunities in Windows that you do not have enough time to do everything, and you must, therefore, do everything you can to optimize the time that you do have. If I can get a tool kit that saves me several weeks or months of work, the cost of the tool kit is insignificant. Likewise, if I can use a routine I have already written, I am saving time. I suppose this is obvious, but it quickly moves into the realm of subtle art when Visual Basic is involved.

After spending a weekend with Visual Basic--which should include going through the tutorial and experimenting with the sample applications--you will find that (1) screens are called *forms*, (2) *forms* have *controls* on them, (3) *controls* have *properties* and respond to *events*, and (4) *controls* come from the tool box. That is basically all there is to it---no pun intended.

However, after programming with Visual Basic for a few weeks, you will find that if you place most of your code in the *event* procedures for the controls you will be doing a lot of *repetitive* coding. There is a better way to do this. Put most of your code into *generic* functions and subroutines that are called from the *event* procedures. This is very important because one thing which is unique to Windows is that there are many ways to do the *same* thing in an application. It is infinitely easier to code an operation one time than to keep coding it over and over for each control. This introduces a Windows *style* concept that requires further explanation.

In traditional mainframe and to a certain degree PC application programming the general approach to doing things is to guide the user through a complex sequence of events in a very controlled way. In mainframe transaction programming you do not let the data entry person do foolish things because it costs too much to pay people to do foolish things. In Windows, one *style* is to let the user do anything he wants to do at any time and somehow deal with it internally. On the other extreme of this is the *style* of entirely controlling every single thing that the Windows user does and sees.

Practical reality is somewhere between the two, but in Windows you must provide some *flexibility* of action as a general rule. This means that there are generally *several* different paths through a Windows application that produce the same result. Also, because Windows is a multitasking operating system, the user can be expected to *jump* around from application to application. *Jumping* introduces an interesting phenomenon into your application design and programming: you should approach Windows programming in much the same way as you would approach *transaction* processing.

As a matter of fact, Windows really is a *transaction* environment. This may not seem overly significant or surprising, but it is. Windows places itself *between* you and your user and takes care of an enormous amount of work that you would rather not know about. All you have to be concerned with are the *messages* Windows sends to you when it determines that your application needs to do for the user something Windows cannot do (or does not want to do). These *messages* are *events*, and they are triggered when the user of your application does something to one of the controls on one of your forms. In other words, all you know is that (1) you have *forms*, (2) *forms* have *controls*, (3) *controls* have *properties* and respond to *events* and (4) absolutely *nothing* happens that is of any concern to you unless and until the user *triggers* a control *event*.

You will find that each control has quite a few events and that some of these events are really obscure. In Visual Basic, the default *behavior* of your application when an event occurs is *already* programmed and does *not* require you to do any additional programming unless you want to do something special for that particular event. This is a powerful capability in Visual Basic, and it is very important. Learn how to let Visual Basic do most of the work for you.

In general, I only add code for a few events in each control. Some of the events I use make sense only when you know Windows SDK/C programming and are just shortcuts to doing things. I have developed a *style* in which my control event procedures are relatively small in terms of code. I think it is a good practice (1) to limit the number of lines of code in a control event procedure to 20 or less and (2) generally to code only a few control event procedures (one or two on average). This will make sense when you understand the basic *mechanics* of Windows and such things as what a push button is and what it does, what a list box is and what it does, what a text box is and what it does, and so forth.

There are really only six controls in Windows at this time: button, edit, static text, list box, combo, and scroll bar. Everything else is a *derivative* of these six controls. You can create new controls if you are programming in Windows SDK/C; so there can actually be more than six classes or types of controls. Generally, if you need a new type of control and are programming in Windows SDK/C, it is easier to start with one of the basic six control *classes* and modify its behavior *only* where it differs from the way that you want your new control to behave. Called *subclassing*, this is a powerful technique. However, *subclassing* is not generally available in Visual Basic at the control level.

Subclassing or creating new controls by modifying existing controls is done in Visual Basic by adding new controls to the toolbox. You can get these new controls in commercial tool kits, or you can build your own tool kits. Building Visual Basic tool kits requires the Visual Basic Control Development Kit (CDK) and either Windows SDK/C or another language that can build a Windows Dynamic Link Library (DLL).

For all practical purposes, you do not need to know how to do this. However, you will, at some point, want to learn how to make your own Visual Basic controls to add even greater power to your applications (or to do those totally weird things that only you could think of doing or would want to do). At first just stick to the basics and buy any tool kits that you need. If you do not already know how to build a Visual Basic control, then you really do not want to learn how to do it at this time--let it happen naturally.

This introduces another new concept which I think is unique to this book: I have found that I can build *hybrid* controls in Visual Basic by using the existing Visual Basic controls as building blocks. After all, Visual Basic gives you all of the six Windows controls: button, edit, static text, list box, combo, and scroll bar. In fact, Visual Basic even gives you a few new ones (most notably: picture and timer). It took me a few weeks to realize this, but once I did it was like getting hit on the head because it got my attention. I stumbled on this quite by accident as a result of needing a spreadsheet control and looking through messages in the MSBASIC forum in CompuServe.

There is a control called GRID (available in the MSBASIC forum in CompuServe) that is a very nice spreadsheet control for Visual Basic. I downloaded it, looked through the documentation, and (somewhat quickly) came to the conclusion that using it would require me to *think*. Now, *thinking* is something that makes my head hurt and is therefore to be avoided at all costs--this is a Southern trait and is most definitely inherited. In fact, *not thinking* is the *basis* of *common sense*. If you are born *knowing* something then you do *not* have to *think* to do it. You can spend more time doing meaningful work when you do *not* have to *think* about what you are doing.

Therefore, when I realized that using the GRID control would require me to *think*, I looked for an alternative which would *not* require *thought*. After putting on my *thinking hat*, it occurred to me that (1) I already knew enough about Windows SDK/C programming to understand the internal mechanics of the GRID control and (2) I could build the same control with the Visual Basic tool box controls that I already had (and knew how to use). That is what I did, and it worked just fine.

7

There are some differences, of course, between the GRID control and my *hybrid* control--primary of which is that I did not program any resizing into my spreadsheet control because it seemed to be a lot of work and definitely more trouble than just resizing the controls manually on the form when necessary. I do not think that this makes me a Luddite (or lazy), but it does show that there are more ways than one to do things in Visual Basic and that some of the ways of doing things require a slight *readjustment* of the way in which you view the world. The fact that this capability is present in Visual Basic and the fact that I stumbled upon it so easily is another example of the subtle power of Visual Basic--combined with common sense.

Since I mentioned the *thinking hat*, I should explain what it is lest you become confused: you put on the *thinking hat* because you are *thinking* too hard (and are therefore *thinking* yourself into *stupidity*) and need to get back to using *common sense* (which does not hurt your head as much). If you Southerners a question and receive the reply that this will require thought, then what they are really telling you is that you have just asked them something so *extremely* stupid that out of courtesy to you (and not wanting to embarrass themselves further by having to explain that to you) they will have to wait until they can get home and put on their *thinking hats* so they can keep from *thinking* and thereby help you find a *common sense* answer to your real question.

For example, consider the case where you are from New York, have just moved to a small farm in Texas, have bought a few chickens, and are talking to your new Texas neighbor who happens to be a farmer. In the course of the conversation, you mention the fact that you are planning to get into dairy farming but are not sure just exactly which kinds of equipment you are going to need to milk your chickens. If, in seeking advice, you ask the Texas farmer, "What's the best way to milk a chicken?" then I can almost guarantee you that the Texas farmer will reply, "Well, (*long pause*), I'm gonna have to *think* about that for a while!"

I know this is getting into an abstract area, but if you watch children (or remember being one) there are times when you will observe them wearing hats (or remember wearing one yourself). That is something interesting to contemplate (preferably with a hat on your head). Also note that soldiers wear hats on their heads. They do this because they cannot afford to think rather than because they want to protect themselves from bullets.

Before we jumped, I was explaining my discovery that when I needed a special control I could most probably build it from existing Visual Basic controls, and that the entire process was relatively easy, not requiring much work other than determining what I wanted the control to do and then programming it to do it. From that small leap in Visual Basic knowledge I then had the ideas that, most of the time (in fact, nearly all of the time), (1) controls are on forms and (2) you work on one form at a time.

Here we are getting back to the four fingers and a thumb type of observation that evokes a general response of, "Duh," from most people. This is a natural response but does nothing more than indicate that the underlying *concept* is not obvious to the responder. I have always thought that replacing a knee joint was one of those surgical procedures beyond the capabilities (or imagination) of most human beings, such an amazing feat that it is better not to *think* about how one would do such a thing lest it hurt one's head too much.

However, I recently watched a special on this procedure in which an orthopedic surgeon explained and performed just such an operation and was struck by the observation that, aside from all of the medical considerations and complexities, it was a lot like watching a cabinet maker and did not really appear to be very complicated. I also noted that the surgeon was wearing a hat---probably to keep him from *thinking* too much. The whole procedure made good *common sense* and appeared to be very simple.

Combining complexity with simplicity is a feature of forms that I have discovered. Specifically, you can look at a Windows application as being a series of *forms* in which you *jump* around from one to another to do the things that you want to do. That should be obvious, but what may *not* be obvious is that by using a little *common sense* you can identify (or become aware of) the fact that you do *not* really need many *different* types of *forms* if you *design* them correctly.

I am writing this book in Word For Windows, and Word For Windows has one major form in which most of the work is done. The remaining forms are used to get more specific information about the actions I want it to perform. If enough information is available, then no additional forms are needed and a button or list box is sufficient--otherwise, a form pops-up and I supply some more information. Again, nothing *apparently* amazing about that observation, but then there really *is* something important to be observed.

Windows grows on you. Although this will come as a shock to some people, Windows is *not* very easy to use at first. If you give people who have never used a computer the task of learning to use any Windows application, I can guarantee you that they will be completely overwhelmed for some time.

Nobody is born knowing what a menu bar is or what in the world one does with a mouse other than get a cat or move. How many people know what a hot key is, what a scroll bar does, or what the difference between a drop down list box and a list box is? Yet, after you learn how to use just one Windows application (even if it is nothing more sophisticated than playing Reversi), things just seem to fall into place, and Windows is easier to use.

Once you can use Excel, Word For Windows, PageMaker, CorelDraw, or any similar caliber applications, then you can use almost any Windows application--probably without reading the instruction manual--provided you have a basic understanding of the work the application is doing for you. If you do not have the slightest idea what project management is, then knowing what to do in Microsoft Project For Windows is not intuitive--but using it is! This is an interesting *phenomenon* which is somewhat unique to Windows--primarily because every application in Windows is going to be built with the same six basic controls and the same graphical user interface. It means that the real key to Visual Basic programming is understanding form *design* and form *programming*.

If you put on the *thinking hat* and make an effort not to think, then you will realize that you probably cannot think of very many truly original forms. In other words, pretend that this is school, you are the student, I am the teacher, and I give you the assignment to make a list of all of the forms you need to do things in Windows. How many forms are going to be on your list? Is it going to be a long list? Probably not, if you have to give me the list tomorrow. If you spend five hours on this homework assignment and if it takes you five minutes to identify and draw each form, then (at most) you will come up with 60 forms.

I would be very impressed if you could in 24 hours identify and draw 60 generic forms such that there is only minimal functional repetition in any two forms. In fact, if you can do this homework assignment, then you can design a new Windows application and make a lot of money--provided you can program it before someone else does.

As an example of this, I suggest you purchase a copy of an interesting book I recently found: **CORELDRAW 2: Visual QuickStart Guide** (Peachpit Press, Inc., 1991) by Carrie Webster and Paul Webster. This book is like a road map for CorelDraw and includes a dialog box diagram (12 pages) that is similar to a high-level flowchart. Actually, this book is very close to a perfect design specification for CorelDraw and will give you some idea of the way you must visualize a Windows application during the design process. It will also give you a better understanding of the fact that the CorelDraw interface appears simple but is really complex and powerful. I really like this book because it provides a tremendous amount of information about designing a Windows application but does so in a way that requires you to do nothing other than look at the pictures to understand the concepts.

Think about designing a Windows application for a minute, and make a list of forms that seem obvious: file open, file save, messages, data entry, data display, spreadsheet, text editor, printer control, file viewer, and a few more come to mind. You can probably think of a few more, and (probably) one of them is something nobody else will think of until they see your form. When they see your form, it will make so much sense to them that they will want to buy it from you. Such is the way of the world, and Visual Basic makes it easy for you to turn your ideas into reality.

Some of the forms I mentioned above come with Visual Basic and are therefore already coded and available for you to use once you learn how to make them *generic*. Put on the *thinking hat* and contemplate the word *generic* because it is particularly important when used in conjunction with forms. Ordinarily, you would view a form as being part of a complex sequence of events and therefore not particularly independent--but that is a mistake. The entire purpose of this latest *sojourn* has been to make you realize that you should view Windows applications as being nothing more than a series of forms and that (since you are wearing the *thinking hat*) you should understand that forms can be *independent* if you make them *generic*.

Well, that sounds intuitively simple but how do you make a form *generic*? The answer is that you do not think of the form as being a form. Instead, think of the form as being a visually basic function (pun intended). In other words, (1) declare some global variables that apply to the form and supply the form with all of the variable information it needs to get started, (2) load (or show) the form, and (3) let the form take care of everything else it has to do from that point forward (or backward). You would not normally think of a screen or form as a function or subroutine--but you certainly can now. I think you can see that (1) you can get from one form to another by putting a few lines of code in a button and (2) if you choose your global variables carefully then you will not have to do much preloading of global variables prior to jumping to another form.

This will probably be a new technique for many programmers (especially for programmers who think anything global should be avoided whenever possible). Some thought will produce rewarding results when you pursue this approach to designing and programming Windows applications. Visual Basic will almost force you to do this, even though you may not be aware of it until some later time. Each form has (1) a *general* topic which has no *visual* form and (2) a *declarations* procedure (whether you want it to or not). Each Visual Basic application has at most (and at least) one global module.

In other words, if you read the writing on the wall, then Visual Basic is telling you to do the following:
(1) Put global variables in the global file.
(2) Put type definitions in the global file. (They cannot go anywhere else!)
(3) Put general variable declarations and procedures in the general section.
(4) Let Visual Basic take care of the things you do not care about.
(5) Do everything else you need to do on forms with controls.

It is similar to using a road map. All you have to do is follow directions (even when they are subtle).

After reading the writing on the wall and giving it some thought, I have two more rules to add:
(1) If there is any possibility that you will be doing something more than once, then put it in a function or subroutine and make it generally available.
(2) Minimize the lines of code in control event procedures by calling functions and subroutines to do complex tasks rather than simply putting the code for the complex tasks in the control event procedures themselves.

To a certain degree, what I am telling you to do is to use some C++ concepts in your Visual Basic programming (but only in the sense that if you can make a function or subroutine *independent* and as *generic* as possible, then you can reuse it later--a concept that brings us back to the topic of making something *generic)*.

A function or subroutine is *generic* (1) if you can give it all of the special information it needs via parameters, (2) if it can do whatever you need it to do *independently* of whatever you are currently doing, and (3) if it can send the *results* back to you in some general way. I suppose someone will say that a subroutine does not send results back to you, but that is a semantic argument and does not apply because the subroutine does something. Whatever it does *produces* some result whether you *see* the result or *receive* the result in a variable.

The important point is that once you code a *generic* routine you can use it without having to do anything else to it. In this sense, all of the Visual Basic functions and subroutines are very *generic* in that you can, for example, call **Mid$** just about anytime and it will do what it does with no more information than the information you send it via its parameters. In other words, you just need to invent some more functions and subroutines to do the other things you need to do. These functions and subroutines are meant broadly to include *forms* (as well as more traditional groupings of code).

Really, none of this is particularly revolutionary in and of itself and is certainly not unique to Visual Basic. What is so great about Visual Basic? Well, several things, most notably the fact that a great majority (if not all) of the graphical user interface is handled entirely by Visual Basic without your having to do anything. GUI work is the great majority of what takes so much time in traditional Windows SDK/C programming. Clearly, in just about every language *except* Visual Basic, you spend (or waste) an enormous amount of time doing GUI work (and *message* routing) before you reach the point at which you can begin to do what I call *real* application programming. With Visual Basic it is simply a matter of, "You wanted Windows GUI, and you got it." So, now that you have it, start doing some meaningful work. Microsoft built the road (i.e., Windows), and now they have built *the* car (i.e., Visual Basic). All you have to do to get someplace is drive it.

That seems really simple (and it is), but *everything* is not really so simple. There are a few more things you need to know, and the real purpose of this book is to help you learn them. I am presuming that most of the readers of this book do not know Windows SDK/C programming and do not have either the time nor the desire to learn it.

If you do not know Windows SDK/C programming, this book will definitely save you some time and frustration because there are little problems in Visual Basic that will not make any sense to you unless you either know Windows SDK/C programming or ask someone who does. That is where I can help you because, internally, Visual Basic is a Windows SDK/C application (at least, it *behaves* like one). I qualify this statement because it is entirely based on observed *behavior,* since I have not examined a single line of Visual Basic's internal code and do not ever expect to have the opportunity to do so (or the desire to do so, for that matter).

If you do not know what a C string is, you will need to learn what one is, and the best time is now because (whether you know it or not) Visual Basic is going to use C strings some of the time (either internally, or when you call an external DLL). There is absolutely no way you can avoid C strings. Actually, there is nothing more simple than a C string: **a C string starts somewhere and contains *none* or more *non*-NULL characters and is terminated by a NULL character.** That is the long and the short of it. What could possibly be more simple?

By definition, a string in C ends in a NULL character. If there is no NULL terminator, then it is not a string. Therein lies the first major problem in Visual Basic, because nearly everything you do in Visual Basic is going *eventually* to involve a function written in some language (probably Windows SDK/C) that is going to do something with or to a C string. If the NULL is missing, then you get to pass GO and immediately jump into *Never-Never Land* (a.k.a., UAE).

Further compounding this problem is the fact that the NULL character, or Chr$(0), is a completely *valid* character in a Visual Basic string. The effects of this bit of madness are so subtle that even Visual Basic, itself, cannot handle its own strings (in certain cases) when those strings contain NULL characters at *inopportune* locations.

For example, build a Visual Basic string consisting of **"I am out" + Chr$(0) + "to" + Chr$(0) + "lunch"** and add it to a Visual Basic list box and you will find that while you are out, you are not out to lunch because something happened along the way to the list box. So, what happened? Well, put the *thinking hat* back on your head, and I will tell you.

The fact of the matter is that there is only *one* way to load a list box in Windows that I know about, and it is a Windows SDK function. All Windows SDK functions that do something with a string are going to expect and operate on that string as though it is a C string or some equivalent thereof. So when you send a perfectly valid Visual Basic string consisting of some number of characters--one of which happens to be a Chr$(0)--to the list box, then that string absolutely must and does end *precisely* at the first Chr$(0) it encounters. OOPS. Welcome to Object-Oriented Programming Systems. In other words "Hell<NULL>o World" is just

"Hell" in Visual Basic (Please accept my apology for this but I just had to do it!)

However, this is not really a problem because now that you know about it you will just do a few things that C programmers do to insure (1) that you have a NULL where you need (and want) it and (2) that you do not have any undesirable NULL characters floating around where they can have interesting (and usually disastrous) effects on the behavior of your application. This is not a big deal, but it comes as a bit of a surprise and is something that will make absolutely no sense to you unless you know Windows SDK/C programming--which I am presuming that you do not.

Even if you did know Windows SDK/C programming, it would still not be very obvious, although you would eventually deduce it from the behavior of list box loading (which is how I discovered it). When you discover this, you learn something very important about Visual Basic: if it does stupid things like this (because deep inside it is the powerful Windows SDK/C), then maybe you can make it do really brilliant things, too. You can, when you know the real rules.

While on the subject of C strings, let me introduce you to another bit of C weirdness: the pointer. Now, some programmers will tell you that pointers are really neat and are the greatest things in the world, but they are somewhat confused and probably need to put *thinking hats* on their heads. I programmed quite successfully in C for years without ever using a pointer but finally found a useful purpose for a pointer about a year ago, put a *thinking hat* on my head, and learned enough about pointers to use them proficiently.

I still avoid using pointers whenever possible but there are some Windows SDK/C techniques that require pointers and--although you can generally avoid them--there are times when you need to get a pointer or send a pointer to a Windows SDK/C function. Obtaining and using pointers in Visual Basic requires a few extra steps. Nearly every DLL you use in Windows is going to use pointers somewhere and will most likely use at least one of them as a parameter. If the DLL is coded correctly, then you can send it either a pointer to a string or the string itself, and the results are identical. This is precisely what happens when you send a Visual Basic string to a DLL--even though you are not directly involved in the process.

When you declare a function or subroutine parameter contained in a DLL as being ByVal <varname> As String, you are telling Visual Basic that you are sending a Visual Basic string which is not NULL-terminated to a DLL that is expecting a C string which is by definition expected to be NULL terminated. Visual Basic will then append a NULL to your string so that everybody is happy and will then proceed to send the DLL a pointer to your now NULL terminated Visual Basic string. On the one hand, this is somewhat bizarre. But on the other hand, it is the only way to proceed *intelligently* in this situation. You can even insert your own NULL a little earlier, thereby enabling yourself to use a few global strings set aside just for use as DLL parameters.

There is something else you need to know about sending strings to a DLL. A DLL function or subroutine will most likely want to *modify* your strings. Therein lies another problem because if you happen to send a variable length string that is not quite so big as it should be, then the DLL function (having all of the power of C at its disposal) will most likely fill up your variable length string and just *keep on trucking* right into (1) a critical internal Visual Basic control table, (2) a Windows control table, or (3) *Never-Never Land*--whichever is the most disastrous. You can cause some really interesting lockups this way--but it gets boring after a while and I do *not* recommend it.

The way to avoid this is always to use *fixed length* strings to send to DLL functions and to make sure that the *fixed length* is *greater* than whatever the DLL function will decide to put into the string. If you fail to do this, it is a guaranteed UAE (in most cases). Also, please note that I never send a *literal* string to a DLL function or subroutine [e.g., <function> ("this is really stupid", 1, "bye bye")]. I never try to make Visual Basic do explicit string concatenation in a DLL function or subroutine parameter [e.g., <subroutine> ("this is even" + "more" + "stupid", 1, "bye bye")]. It might work occasionally, but then it might not---so why do it?

There are times when you can send a variable length string to a DLL and everything will be just fine, but there are more times when variable strings will jump you into *Never-Never Land*; so I just do *not* use them. It requires very little additional effort on your part to guarantee that you are sending a DLL what you want to send it and that you are sending it in a *format* it can correctly use. The world seems to run better if you follow this rule. Sometimes, you can cause a UAE so major that DR. WATSON cannot handle it; so you cannot even prove to anyone else that it happened.

In a special chapter devoted entirely to **Strings, Structures, and Other Strange Things**, I will show you exactly how to send strings to a DLL and will explain, step-by-step, *what* is being done and *why* you want to do it I will also explain and show how to create and send a structure to a DLL. When you can send a structure to a DLL, then you can use any Windows SDK function. In fact, you can even send a structure consisting of items that are pointers to functions--something which is really approaching the outer limits of

20

absurdity, in my humble opinion (although I realize that the C++ people would consider a structure of function pointers to be a rather trivial building block for something really useful).

This concludes the introduction, and I hope you have enjoyed it. I introduced you to some new concepts (and some unusual observations). Now, we can begin discussing when, where, and how to start using Visual Basic productively and efficiently.

The Basics

Everything has a beginning, and the best place to begin with both Windows and Visual Basic programming is to learn how to use Windows. If you are new to Windows, then take some time and learn how to use one of the applications included in Windows. You absolutely must know the general functioning of Windows itself before you can start programming in Visual Basic.

One good way to start learning about Windows is to play one of the two games that come with Windows: Reversi and Solitaire. Some people will think that playing a game is an extraordinary waste of time. While that may generally be the case, in most situations it is useful to play one or both of these games when you are learning about Windows, and this is probably why Microsoft decided to include the games.

Reversi and Solitaire are relatively easy to play once you learn how to use the Windows interface; that is precisely why you should play these games. They are designed specifically (1) to make you learn how to use the mouse, (2) to accustom you to selecting items from the menu bars, (3) to cause you to interact with a Windows application via a dialog box, and (4) to teach you a few other things that generally have nothing to do with playing a game. After you can work your way around the games, start using one of the more serious applications like Write and Paintbrush. Then, when you can write a letter and draw a picture, you are not too far from being able to start programming in Visual Basic.

I am not going to lead you step-by-step through the Windows interface because this book is not an introduction to Windows. If you need an introduction to Windows, then go to your local bookstore and buy one of the many good books on the subject. You must already know at least one real programming language for any of this book to make much sense, although it does not matter whether it is COBOL, Pascal, Clipper, dBASE, FORTRAN, Ada, PL/1, C, or any other serious programming language, including Basic. Contrary to rumors you may have heard, Basic is a serious programming language and has been serious for many years.

Basic is a simple language. If you can read, write and think logically (with or without a *thinking hat* on your head), then you can learn Basic. Basic lends itself very well to trial-and-error learning because Basic is (generally) available as an interpreter. Interpreters do not let you get very far when you are making mistakes. Visual Basic is also an interpreter when you are in design mode. Although you can disable syntax checking, the syntax checking feature in design mode will quickly turn you into a proficient Visual Basic programmer (if it does not drive you *bananas* first).

After making the same mistakes over and over and having to read the numerous syntax warning messages, you will learn to get from one line to the next without getting *beeped* very often. There are really not that many functions and subroutines in Visual Basic, so you do not have very much to learn anyway. There are only a very limited number of elaborate string manipulation functions and subroutines, and they are not really very elaborate. However, Visual Basic's string manipulation capabilities are more than sufficient to enable you to write sophisticated interpreters and parsers (much easier than using C!).

In fact, Visual Basic is a very basic language, and therein lies its power. From a small number of functions and subroutines, you can build elaborate and complex functions and subroutines. You will find that, even though Visual

Basic is a little more verbose than C, you can do most of what you want and need to do.

There are many new tool kits and function libraries available specifically for Visual Basic. Tool kits greatly extend the power of Visual Basic and can make your programming much easier. **QuickPak Professional for Windows** (Crescent Software), **VBTools** (MicroHelp), Inc.), **ChartBuilder For Visual Basic** (Pinnacle Publishing, Inc.), **3-D Widgets** (Sheridan Software Systems, Inc.), **ButtonTool** and **EditTool** (OutRider Systems), **The Custom Control Factory** (Desaware), **DataLIB** (Everest Enterprises), and, of course, **PowerLibW** and **PowerShoW** (ETN Corporation) are very good additions to your Visual Basic tool box. **Word For Windows V2.0** (Microsoft) and **Doc-To-Help** (WexTech Systems, Inc.) will make building Windows Help files for your application an easy, quick, and pleasant experience.

You will find that sophisticated editing functions for edit controls are necessary, but are, unfortunately, missing from the standard Visual Basic tool box. I have not found a complete editing tool for Visual Basic, but I am looking for one. **QuickPak Professional for Windows** (Crescent Software) does the best job and is actually very complete. An alternative is to write your own routines to do text box editing, but it takes a lot of time when you have to do edits like date, time, social security number, telephone number, and just about any other type of mixed character or specific value editing.

The most difficult types of editing functions are the ones that dynamically reformat data as it is being input. It is perfectly acceptable to do the reformatting after the data is input, but, in either case, it requires a significant amount of code. A good example of this type of editing function is a function that reformats numeric data into '$ZZZ,ZZN.NN' format. In this type of edit field, you can enter '2001.5' and it will be displayed as '$002,001.50' when you press enter, tab out of the field, or click on another control. Another variation of this type of edit function is one in which leading zeros are dropped. In that case, '02001.50' would be displayed as '2,001.50' when the data input was completed. I have written many of these in Windows SDK/C and know that the subclassing is not trivial. But, I also know that it is not overly complex. I am writing a second book on Visual Basic, devoted to custom controls and Dynamic Link Library (DLL) development, and plan to include detailed code for doing these types of edits (and more!). Even something as trivial as making a field *numeric-only* or *alphabetic-only* can take a few lines of code. Converting lowercase to uppercase also takes a few lines of code. In general, anything that requires more than one line of code is going to waste your time if you are doing it over and over (which is generally the case with editing).

If you want to do everything yourself, then buy the Windows SDK and C, and really do it. Otherwise, take as many shortcuts as you can afford or invent. Most of the better tool kits do not charge runtime royalties and are designed for you to release with your Visual Basic application. Visual Basic, itself, is a tool kit in the sense that it also has a runtime driver that you release with your application (in case your customers do not have a copy of Visual Basic on their machines). However, your customers *must* have a copy of Windows: Microsoft is not foolish, so Microsoft is not going to let you give out free copies of Windows. I would generally avoid anything that charges runtime royalties unless it is specifically designed to run on a network.

I need to clarify some terminology so that you will not be confused. I use the term *edit control* and *text box* interchangeably although I am not entirely certain why at this point. Probably this is a result of teaching myself Windows SDK/C programming. Anyway, the two are identical and both are the type of control into which you can enter data via the keyboard. Do not confuse edit controls and text boxes with *labels* and *static text* controls because they are *very* different. *Labels* and *static text* controls do not let you enter data: they are used *exclusively* for displaying data that your program already has (or knows about).

I will also refer to labels and static text controls as just *static* controls because that is what they really are. *Static* controls (generally) do not do anything other than display data. They do have one very important capability in Visual Basic that edit controls do not have. Their ability to respond to *clicking* (either single or double) makes them special, as you will learn. *Edit* controls also respond to *clicking*, but not in the same way as you would like in situations where you need to use the *Click* and *DoubleClick* events to *trigger* a special action. We will discuss *clicking* and *double-clicking* later because they are important mouse actions.

Since we are talking about the mouse, please be aware that, as you become more proficient in the use of the Windows interface, you will use the mouse more frequently. It is therefore important that your application be designed in such a way that experienced Windows users can do as much as possible with the mouse. In the Windows interface, nearly everything is done from either the keyboard or the mouse (or both). Switching from the keyboard to the mouse requires learning several new motor skills.

When doing something is most *logically* done with the keyboard, then make it possible for your customer to use the keyboard. If tasks are better suited to the mouse, then use mouse actions. When doing something requires both the keyboard and the mouse, then try to group actions in such a way that switching from keyboard to mouse and back is not a constant process. The mouse is provided to make life easier, not more complicated. There is an art to designing your interface in such a way that your application is easy to use and does not irritate people.

Another thing to consider when designing your application is that some people cannot use a mouse and some people cannot use a keyboard. Most of us would not even consider that such a thing is possible, but it is. One of the subtle powers of the Windows interface is that it does not actually require *both* the keyboard *and* the mouse. You can, for example, make a form which is nothing more than a small, visual keyboard. Then, someone who can only use a mouse can use your application. Conversely, you can do anything with the keyboard that you can do with the mouse.

In general, you do not find as many applications that are keyboard and mouse *independent* as you would expect, but the Windows programming *standard* is really such that you should be able to use *any* Windows application without a mouse. If you want to build a *perfect* application, then one *standard* for you to follow is to make your application keyboard and mouse *independent*. You will also find that your customer base will then include some very grateful and loyal customers and that you will be helping to make life easier and more productive for a lot of people.

Making an application *mouse-independent* is easier than making it *keyboard-independent*, but the overhead in doing either is really minimal. If you want to learn some of the finer points of Windows programming, then set yourself a standard that includes being able to run your application with either a keyboard or a mouse. When you can do that, you really know Windows programming. Experienced Windows users and programmers will be impressed with the fact that you are a thorough programmer when they discover your application.

I am particularly enthusiastic about the capabilities for using sound in Windows. Windows can also be an Audio User Interface. The technology for doing sound in Windows is available now. Using sound in Windows applications is a relatively new aspect of Windows application development, but is something with a notable future. Musicians make *excellent* programmers (especially in Windows); so I expect to see *and* hear some good Windows applications in the next year.

While on the subject of standards, let me tell you that there are generally two standard Windows applications, one older and one newer. The first and *original* standard for a Windows application is Microsoft Excel. For a very long time, if you were a Windows SDK/C programmer and wanted to know what the standard way to do something was, you ran Excel and found out how Excel did it.

Excel continues to be a standard, although Microsoft Word For Windows V2.0 has extended the Excel standard and broken new ground in the area of word processing. I highly recommend both products and, in general, anything from Microsoft. I have at least one copy of nearly everything that Microsoft sells and have never been disappointed in a Microsoft product. Microsoft products work, and that is very important to me. I am writing this book in Word For Windows V2.0. With the exception of a few diagramming tools, Word For Windows is *all* I am using for everything, including typesetting and layout.

The other, newer standard is CorelDraw. In one sense, CorelDraw may very well be the *ultimate* Windows application at this point in time (at least with respect to the pure beauty of its interface). However, it looks like Word For Windows Version 2.0 may be a strong contender for this position.

CorelDraw is a very powerful graphic design and production program and can do things with graphics that most people simply cannot comprehend. Yet, its interface is one of the most *simple* that I have seen in Windows. That is precisely what makes it a standard for *excellence.* A well-designed Windows application does *not* need a complex interface and should be as simple to use as is *humanly* possible.

I use CorelDraw for doing full-color artwork for book covers, packaging, and magazine advertisements. I still find it utterly amazing that I can design something in CorelDraw, look at it on the screen, make a POSTSCRIPT file, take that file to a printer, get film that looks even better, and *not* have to know much about what I am doing. If you want to study two applications and learn how to do things the *correct* way in Windows, then get copies of Excel and CorelDraw and study them.

It would not hurt you to get Word For Windows, and it is probably a good idea [if for no other reason than the fact that Word For Windows uses *Rich Text Format* (RTF)]. RTF is the format that the Windows Help program uses--what a coincidence! If you are planning to provide Windows Help for your application, then you should get **Word For Windows V2.0** (Microsoft) and **Doc-To-Help** (WexTech Systems, Inc.) for use with Visual Basic. The Windows Help system is a very robust *hypertext* system and is not very difficult to use. However, it generally lacks the abilities to modify and to add new data interactively . The Windows Help Compiler comes with the Windows SDK, but is also available from Microsoft as a separate utility for Visual Basic developers.

Doc-To-Help is a set of expert system macros that guides you through the creation of Word For Windows Version V2.0 document files for you application and then converts them *automatically* to Windows Help files (including doing the Windows Help Compiler step). I use Word For Windows V2.0 proficiently, so have no problem with creating the Help documents. The extra work that the Windows Help Compiler requires can now be avoided by using Doc-To-Help. Here is a good example of the way things work in Windows, regarding Microsoft creating new opportunities by not eating all of the pie.

Prior to Doc-To-Help, and dreading the amount work that would be required for me to build a Windows Help file, I just decided that my applications would not have any Windows Help. Now that I have Doc-To-Help, all of my new applications have Windows Help. The first time I used Doc-To-Help to generate an RTF document and then compile it with the Windows Help Compiler, I knew that I had easily done something that was even more complicated than I had previously imagined. I am ever so grateful that I do not have to understand it. I do my part and then Doc-To-Help takes over and does the rest.

I have come to realize that each Microsoft product represents an opportunity for consulting, contracting, and new product development. There are so many new things to do that Microsoft cannot do them all (and does *not want* to do them all, either). In fact, Microsoft wants *you* to do some of them and will be greatly disturbed if you or someone else does not do them. If the only company that did Windows work was Microsoft, then Microsoft would quickly disappear, and Microsoft knows it.

I do not know if there is any actual plan or reason for this, but I do know that Microsoft always leaves plenty of work for everyone else to do. When you get to know the Windows market, you will find that there are so many opportunities that no single person or company can do them all. At just about the time when I begin to think that I am current on Windows technology, Microsoft announces something new.

I am continually scrambling to learn everything I can about Windows in an effort to be current in my understanding and use of new Windows technologies. It is not easy, but it is *rewarding*. I cannot overemphasize the fact that Microsoft is an *opportunity factory*. Microsoft *creates* new opportunities for Windows developers and Microsoft makes a very *diligent* effort to *help* Windows developers bring new products to market. You do not even have to ask them to help you; they do it *automatically*. If you want to help Microsoft help *you*, then join the Microsoft Consultant Relations Program.

If the Federal Trade Commission (FTC) needs to do anything regarding Microsoft, it needs to give Microsoft an *award* for creating new opportunities for small businesses. I am working because Microsoft has *created* opportunities for me in Windows. My friends are working because Microsoft has *created* opportunities for them in Windows. We all have companies that sell Windows products, and we all get significant *help* from Microsoft.

In the ocean of computer software, Microsoft is a big fish, and I am a little fish, but Microsoft is a *friendly*, big fish and *likes* to have company. From my experience over the past 15 years, most of the other big fish are sharks. Borland is another *friendly*, big fish, and they, too, are creating new opportunities in Windows software development and consulting. Look at who is suing whom to get a good idea of who the *friendly*, big fish are and who the sharks are. Microsoft and Borland do not maintain their presence in the marketplace by going to court. They devote the majority of their time and effort to creating new products and innovations. It is my opinion that Borland now *owns* Ashton-Tate precisely because Borland *jumped* wholeheartedly into Windows rather than into court.

If you have ever read a Microsoft or a Borland software license, then you know (1) that these companies are *fair* and (2) that they genuinely want you to be successful and happy when you use their software. When I read about some big company suing somebody, I automatically add that big company to my list of big companies that are going *nowhere*. In addition, I do *not* buy any of their products from that point forward because I know that they are devoting most of their time and effort to winning legal battles rather than to making their products better. In a capitalistic economy, you compete in the marketplace, *not* in the courtroom. When a company *relegates* its competitive efforts to the courtroom, it sends a very clear message to me that it has lost its *imagination*.

I guarantee you that if you stick with Windows, you will never be alone in the marketplace: there are plenty of customers. Their number is increasing at the rate of approximately 10 to 20 thousand (or more!) each day. I expect this rate to accelerate dramatically. I also know that every one of these new Windows customers needs and wants something very important: *application software*. If you have Windows application software to sell, then you will have ready, willing, and able customers for your products.

Windows is going to be around for a long time. If you are putting all of your eggs into any one basket, then you can choose no better basket than Windows. Once you have a good, commercial Windows application you can sit back and look at new versions of Windows as being nothing more than a little additional work, an opportunity to improve your products, and a guaranteed dividend on your investment as a result of version upgrade revenue. Unless I am terribly mistaken, every company that sells Windows applications cannot wait until the next major version of Windows because it virtually guarantees them a nice big bunch of money. (Both they and Microsoft know it.) With a long term financial plan like that how can you go wrong?

So what do you do next? First, you have to learn how to use Windows, and you have to learn the names and functions of the controls that make up a Windows application. I am not going to explain any more about this, but once you know it you can proceed to do the next logical thing: run the Visual Basic tutorial. It will take you about six hours to go through the Visual Basic tutorial and become reasonably proficient in the Visual Basic programming techniques it teaches you.

Normally, I would say to skip the tutorial, but do not skip the Visual Basic tutorial because you will find it very helpful in a rather unique way. It is not going to teach you how to program in the Basic language and may not do anything else except one *important* thing: it will get you pointed in the right direction for using Visual Basic as a programming language for developing Windows applications. What you get from the Visual Basic tutorial is *style*.

Style is one of the most important things to know if you are going to use Visual Basic successfully. There is a special *style* to Windows applications. Visual Basic has a unique *style*. Once you learn the correct *style* of programming, then learning either the Visual Basic language or the Windows interface is either trivial or automatic (or both).

I cannot say enough about *style* and Windows application development. *Style* and using something either you or someone else has already done (cloning) are the true secrets of successful Windows application development. This is more true of Windows than of any other system I have worked on in the past 15 years. More often than not, you will find that if you just start somewhere, you will find yourself needing to do something you have already done.

If you know the *style* of doing things in Windows and Visual Basic, you will find that with just a few additional lines of code you can reuse something you have already coded. That is *working smart* (as some people call it), and you definitely want to *work smartly* in Windows. If you work foolishly in Windows, you will be *overwhelmed* with complexity. When you *work smartly* in Windows and Visual Basic, you will be astonished with the ease at which you can produce meaningful and impressive applications.

That is basically all there is to the basics. "But wait a minute," you say, "you have not really told me anything technical, yet!" If that is what you think, then you need to read this chapter 20 times. I have just given you an enormous amount of technical information, even though the importance of it may not be so obvious as it should be. Continue reading, but come back to this chapter at a later date. As you learn more about Visual Basic, I think you will find that some of the things I have discussed in this chapter will begin to make more sense. You will see that some of the simple statements in this chapter are really not so simple.

I do not mean to imply that I think you should inscribe the text of this chapter on a block of marble and *ponder* it for the rest of your life (or until one of the major networks starts showing reruns of the **Pee-Wee Herman Show**). However, some technical information does not immediately *appear* to be very technical. We have time for *annotated* Visual Basic code (and there will be plenty of it in later chapters), but it is useful at this point in time to start *thinking* about the general *flow* of things in Windows and Visual Basic--rather than to get into the specifics of all of the little things. So, *think* about this for a while. (Put on your *thinking hat!*)

More Basics: Windows

As you will quickly discover, there are really a lot of basics involved in Visual Basic programming. However, the great majority of them are more Windows basics than Visual Basic basics. The previous chapter was a guide to what you should do to get started (with a few hints about some things that are worth contemplation during the getting started process). This chapter is about the *true* basics of Windows applications and how the *true* basics apply specifically to Visual Basic application design and programming.

In Windows, everything is presented to the user as *screens*. In Visual Basic, *screens* are called *forms*, and *forms* begin with *nothing* on them. This is probably not an astonishing bit of information, but it is, nevertheless, important on some level (in the sense that you have to start *somewhere*) because everything in Visual Basic really starts with *form design*. One of the nice things about Visual Basic is that you do not have to be aware of the fact that, when you create the first form of an application, Visual Basic has *already* created a tremendous amount of code for you. This is where Visual Basic is a subtle powerhouse.

In Windows SDK/C programming, you have to create a main program (and a somewhat enormous amount of other supporting code) before you ever get to the point at which you can actually display a screen or form. By reusing this startup code, you learn to make the process quicker each time you do it. Nevertheless, it can still take several hours to create a main program when you get to the expert programming level. Even then, you have to use the Dialog Editor to build the screens, and you have to do a lot of additional coding to *empower* the screens with the ability to do not much of anything. Visual Basic does all of this for you automatically. More importantly, Visual Basic does it in such a way that you would not even know about it if you had never programmed in Windows SDK/C.

Having done this more times than I would prefer to count, I can tell you that you do not want to know how much time this saves--you do not want to know about it at all. Just take my word for the fact that Visual Basic has already saved you an enormous amount of coding when you do nothing more than *click* on the New Form menu item.

If you hired me to do the coding that is done automatically by Visual Basic when you create a new form, I would charge you several thousands of dollars--it is that much work. Visual Basic does it virtually for free. In addition, Visual Basic continues to maintain all of the code (code that you never see) as you add more forms and features to your application. Just the fact that you *use* Visual Basic is saving you significant amounts of time and money, even though you would never know about it unless someone who *does* know about it *told* you about it.

It is not really fair to say that you do not want to know about it, because at some point you will (and may even be reading this book to find out about it). If you are interested in learning about all of the things that you would have to do if you were programming in Windows SDK/C , then read one of the numerous good books on Windows SDK/C programming. You will be impressed at how much work Windows programmers had to do *before* Visual Basic was available.

So, where are we in terms of basics? Well, we have a *form*, and we have some *internal code* about which we know little other than that it exists (and it takes a certain amount of faith for us to believe it). Where do we go from here and what is next? Well, the next thing we do is add *controls* to the *form*.

Any discussion about basics eventually becomes a discussion of *controls* because *controls* are the real *basics* of Windows programming. *Controls* are things like push buttons, radio buttons, check boxes, frames, edit boxes, labels, list boxes, combo boxes, and all of the other individual components that you put on forms. Something that is useful to know is that all *controls* are windows. In fact, everything in Windows is a window. This is something that is truly *profound* in its near *obscurity*.

In learning about Windows SDK/C programming, much time is devoted to various kinds of *windows*: parent windows, child windows, sizable windows, dialog windows (modal and modeless), and many more kinds of windows. In general, the discussions about these types of *windows* are concerned with *control* and appropriateness of *use*. Later, you learn that the things that appear in *windows* are themselves *windows* and that nearly everything is a *window*.

At this point, let me introduce you to some new terminology and a convention or two: **Windows** is the product that you get from Microsoft, but *windows* are the *objects* that **Windows** uses. Note the difference in these two words because it is *important*. Everything is not **Windows**, but everything *in* **Windows** is a *window,* belongs to a *window*, or is associated (in one way or another) with a *window*.

The term, *window*, and its implications are so *profound* that, even though it may appear to be foolish to discuss it any more, it is even more foolish *not* to know what a *window* is and what it does. All *controls* are *windows*. A push button is a *window*. A list box is a *window*. A label is a *window*. **Nearly everything is a *window* in Windows.**

When you know that, then you can begin to look at **Windows** programming as nothing more than programming the *behavior* of *windows*. Since nearly everything in **Windows** is a *window* and *windows* have a lot in common, you can carry this to an extreme and state that **Windows programming is really** *nothing* **more than programming one** *window* **many times.**

This is something to which you may not have given much thought (nor even considered important), but it is the single *most* important fact about **Windows** programming: *everything* is a *window* in **Windows**. If you can program one *window* and if all *windows* are similar, then you can program all *windows*. If you can program all *windows*, then you can program *all* **Windows** applications. If you can do that, then you *really* are a **Windows** programmer.

Well, it is not quite that easy, but looking at it that way at least gives you a basis from which to proceed and will prove to be a cornerstone to your *sanity* when things start becoming complex. **Windows** programming is really simple, but it is not easy to discover that fact. Anyway, we are talking about *controls* and I just wanted to make it *clear* that *controls* are *windows*.

As previously mentioned, in **Windows 3.0** there are six standard *controls*, or *windows*, and they are the following: *button, static, edit, list box, combo box,* and *scroll bar*. These are the standard *controls*, and you can do an enormous amount of work in a **Windows** application with nothing more than these six *controls*.

By *subclassing* (an *advanced* technique), you can *modify* the *behavior* of standard *controls* and thereby *create* new *controls*. You need the Windows SDK/C (or some derivative thereof) to do *subclassing* but probably do not want to spend the time and effort associated with *subclassing* if you are programming in Visual Basic. It is much easier to purchase tool kits that contain *subclassed controls* than to build them yourself.

So, where are we now? Well, we know that (1) we start with a *form*, (2) Visual Basic has already done a lot of *coding* for us, and (3) we have *controls* that can be put onto the *form*. The next step in learning the basics is to learn more about *controls* and what happens in Visual Basic when we put a *control* onto a *form*.

In Visual Basic, every control has two things: (1) *event procedures* and (2) *control properties*. These two things are very important and comprise approximately half of what you need to know about programming in Visual Basic. At this point (even though I would rather avoid it), I need to say a few things about Object-Oriented Programming Systems (OOPS), Windows, and *transaction processing* because that is really where *events* and *properties* belong.

Everything in **Windows** is a *window*---we already know that---and everything in **Windows** is an *object*. So, in general, a *window* is an *object*. What is an *object*? Well, an *object* is a *window*, and it is one of those things that you *see* on forms. I suppose that this is not a sufficiently clear definition of an *object,* but it will do for now. An *object* is something, but it is also something that *does* something. Another way to state this is to say that *objects* can *do* things. In other words, **objects are capable of *acting*.** *Objects* and *actions* go together.

Windows applications perform *work* for you, and the *work* they do for you can generally be called *actions*--whereas the things that initiate *actions* are called *objects*. If you were confused, you probably still are; so let me clarify this for you by changing the terminology to match Visual Basic. *Controls* are *objects*. The *actions* that *objects* perform are triggered by the *events* that the *objects* recognize. Everything should really be clear now (*for sure*).

For example, a push button is a *window*, but it is also an *object* because *windows* are *objects*. A push button does not do much, but it does do a few things. Most notably, a push button goes *up* and *down* when you *click* on it (provided it is *enabled*). Forget about the *property* of being *enabled* for the moment. Also, forget about going *up* and *down*. Just remember that you *click* on a push button and it *does* something.

What does it do? Well, it goes *up* and *down*. (Do you get the impression we are going around in *circles*?) In Visual Basic, a *click* is an *event* and a *click* is (conveniently) an event that the push button is *programmed* to *recognize*. Note that **every Visual Basic *control* is *programmed* to *recognize* certain *events*** (you cannot change this one bit). You can, however, simply *ignore events* that are not significant. Being able to ignore *insignificant events* is a very important *power*.

The *events* associated with a Visual Basic *control* are *already* coded for you (at least in terms of their *default behavior*). This is important because if you do not care about doing anything particular when an event happens, then you do *not* have to code that fact. Consequently, the more things that you can *ignore*, the more things about which you do *not* care, the more work you can *avoid* doing. I need to say a little more about *events* at this point.

Events are the set of *actions* that occur as a result of *doing* something in the Graphical User Interface (GUI) and include things like pressing a key on the keyboard, clicking a mouse button, moving the mouse, and other similar types of actions. There are many *events* in **Windows**. Some of the *events* are important, but many more *events* are unimportant. *Events* are Windows *transactions*. The *events* (or Windows *transactions*) that are important to *you* are the ones that you *must* program. It will prove to be very *productive* to keep the *number* of important *events* (or Windows *transactions*) to an absolute *minimum*.

If you are coming to Windows from DOS (or some other *non*-transaction environment), then you are probably accustomed to *thinking* about application development and programming in terms of functions and subroutines that do something (a truly obvious fact). One of the first things that you discover in Windows is that you do a lot of programming and *never* get to the point at which you really do something *meaningful*. This is excruciatingly true about Windows SDK/C programming. In Visual Basic, it is a little true but it is generally more *transparent* than *apparent* (but not completely). When you add *controls* to your *form*, you are really *not* doing traditionally *meaningful* work. You are drawing pictures, but (this may come as a surprise) *you are really doodling*.

Even more *surprising* is the fact that someone is probably paying you to *doodle* and considers your *doodling* to be critical to the success of their business or project (or both)! Who would have ever thought that it would be possible to invent a way to get paid for *doodling*? Certainly not me. But that is what you are doing (in a philosophical sense) when you are building your forms. Of course, you are not *really doodling*, but it makes it more *fun* when you *think* that you are. What you are *really* doing is *thinking,* and we know that *thinking* can hurt your head. So, I recommend that you get out the *thinking hat* and put it on your head when you start *designing* forms.

While you may be *doodling*, Visual Basic is quietly adding code. Every time you add a control to a form, Visual Basic automatically *generates* all of the code necessary to handle the default *behavior* of the control. So, you are *doodling*, but Visual Basic is *coding*. Visual Basic is *coding* the default *behavior* of quite a few *events* associated with the control. This means that you are getting a lot of work done for free and are producing a lot of code with *nearly* no effort or knowledge.

The *meaningful* work is not too far away, and actually begins when you decide to make something other than *default* behavior occur when an event is triggered. If you do not want anything special to happen when a push button is clicked, then do *nothing* when the click event occurs. On the other hand, if you want the fact that the user *clicked* a push button to cause something meaningful to occur, then you have to *do* something in the *Click* event procedure. Specifically, you write a function to do something *meaningful*. *Now* you are where you are used to being, except that you need to know more about *events* because, as you will learn, **events are related, and one *event* can *trigger* another *event*.** (Be careful that event triggering does not become recursive or you will run out of stack space!).

In fact, *events* and *event chains* (or *loosely coupled events*) are an areas in which Visual Basic programming becomes an art. You will find that if you pick your *significant events* carefully, then you can use them as a **control language *within* a language**. In other words, you can cause a very complex *action* to occur by causing the *event* that *triggers* the *action* to occur.

For example, if *clicking* a push button causes a list box to be loaded and if you need to load that list box in another event, then you do *not* need to code loading the list box two times. All you need to do is *trigger* the push button that loads the list box. This is really *slick*. When you understand it, you enter a new realm of Visual Basic programming. In this sense, the *key* to everything is to do each thing *one time*. When you do it *one time*, do it in such a way that it is completely *generic* because if it is *generic* then you can *reuse* it. Also, note that (1) there are event procedures and (2) there are *non*-event procedures.

Event procedures are directly and explicitly associated with controls and forms and cannot be separated from them (well, not really anyway). *Non-event procedures* are just functions and subroutines that are separated from forms and controls---although they quite frequently refer to and use forms and controls. **Never put code in an *event* when you can put it in a *non-event*.**

Event procedure code is *stuck* to its control like glue and you cannot separate the two (for usual purposes). This means that it is very difficult to make an event procedure *generic* (in a practical sense). You do not want to use the event procedure of one control as the event procedure for another control, even though (1) you actually can and (2) it can be a useful technique. If you need to *share* event procedures, then consider using a *control array*.

You can, however, *move* most of the *meaningful* code *out* of the event procedure, put it into a *non*-event procedure, and then *reuse* the *non*-event procedure with many controls: that is the *smart* way to do things in Visual Basic. I set an arbitrary rule for myself that **no *event procedure* should contain more than 20 lines of code.** I also *ignore* this rule when it is *inconvenient*. Put only the code that *absolutely* must be in the event procedure *into* the event procedure. Put the remainder of the code *into* a *module* as a *non*-event procedure. Keep the code in a form to a *minimum* by putting most of the code into a *module* with the same name as the form.

This means that you will have two files associated with each form: FORMX.FRM and FORMX.BAS. Make the .FRM file contain *only* the event procedures (and the form itself), but put everything else in the .BAS file that is *associated* with the form. This provides an additional benefit because you can edit the .BAS file with a traditional programming editor [e.g., **Brief (Solutions**ystems)] and thereby gain some of the advantages that come with having more powerful text editing capabilities (but at the cost of interactive syntax checking).

Using a traditional text editor to do most of your Visual Basic coding is powerful, but it means that you have to be *proficient* in Visual Basic and is therefore reserved for a later date. Separating the form (i.e., the screen as it is displayed and its event procedures) from the *non*-event procedure code is very important when you are building an application that consists of more than a few forms. There are some very definite limits to what you can do in Visual Basic regarding the size of your application and how big it can get before you start to have *size-related* problems.

In Windows SDK/C programming one quickly learns that when an application approaches a certain size it becomes important to be concerned with the amount of Free System Resources that are available. Free System Resources refers to the amount of available data segment memory (or local heap) that is available for use by two of the three Windows DLLs: USER and GDI.

A DLL can have one 64K data segment for its internal use. Since USER and GDI are DLLs, they too have their own 64K data segments (or local heaps). At 100 percent availability, there is 128K of Free System Resources, but there will *never* be 100 percent availability. Each time USER and GDI use more of their local heap memory, the amount of available Free System Resources decreases. When no more Free System Resources are available, Windows *stops*. There is a very good explanation of Free Systems Resources in one of Fran Finnegan's *Windows* columns in **PC Magazine** and I suggest that you read it. Finnegan also has a column in **Windows Magazine**--another excellent source for technical information about Windows.

Although I do not know this for a fact, I am guessing that USER and GDI primarily use their local heap to maintain tables which contain information about the current and previous states of various aspects of Windows. For some unknown reason, not unloading Visual Basic forms causes USER and GDI to use considerable amounts of their local heap and will eventually result in making Windows stop or lock. The 128K Free System Resources limit is particularly troublesome for Visual Basic applications, but can be managed with a little extra work.

For Visual Basic, Free System Resources is primarily associated with the memory used by screens when the screen is *not* discarded (or unloaded) but rather is simply left in an *invisible* state. Windows SDK/C programmers use a technique to force Windows *not* to keep a copy of screens that are *not* currently displayed that involves setting a bit or two and then manipulating these bits at appropriate times when *jumping* from one screen to another. This technique was more necessary when Windows only ran in REAL mode, but it is still a good and necessary thing to do in Windows 3.0+.

This carryover from Windows Version 2.1 is not handled very well in Visual Basic (which is also written, at least in part, in Windows SDK/C). It is not immediately intuitive (at least to me) that one should concern one's self with Free System Resources when programming in Visual Basic. Consequently those concerns do not appear very important--*probably because they cannot appear to be anything if they are not present*--so one does not, therefore, devote much time to *unloading* screens when *beginning* to program in Visual Basic.

Further compounding the problem, the Visual Basic documentation actually goes so far as to *recommend* that you do *not* unload forms. The Visual Basic documentation even suggests that *loading* forms in *advance* is a *good* idea. I have not seen anything in any other books that contradicts this belief. This is a strong indication (at least to me) that nobody writing books has ever actually programmed a large Visual Basic application. I guarantee that if you preload forms and *never* unload them, then you will most *definitely* incur *problems* that could be easily avoided by doing a little additional work and explicitly unloading forms when they no longer need to be visible. You will have to do this (eventually) so you might as well do it the right way from the beginning and save yourself a big hassle.

However, these concerns will not surface until you get into the realms of (1) *REALLY BIG* screens or (2) *TIGHTLY COUPLED* screens. These types of screens are the ones that (1) are either at or near the upper limits of what Visual Basic can handle in terms of quantity of controls (and other considerations) or (2) are more *mundane* screens that are *numerous* in *quantity* rather than in *complexity*, but are *tied* to each other by *interdependent* action. If doing something on one form causes something to happen on another form, even when the other form is not visible (i.e., is *hidden)*, then those forms are *tightly coupled*. *Tight coupling* is something to *avoid* as a general rule, but it can be very useful when used appropriately.

The primary reason for *hiding* forms is *laziness* (to a certain degree). It is a little more trouble to save the current values of variables used in the form. But, if you save the current values, you can (1) unload the form, (2) then (at some later time) reload it, and (3) restore the variables used by the form to their current values at the time you unloaded the form. It is *not* much extra work to save variables, either in global variables or in a DOS flat file (i.e., a Visual Basic sequential file or a binary file). The *reward* for doing the extra work is that you do *not* have to do it later when your application is more complex. If your application is going to be *big*, then I guarantee that this will occur. It is an absolute fact; so you can either (1) *believe* me and do it the correct way or (2) *not believe* me, do it the *wrong* way, and then have to *change* a lot of your code (probably at precisely the moment when your application is due to be delivered and when you do *not* have any more time for coding).

It is better to use *loose coupling* than *tight coupling* and that means that any *coupling* should be done by *non-event procedures* that are invoked when you show (or make *visible)* one form that is *dependent* on another form. Put the *coupling information* into global variables or binary files, and then use the *invoking function* to get that data and refresh the new form with any *coupled data*.

In order to make everything in your application *flow* smoothly from screen to screen (from form to form) it is very convenient to *tightly-couple* controls and events in such a way that when you do something on one form it will update the appropriate objects on other forms. This works, but at some point it causes all of the *tightly-coupled* forms to be *loaded* and will *eventually* cause either a low memory condition or an undesired (and quite abrupt) termination of your application (accompanied by an "Out Of Memory" message).

Note that there is a difference between a form being *loaded* and a form being *unloaded*. Also, note that the difference applies *only* to the actual screen, *not* to the *code* associated with the form. *Code* does *not* generally cause much affect on Free System Resources, but the screens *do*. Windows manages code segments quite well, provided the code segments are marked as discardable. You do *not* have any control over the way in which Visual Basic *marks* the code segments it *generates* for you. You can only *hope* that it generates *code* segments that are primarily *discardable*.

For reference, when you click on the About item in Help List for Program Manager, the percentage given for Free System Resources is an *indicator* of how much of the 128K of USER and GDI local heap is currently available. You may, as I do, have over 16MB of extended memory (*virtually*), but still be at the mercy of the 128K limit regarding *invisible* screens. Windows 3.1 does a much better job of managing Free System Resources, so you can expect some *very* nice improvements in Windows performance in the near future. However, the problem will not disappear (it just occurs at a later point).

The solution to this problem is explicitly to *unload* screens when they are not visible. This requires a little additional programming because you must reinitialize or restore control states (and other things) that are cleared when you unload the screen. (It is a bit of a hassle, but it is the *method* of doing things that *must* be done in Visual Basic if you are going to have applications with more than a few screens!)

I suppose this is generally obvious, but it was *not* obvious to me. In fairness to the Visual Basic designers, this would have been obvious to me if I were coding in Windows SDK/C; so it more of a lapse of *awareness* on my part than a deficit in Visual Basic, itself. There is a definite style to programming in Visual Basic (particularly with respect to applications with more than a few screens), and there are not really many different ways to do things. At most, this is only a *minor* inconvenience. When you consider the profoundly astonishing amount of *meaningful* work that you can do with Visual Basic, it is just not very important.

If telling you that you cannot *hide* forms causes you not to use Visual Basic, then I should not have told you about it, and I have done you a great disservice. Visual Basic is a productive *dynamo*. When I use adjectives like *amazing*, *astonishing*, *astounding*, *incredible*, *phenomenal*, *fantastic*, *wonderful*, and so forth, I am doing so with the intention of conveying an *important* fact to you about Visual Basic. I have been working on computers since 1975, and (with characteristic exemplary modesty I say it) I am very good at it, but I have never been able to do so much, so quickly, and so easily, as I can now do with Visual Basic.

Developing with Visual Basic is at least 10 times faster than developing with Windows SDK/C or any other language or system that I know. You have to *think* when you use Visual Basic, but when you learn *how* to *think* in Visual Basic (and it *does* require some learning), you will find that you can do almost anything you want to do. If you cannot do it with a Visual Basic function, then you can do it with a Visual Basic Add-On Tool Kit or with a Windows SDK/C function.

When you become proficient in Visual Basic programming, something even *more* important happens: your ability to *imagine* improves dramatically. When I programmed with Windows SDK/C, there was such a tremendous delay between having an idea (*imagination*) and implementing the idea (*implementation*) that I spent more time *coding* than *imagining*. In other words, it was very easy *not* to want to have new ideas because having new ideas just meant an increase in frustration due to not being able to code them.

Knowing how to design and program Windows applications with Visual Basic is *power*. I now have the *power* to look at an application like Microsoft Money and know that I could clone it in less than three months *and* continue to do full-time contract work on other projects. Microsoft Money is not in the same category as Excel or Word For Windows, but it is a complete and useful Windows application (at the high end of the Windows applet scale). I have no desire to clone Microsoft Money, but knowing that I really *could* clone it gives me the *power* to *imagine* applications that I do want to code.

This is a somewhat *subtle* ability to recognize, but it is basically a matter of *positive* feedback. It is easy to have ideas, but if you never *do* anything with your ideas, you tend to begin having fewer and fewer ideas. In contrast, if you have an idea and can then code it very quickly, you receive *positive* reinforcement (a *cookie*) for having the idea, and you *feel* good. Then, you have another idea, and another idea, and another idea, and so forth.

When I worked on Windows SDK/C projects, I would often have an idea and then discuss it with some of my friends (who were also Windows SDK/C programmers). We would think about it for a few minutes and then realize that, even though it may be a good idea, it would take six months or more to code it.

In reality, therefore, it was not a good idea--it was a waste of time because it was *not* practical. Just as often, my friends would have ideas and discuss them with me. The result was the same, and it became so frustrating to have good ideas but not be able to code them that everyone *nearly* stopped having ideas. It is *impossible* for me to stop having ideas; so I just *deferred* the time to begin coding my ideas until several years in the future (but this also became a source of frustration).

I recently completed a Visual Basic project (for a Fortune 100 corporation) that involved porting (and enhancing) a mainframe-based, human resource system to Windows and Microsoft SQL Server. This project was completed in *less* than 90 days with a total staff of one client requirements specialist, one manager/programmer, one SQL Server DBA, one mainframe programmer, and myself. If you do not *understand* how completely and totally *incredible* it is to be able to do so much work so quickly with so few people, then you have never been involved in a Windows SDK/C project.

There *are* limits to what you can do in Visual Basic, but they are more *structural limits* than feasibility limits. As you approach the *structural limits* of an application, *another set of rules* applies. It is much easier to follow those rules from the *beginning* than to have to go back and make a significant number of changes later. The *primary* difficulty associated with structural limits is *discovering* them. There are two ways to discover *structural limits*: (1) trial-and-error and (2) reading a book written by (or talking to) someone who has discovered *structural limits* by trial-and-error. *Structural limits* are almost *never* documented, especially in Windows, so can only be discovered through either (1) your *experience* or (2) someone else's *experience*.

When I use the term *structural limits*, I am referring to the fact that, at some point, you can build a Visual Basic application that is simply TOO BIG (no matter what you do to streamline things). When you reach a *structural limit*, you have to *split* the application into *separate* applications that are *connected* by a main menu application. When you do this, you can use (1) Visual Basic's Dynamic Data Exchange (DDE) capabilities or (2) *state* files (binary data files) to solve the problem of *intertask communication*. However, this will require you to understand (1) the *architecture* of Windows, (2) what you are really doing, and (3) how to do it.

You should also be aware of an important fact regarding the difference between what *you* do in Visual Basic and what Visual Basic does *for* you. *You* have *direct* control over what *you* do, but only *indirect* control over what Visual Basic does *for* you. In the case of Free System Resources, *you* have to adjust the way *you* do things in order to *cause* Visual Basic to adjust the way *it* does things. *Indirectly* controlling Visual Basic is *not* an *intuitive* process and requires that you *understand* Windows SDK/C programming in *considerable* detail. Otherwise, you have to find *expert* help or rely on *experimentation*.

Events, Properties, and Methods

In the last chapter, I introduced you to the concept that everything in Windows is a window and extended the concept to encompass the following facts: (1) *controls* are *windows*, (2) *windows* are *objects*, (3) *objects* perform *actions*, (4) *actions* are *events*, and (5) *events* are associated with *controls*. From this you can see that there is a considerable amount of redundantly-equivalent terminology being used when discussing Windows and Visual Basic programming. It would probably be nice if everyone used the same single term for the same thing--but nobody does, so you may as well learn the *jargon*.

Objects, *windows*, and *controls* are generally identical and can be considered equivalent for most practical purposes. For reference, the term *object* is also used to refer to database items (and several other types of things which are somewhat context dependent) but we are not discussing databases. For the present, an *object* is a *control*. Another term that will eventually appear is *entity*, and it is generally used when discussing database or system design.

At some point, I will discuss system design and introduce you to an interesting way to flowchart Windows and Visual Basic screens and applications. Since I have mentioned flowcharting, let me say that you *cannot* flowchart a Windows application very well by using traditional, structured flowcharting techniques.

Windows is not the least bit structured in the sense that there is a *single* path leading from one step to another step. Windows is more like a *Mobius Strip Maze* than a line (if you remember that a line is generally defined by two points and connects them in a usually straightforward manner). We may as well talk about flowcharting Windows applications for a while because it will help you understand control events and some aspects of control properties.

In traditional, structured flowcharting you start *somewhere* and proceed from *somewhere* to the *next* step. Then, you continue the process by proceeding from the *current* step to the *next* step, and, finally, stop when you are done. This method implies that (1) the program follows a *predefined* structure and (2) there is (generally) *one* path from point A to point B (with a few detours that are dependent on various program-related conditions). This method is *not* very appropriate for flowcharting a Windows program because it is inherently *limited* by the *presumption* that there is a *single* path from one point to another.

In Windows applications, the major components of design are *objects,* and each object is generally *independent*. This is due, in part, to the *transaction processing* nature of Windows. With a few exceptions, Windows applications behave in a manner that is best described by the term *random*. This will take some explanation, but it is, nevertheless, true.

When you start a traditional program, you begin by doing *something* and then proceed (in a controlled manner) from one step to another step. In a Windows application, you start and are presented with a *set* of *objects* contained within a *screen*. Then, you proceed by *using* the *objects* to *do* things for you. Although there is an *embedded control system*, it is *not* very *obvious*. Actually, Windows applications *appear* more like *calculators* than like traditional screens.

For example, if you are one of those people who use Automated Teller Machines, then you are accustomed to using a traditional application: (1) insert your card, (2) select what you want to do from a small list, (3) enter an amount, and then (4) wait for something *intelligent* to happen. You do *not* have many choices at any given step in the process, and you are guided--*actually controlled*--at *all* times. In this type of system, the application is *designed* to *control* everything you do and not to let you do foolish things--including getting all of your money. (Someone at the bank decided that it would be foolish for you to withdraw all of your money, and, therefore, you cannot do it.)

In a Windows application, you start, and from that point forward how you proceed is generally up to you. Windows applications do not provide much *guidance* as a general rule. At the beginning, the lack of *guidance* in Windows applications is rather frustrating, but once you learn how to use one Windows application, then you quickly learn that there *is* guidance, but that it is *disguised* as the *menu bar* and Help. Coming from a traditional, mainframe background, my first impression of Windows applications was that they were more like a *wild party* than a formal event. It was more like you could do anything you wanted to do anytime you wanted to do it, rather than doing what you were told to do at appropriate times.

I found it irritating to be presented with a screen and left to myself to determine what to do next. That is just not the way you do things on a mainframe. In mainframe programming, you *control* every single step and do everything you can (1) to eliminate any doubt as to what to do next and (2) to eliminate any possibility of making mistakes. In effect, as a programmer, you *presume* that the people using your program have a *tendency* to do foolish things. You do everything you can to *force* them to do exactly what you *want* them to do. This will probably sound *totalitarian* to some people, but that is the way it works in traditional, mainframe programming.

In Windows programming, you still *control* everything, but you do it in such a way that there is an *appearance* of complete *freedom* of action. This implies that several things have to occur in order for this approach to be successful. The most important thing that must occur is that, whenever you *allow* an object to do something, then whatever it does must be mostly *independent* and definitely *not* wrong.

There is no particular rule against letting people do foolish things in Windows, but it is a good idea to make them *aware* of the *possibility* of doing something foolish *before* you let them continue with a *possibly* foolish action. What this does is require you to be actively *cognizant* of the current state of the world at all times. In the beginning this is a difficult thing to do, but, after a while, you learn to maintain two *lists* as you program: (1) a *list* of what you *have* and (2) a *list* of what you can *do* with or to what you *have*.

The first *list* is generally composed of your input and your output (either of which may or may not be visible). The second *list* is generally composed of the controls that can or cannot *modify* the items in the first *list*. I suppose that this is beginning to become *abstruse* but hope that it will become clearer as we proceed. It will help to examine an example application, and a word processor is a good choice for an example application.

In designing a word processor for Windows, you know that you need some *objects* that perform *actions*. You also know that the *purpose* of the word processor is to produce *documents*. So, in the case of a word processor, your first *list* contains (1) the *data* you are entering into the document and (2) the *document* itself. The second *list* contains all of the *tools* that you use to do things to the items in the first *list*. In other words, the *document* and the *data* that goes into it are the input and the output. The tools that you use to create the input and the output are the keyboard, the editing functions, the fonts, and a few other things.

You can look at the *process* of programming your word processor as being one of (1) *creating* the tools and then (2) tailoring the *behavior* of the tools in such a way that they do useful work that results in the production of a document. The nice thing about Windows is that you can begin *anywhere* you desire.

A good place to begin is with the tools because the document is just a piece of paper in the beginning (a piece of paper does not require much programming at first). What do you know about the process? Well, you know that people generally enter data into a document by typing. Typing usually requires a keyboard and some way to get the keystrokes into memory. You also know that once you have the text, you will probably need to do things to it (e.g., give it a particular appearance and format it).

Appearance and formatting involve typography and editing; so you can use your knowledge of typography and editing to provide some *clues* as to what types of tools you will need. You will need a way to list the available fonts and, since fonts have point sizes, you will need a way to list the available sizes for each font. You will need a way to specify such things as whether the font is bold, italicized, uppercase, underlined, raised, lowered, and so forth.

For editing, you will need tools for such things as single-spacing, double-spacing, left-justification, centering, right-justification, indenting, and so forth. To make the interface easier to use, you will probably want to provide a mechanism that enables the word processor to use styles to specify predetermined settings (or states) of certain tools. You will also want to provide information regarding location within the document by using *metaphors* like rulers and visual tab settings.

Metaphors are important in Windows programming and are used to describe the way in which you *visually* present things to the user. For example, a ruler and scroll bars are good *metaphors* for providing the user with information about the current location within the document.

So far, most of the things I have described are *visual* in the sense that they are things you can *see*. Some of the other tools you will need in your word processor are not very appropriate for visual presentation. These types of things generally fall into the category of *functions* and *processes*. This does *not* imply that you cannot make them visual, but that they may be more *appropriate* for inclusion in the *menu bar* than for inclusion in the *visual* tool kit or *tool bar*. However, please be aware that there is no reason why *everything* cannot be *part* of the *tool bar*.

In general, people are more likely to understand things in the beginning if they are *not* represented in *symbolic* form, and that is the *primary* reason for having a *menu bar*. A picture is worth a thousand words (or more), but if you do not understand the picture then there is no telling what the thousand words are (other than, "Duh!"). That is, in part, due to the fact that, as children, we are *taught* to think with *words*, rather than with *pictures* or *symbols*, at precisely the time when we do *not* know any *words* and can only think *symbolically*.

Later, after we have *learned* to think with *words*, we are introduced to *mathematics*--a *symbolic* language if there ever was one--and then find *mathematics* difficult to understand. I think this is the *wrong* way to approach *teaching* and *thinking*. As a consequence of this, many people find it very difficult to think with *symbols*.

If you present a word processor to your user in such a way that all of your *metaphors* are push buttons (with *symbols* on them), then it will be difficult for anyone to use your word processor in the beginning unless (1) you are very *adept* at picking symbols and (2) your users are very *perceptive*. However, as you become more proficient in the use of a word processor, the use of *symbolic* push buttons becomes *invaluable* and can make everything tremendously *easier*. An excellent *tool bar* is the *key* to a successful application. People *like* buttons when the buttons do useful things for them. The *tool bar* is really a *button bar*.

I think that *symbols* and *pictures* are an excellent way to *represent* tools, but I know that providing *symbolic* tools requires a considerable amount of design work and mandates an initially complex (or somewhat complex) learning curve. However, once you learn to use the *symbolic* tools, they are much quicker than the corresponding text commands. The fact that you *can* use *symbolic* tools means that your *knowledge* of the application and your *expertise* in using the application are much greater than would otherwise be the case. In truth, I think that (1) *programming* should be done with *symbols* and (2) Visual Basic is one of the first *practical* languages to provide some *symbolic programming* capability (even though it is very rudimentary).

In Sigmund Freud's classic book, **The Interpretation of Dreams**, there is a small diagram of the architecture of the mind. It is a very simple diagram and is, therefore, easy to remember. When I first read the book and saw the diagram, I knew absolutely nothing about computers (and probably did not even know that they existed). Later, when I began studying Computer Science, one of my professors drew a simple diagram of the architecture of a computer and I noticed that the diagram of the computer looked almost exactly like Professor Freud's diagram of the mind.

For me, this was a profoundly significant observation. In fact, I find computers (and computer programs) to be very *Freudian*, in the sense that when we create computers, we are really creating physical analogies of our *minds*. If you really want to understand how *computers* think, then you must first understand how the human *mind* thinks. Windows is a software analog of the human mind. Your *mind* is not restricted to thinking only with words, and there is no reason why Windows programs (or programming) should be *restricted* to words, either.

In this regard, I think that Microsoft's vision of *Information At Your Fingertips* should really be *Thinking At Your Fingertips*. Windows is *like* your *mind*, but Windows is actually an *enhancement* to your *mind*. Because you *think* that you are fascinating, you *think* that Windows is fascinating, and you are *correct* in both thoughts. You *and* Windows *are* truly *fascinating*. When you design and program a Windows application, you are *creating* a software analog of one or more of your thoughts or ways of thinking. More than likely, if thinking in a particular way is *useful* to you, then it will be *useful* to other people. A *programming* language is, therefore, just a *language* for defining and describing ways of *thinking*.

It has been my feeling for quite a while that it is *possible* to invent a programming language that *looks* something like *hieroglyphics* and *operates* at such a *high* level that writing a program would be no more involved than picking a *set* of *symbols* and *compiling* them. This is what occurs *internally*, today, but the *process* of *creating* the *symbols* is so *rudimentary* that it borders on being crude.

The primary hindrance in the production of a *symbolic programming* language is more a problem of *selecting* (1) a useful *set* of *symbols* and (2) a *set* of *rules* that programmers can *understand*, rather than a problem of *designing* the internal *behavior* (or *mechanics*) of the language. It is less important that the *understanding* process be *simple* than that it be *possible*. The current way of *understanding* how to program is everything *but* simple. The *metaphor* of the Visual Basic *tool box* has great potential and will become very powerful when people learn how to build new tools that not only do useful things but also are *already* programmed (i.e., are *smart*).

The concept of *preprogrammed* tools relates to my idea of creating *generic* forms and using *them* as tools. There is no reason why there cannot be a tool that manipulates *generic* forms, except that it does not make sense to put forms onto forms. You can, however, put frames onto forms, but Visual Basic, unfortunately, does *not* recognize frame boxes at the same level of *independence* as forms (at present).

I think that, as Visual Basic *evolves*, programmers will want more and more powerful tools and hope that *encapsulation of frame boxes* will become available. It will require some kind of data dictionary (and quite a few other *constructs*), but the *foundation* already *exists* and will become more *obvious* as Visual Basic *evolves*. In this regard, it is very important for you to tell the Visual Basic designers what new features and capabilities you would like to have in Visual Basic.

As you learn to *see* what you can do with Visual Basic, you will quickly reach the same conclusion that I have reached as a consequence of spending the past ten months doing nearly nothing except program in Visual Basic (day and night). Visual Basic has *changed* the *world*. This fact will become more apparent in the next few years, but it is something you can use to your *benefit* today. After seeing what people can do with Visual Basic, almost immediately, I know that I really do *not* know all of the capabilities of this powerful language. Visual Basic is *making* me *think* and I am *enjoying* it.

I think this is simply wonderful! However, I *do* know (1) that I *know* that I *can* do things in Windows with Visual Basic that I have *not even imagined*, and (2) that my *imagination* is *working* overtime at this point. When you add Windows Multimedia and Pen Windows into the equation, then you have (1) a tremendous amount of *learning* to do (and hardware to purchase!), and (2) the *opportunity* to be a significant *contributor* to some truly amazing *leaps* in *thinking* and *productivity*. Visual Basic *is* Thunder and it is enlightening!

I have jumped around quite a bit; so I need to get back to talking about control events and control properties. At this point, we are really working with two things: (1) *objects* and (2) *actions*. It may not be clear how to proceed, having no more than *objects* and *actions* with which to work, but it soon will be when I show you how to group *objects* and *actions*.

The *objects* that I am talking about are really divided into two groups: (1) *operators* and (2) *results*. The *actions* I am talking about (1) apply to the *results*, but (2) belong to the *operators*. Actually, this is a good way to *look* at the processing that occurs in a Windows application. You begin with *nothing* as a *result* and then change *nothing* into *something* by using *operators* as *mechanisms* for causing *actions* to *occur*.

To keep this simple, let us limit the *operators* to being only push buttons. The *result* we produce is *data*, and the *actions* that the *operators* cause to occur are *functions* that *modify* the *data*. With this in mind, each time we need to *modify* our *result*, we can *create* a new *operator* (or push button) and then make it *do* something. For example, in the beginning we have an empty *set* of *data*; so if we want to add some *data* to our currently empty *set* of *data*, then we need to have one or more buttons that provide the ability to input data.

At this point, we can jump forward a bit in the philosophical *creation* of *metaphors* and make a very useful observation. Keys on the keyboard are buttons, and there is no reason why they cannot be push buttons (because that is what they *really* are). We can even carry this a few more steps and create a push button for each of the alphanumeric keys. Then, we have a nice *metaphor* for a keyboard on our form.

The alphanumeric push buttons are *operators* that cause the *action* of adding the appropriate alphanumeric character to the *set* of *data* that is our current *result*. In this case, the important *event* associated with the alphanumeric push buttons is the *Click* event that occurs when the user *metaphorically* presses the push button. The *action* that *occurs* as a *consequence* of this *event* is the addition of the appropriate character to the current *result* or *set* of *data*.

Another useful thing to note is that we know everything (or nearly everything) we need to know in order to proceed. We know which character to add as a consequence of knowing which push button was pressed. We know the *event* in which to *cause* the *action* to occur. We know *where* to add the character, and we know something else that is *not* so obvious. We know *when* to do all of this. However, we do *not* have to program for *when not to do this*, because we do *not* care about *not* doing this, at the present time.

Nevertheless, there may come a time when we *will* care about *not* doing something. *Conveniently*, Visual Basic has provided a way for us to control the condition in which we do *not* want the user to be able to do something. If we do *not* want the user to be *able* to do something, then we can *disable* the push button that causes the *undesired* event to occur.

One property of controls is called *Enabled* and it has two values: (1) True and (2) False. If the value is True then the control is enabled and can be operated. If the value is False, then the control is *not* enabled (i.e., it is *disabled)* and cannot be operated. This *control capability* is enormously *convenient* when we are working with *objects*.

If we want an *object* to be *available* for use, then we can *enable* it. If we do *not* want an *object* to be *available* for use, then we do *not* have to do *anything* other than *disable* it to make it *unavailable* for use. In some cases we would like it to be *enabled*, but we would also like the user to be *unaware* of it. In that case, we can make it *invisible* by setting another *property* of *objects*, *Visible*, to False. If we want an *object* to be *visible*, we can set the *Visible* property to True, and then the *object* becomes *visible*.

When contemplating the *Visible* and *Enabled* properties of *controls*, it is also useful to note that when you begin in Visual Basic with a *frame box* and add *controls* to the *domain* of that *frame box*, then something *interesting* occurs. You can not only make the *frame box* visible or invisible and enabled or disabled, but you can also do the same thing to *all* of the *controls* within the *domain* of the *frame box* by doing *nothing* more than *setting* the appropriate values for the frame box *only*.

This is a powerful capability because it lets you *group* objects in such a way that you can control them with just a few commands. This technique will make more sense in later chapters, but for now just consider that it is useful to make an *object*--that is itself a *set* of *objects*--become visible, invisible, enabled, or disabled with a few lines of code.

Please note that (1) there is a *correct* way to add *controls* to the *domain* of a *frame box* and (2) there is an *incorrect* way to add *controls* to the *domain* of a *frame box*. The *incorrect* way does *not* work and will confuse you. The *correct* way to add *controls* to the *domain* of a *frame box* is to make the *frame box* the *active control* when you add other *controls* to it.

This appears obvious (and it is when you are getting *controls* from the tool box), but when you are pasting *controls*, or moving *controls* from one place on the form to another, it is not *visually* obvious. If you have a *control* on your form but that *control* is not currently in the *domain* of a *frame box*, please note that simply *moving* the *control* on *top* of the *frame box* does *not* put it into the *domain* of the *frame box*.

If you want to move a *control* from a *non-frame box domain-area* of your form to the *domain-area* of a *frame box*, then you *must* cut the *control* from the form (i.e., cut it to the *clipboard*) and then paste it into the *frame box*. When you do this, be sure that you *click* on the *frame box* to make it the *currently-selected* object *before* you do the paste operation. Otherwise, you will *not* be pasting it where you want it to be pasted. (You will be pasting it *someplace* else!)

When using the technique of *grouping* controls *within* the *domain* of a *frame box*, it is important to *begin* with the *frame box* and *then* add the controls. If you do *not* begin with the *frame box*, then you can still do it, but you have to cut and paste each control, and it takes more time (but not that much more time).

Another advantage to *grouping* controls in *frame boxes* is that it is easier to *rearrange* the items on your form because **when you move a *frame box*, *all* of the *controls* within its *domain* follow it and maintain their *relative* position within the *frame box*.** This technique is so powerful that I suspect at some time the Visual Basic designers will provide a mechanism for *encapsulating frame boxes* with respect to code *following* the visual components when you go to the clipboard.

Currently, when you cut (or copy) a *frame box* and its *domain* to the clipboard and then paste it onto another form, the code does *not* follow. The code will only follow the *frame box* if the *frame box* is moved *within* the form that contains its code. However, it seems at least possible that there is a way to work around this in a general sense (and there *may* be), but it is easier just to be aware of it, now, than to spend a lot of time trying to determine how to extend this powerful capability.

You can get the code for each control by an indirect method, but some work is involved. What you do is cut the *frame box* and its *domain* to the clipboard and then make a new form and paste the frame box to the new form. This causes the code associated with all of the events of the *frame box* and its *domain* on the original form to move to the general procedure area of the form and, in effect, to become *detached* from the controls to which it originally applied. You can then save both the original and the new form and then save the original form as text. This will get you a copy of the code in a text file, and you can then use that text file to move the code into the new form.

I am still experimenting with this, and it works, but it seems like a complex procedure (and it hurts my head); so I am *not* very enthusiastic about it. However, cutting and pasting is still *superior* to coding. Even though the process is boring, it is still quicker than starting over. It produces useful results in less time than would otherwise be possible. Using this technique is another good reason for my rule of **limiting event procedure code to 20 lines or less**. When you cut and paste it is easier to work with *small* event procedures.

While on the subject of useful techniques, let me say a few words about *control arrays*: they are extremely powerful. In fact, *control arrays* are so powerful that you *must* learn how to use them. When I first looked at the Visual Basic documentation and saw the section on control arrays, I skipped it because it looked like something that would hurt my head. Later, I discovered that skipping that section was somewhat foolish of me because it was not really very difficult to learn how to use *control arrays* (although it did hurt my head a little, as is generally the case when you have to *think*). The basic way that *control arrays* work is easy to understand, because all you have to program is the *first* occurrence of the *control array*.

A *single control* is transformed into a *control array* when you do one of two things: (1) set the *index* property of the *control* to a numeric value or (2) make a copy of the *control*, paste it onto the same form, and reply "YES" to the message box asking you whether you want to make the *control* become a *control array*. In either case it is easy to do. Then you can have any number of similar *controls* on the same form and only code *one* of them (because that is the only way to do it).

Each unique *control instance* within the *control array* is identified by an *index*; it is with that *index* that you make any general code become specific. For example, when we code the keyboard *metaphor* for our word processor, the best way to code it is to represent the *set* of keyboard buttons via a single *control array*. Each button *can* have a unique *caption* (in this example, nothing more than the alphanumeric character of the key that the push button is emulating), but each push button *does* have a unique *index value*. The identification for the key being pressed is made via a *Select Case* condition within the *Click* event of the *control array*.

All we have to do is assign specific *characters* to specific *index values*. Then, we know which key is pressed and which character to add to the *result* (i.e., to the document). There is an example of this technique as applied to numeric keys in the code samples. It is so *easy* to do that you will soon reach the conclusion that *control arrays* are *indispensable* to Visual Basic programming.

However, please be warned that there is a *limit* to the number of controls that can (*currently*) appear on one form. The limit is 255 controls. Also, note that when you have approximately 75 controls on one form, some bizarre things can begin to happen to Visual Basic when in *design mode*. At some point, as you begin to get into the realm of large numbers of controls on a single form, Visual Basic enters a *gray area* regarding its ability to keep track of what it is doing. The first thing you will notice is that Visual Basic becomes very *confused* regarding painting itself.

For those of you who are new to Windows, *painting* is something that a Windows application does when something on the screen has changed and needs to be visually updated. *Painting* is a very complex procedure. It is further complicated by the fact that Windows *queues* paint messages and then examines them with the intent of getting only the most recent paint messages and discarding the older paint messages. Windows does this in order to avoid having to paint the same screen region more times than is necessary. If this process is *not* handled correctly, Windows and your application can become greatly confused.

It is definitely not a trivial process, and it can become *recursive (*which is what I think happens when you exceed the practical *threshold* of the number of controls on a form). When Visual Basic has trouble painting itself, you have serious trouble. This problem is also associated with having a code window open and displayed on top of the form window. If you close the code window, then the problem occurs. If you make the form window *current* by clicking on it, then the problem does *not* usually occur.

When I have a form with a large number of controls, I always bring the form window to the front *before* switching from a code window. You will learn to do this, and I suspect that at some point this problem will be fixed. For now, just remember that you always bring the *form window* to the *front* by *clicking* on it *before* doing *anything* to any other window. If you do that, then you will *not* have a problem.

There is something else related to this problem that you need to know about. If you do not handle going from code window to form window correctly when the form window contains a large number of controls, then (at some point) you will lock Visual Basic (possibly even Windows) and have to give your machine the *three finger salute* (i.e., Ctrl-Alt-Del). After you reboot, you need to look in your temporary Windows directory (if you have one) or in the directory that was current at the time of the lockup for any files having names like "˜**VBxxx.TMP**". You must *delete* them before restarting Visual Basic.

I am not entirely certain what these files do, but I do know they *appear* to remember that you were *out to lunch* and should probably *continue* to be. This was discovered in a rather lengthy and irritating series of events, but I have never had any problems when I deleted these files *prior* to starting a Visual Basic session. I have also observed that if one or more of them is present, then (at some point) Visual Basic *appears* to want to *know* whether it needs to do something and then goes out and looks in one or more of these files. The data in the file(s) *appears* to tell it to take a trip to *Never-Never Land* or some other place to which you would probably rather *not* jump. (This is not terribly scientific, but it works for me!)

For reference, your Windows temporary directory is declared in your AUTOEXEC.BAT file by the "SET TEMP = <drive><directory path>" command or simply becomes whatever Windows *thinks* is the current directory when it needs a temporary file if you do not declare a specific temporary directory. It is much easier to declare a specific temporary directory than to use the default of *anywhere that seems convenient*. If you are not currently running Visual Basic, then it is my opinion that you do not need the "˜**VBxxx.TMP**" files. I have even deleted these files while Visual Basic was *running* and not had a problem, but when I did so I was *not* editing my Visual Basic application code in *design mode*. You must *not* delete these files when in *design mode*. (If you do, then Visual Basic will *not* be able to save some of your code changes!)

I suspect that these files are used in the dynamic compiling or creation of the **P-Code** that occurs just before you "**Start**" you application when in design mode and in temporarily saving changes in code, but that may not be the case. I look at the "~VBxxx.TMP" files as being a venting area for Visual Basic when it starts to become frustrated. It seems to me that whatever it reads and writes in these files does *not* always result in very good behavior. Considering that I have over 16MB of extended memory (*virtually*), I can find no reason for Visual Basic's needing to write anything to temporary files, but then there may be a valid reason for doing so.

I have previously suggested that you create small binary files for the purpose of *loosely coupling* forms and that doing so is a *valid* reason for using a temporary file that is small. There is no reason why Visual Basic cannot do the same thing without being criticized by me. On the other hand, it is a problem that needs to be fixed. This is one of the traps and pitfalls that I mentioned in the advertisements for this book. If this problem has been occurring in your Visual Basic sessions, I think that you will agree with me that this book just paid for itself by saving you some valuable time. There are a few other bits of odd behavior in Visual Basic, and I will tell you about them when appropriate (actually, I have already told you about quite a few).

In fairness to the Visual Basic designers and programmers, this is the *first* version of a truly fantastic product and I am surprised that there are so *few* bits of odd behavior. I would normally expect a first version of something as complex as Visual Basic to have more problems than it does. Every software product you buy is going to have some number of problems, and there is mathematically no way to prove or disprove that fact.

If you are one of those people who like to read about Computer Science theories and Mathematics then at some point in your reading you will have encountered one of the fundamental theories about proving that a program is perfect. In effect, the theory states rather emphatically that you cannot write a computer program that can determine whether another computer program is perfect. It is associated with Türing Machines and proving that a Türing Machine program will halt (it is called the *"Halting Problem"*). The *"Halting Problem"* demonstrates the fact that if you think you can prove a computer program is perfect, then you are making an assumption based on the way things work in *Another World*.

With a computer program, the best you can do is to do all you reasonably can to prove that it works correctly in as many different situations and circumstances as you can conceive. You cannot prove that it is perfect and you should not guarantee to anyone else that it is perfect. In doing contract programming, when someone asks me if one of my programs works, I always tell them, "I think it does, but then what do I know?" This statement usually results in one of those looks like "*...and what planet did you say you came from?*" Then, I explain the rules and restate the fact that I have done the best I can and that if I missed something I can fix it later.

Normally, the *correctness* of programs is important, but if a program has a problem then it is *not* the end of the world. It probably results in nothing more than a little inconvenience on the part of its user. However, in some kinds of programs you cannot afford to make mistakes and (knowing the rules) you must therefore take extra care to make absolutely certain that your program works in every case it will encounter. This is *patently* different from being perfect. For example, if you are coding a control program for medical equipment, airplanes, trains, chemical plants, nuclear power generation, or any other type of critical equipment or processes, then you must take extra steps to insure that your program works correctly even though you cannot prove that it is perfect.

If your client is not willing to make available the extra time and resources this requires, then I strongly recommend that you either find a way to do what you need to do with the available time and resources or that you decline the contract. In some cases, you may have an *ethical* responsibility to do the work because if you do not do it, the next programmer may be a *real dummy* and just not care about it (or *not* even know enough to care about it).

I try to avoid situations like this, but at some point in your career you will find yourself in such a situation. When it happens, all you can do is try your best to inform your client about what you are doing and why you are doing it; then do it the right way. People whom you do not know (and will probably never know) will appreciate your diligence, even though they may never have the opportunity to tell you that they do. You know about it; so it does *not* really matter if anyone else does.

The fact that Visual Basic has a *few* problems is *not* very important to me when I consider that I can work around them and when I consider that Visual Basic is a wonderful product which saves me much time and makes many more things possible than would be possible otherwise. In fact, I consider Visual Basic to be the most *significant* thing that Microsoft has done since it introduced Windows. I do not make that statement lightly. It may not be obvious to everyone that Visual Basic is this significant, but it is.

Prior to Visual Basic, programming in Windows was an arduous task, not really an activity that a single person could perform; it was simply *overwhelming*. I have known exactly how to do everything that needs to be done in designing and programming a Windows application for several years. For quite a while I have had ideas for applications but could not do anything with my ideas because I knew that there was *not* enough *time* for me to do anything by myself. It was very frustrating and disappointing. Then one day, Microsoft called me to ask if I wanted to evaluate a new product called Visual Basic, *and the world changed.*

It changed because Microsoft had somehow made it possible for me to produce Windows application code at the rate I needed. I do *not* care if strings are a little bit weird or if I cannot put 255 controls on a form without having to be careful about where I *click*. So what! These minor problems are totally *insignificant* (1) when compared to the amount of work I can do and (2) when viewed with respect to the *leap* in productivity that Visual Basic has given me. I can have an idea for a screen and then code and test the screen all in the same day with Visual Basic. I am not too far from being able to design, program, and test a complete Windows application in less than three months. I find that to be absolutely, unequivocally, amazing!

Visual Basic has changed the world of *a cappella* Windows programming forever. *A Cappella* Windows application programming is not trivial, but it is now at least *possible*. The fact that it is *possible* is of such enormous consequence that I think **Visual Basic is the *most* significant event in programming since the introduction of Windows.**

There is a lot of talk about C++ and all of the great things that does, but compared to Visual Basic it is insignificant. I have read several books on C++ but do not understand it (and do not really want to understand it): I am a C++ Luddite (in the sense of being reluctant to adopt a new technology that appears to be of no benefit to me). To me, C++ takes C (which is inherently capable of doing some very *abstruse* things) and moves it into the realm of *abstract* to the *extreme*.

I have enough problems trying to find my *shoes* in the morning. I do not need to fill my brain with thoughts about how I can program with classes that inherit and modify the behavior of structures consisting of function pointer items. C++ is powerful. I will probably take the time to learn how to use it (someday) because enough of my friends tell me that it is a powerful language (and I respect their judgment). But for now, I am more interested in *real power*. The ability to have an idea for a complex screen and program it in a day or so using Visual Basic is *real power*.

If you are new to Windows, it will take you some time to get to the point at which you can do things almost instantly in Visual Basic. You have to learn how Windows works and which objects, events, properties, methods, and techniques to use to do things quickly. Learning that is almost *separate* from learning Visual Basic programming. **Visual Basic makes it possible to do the programming quickly.**

If you are finding it difficult to program in Visual Basic, do not give up. You are on the right path, and all you need to do is keep working on it. There is no easier path. Everything you are learning must be learned, and there is no easier way. You are *not* wasting any of your time. Nothing worth doing is easy. Visual Basic programming is not *always* easy, but it *is* the *easiest* way to program Windows applications. There are some eccentric behaviors in Visual Basic--but it is the *only* game in town. It is truly an *amazing* language. In truth, Visual Basic is a *phenomenon*.

Getting back to the subjects of this chapter, there are quite a few *properties*, but my favorite properties are *Visible, Enabled, Text, Caption, Value, BackColor, ForeColor, Ctl-*

Name, *Index*, *Border*, *TabIndex*, *Style*, and *AutoRedraw*. There are more, but these are the ones I use frequently enough to remember.

There are also quite a few *events* and my favorites are *Click* and *Change*. In fact, I try to *avoid* all of the other events and suggest that you do the same. I am tempted to use the *GotFocus* and the *LostFocus* events because I know how they work in Windows SDK/C programming; but precisely because I know how they *really* work and how truly bizarre coding them is, I do not use them.

In Windows SDK/C programming the real events corresponding to the Visual Basic *GotFocus* and *LostFocus* events are WM_SetFocus and WM_KillFocus, and these two Windows SDK/C messages travel as a pair. Note that I equated the term *messages* with the term *events* and that this is really what happens *internally*.

Windows sends your application messages when something happens (when an event occurs), and these messages are what Windows SDK/C programmers use. *Event* is a higher level, or fancier, term for receiving a message. There is some difference because when you are dealing with things at the message level, you are dealing with *many* messages. There are actually *fewer* events than messages because **an event is really a *set* of messages**. Another way of stating this is to say that **when an event occurs it is accompanied or defined by a *set* of messages**.

Be glad that you do *not* have to start *thinking* about messages. But if you did, and, if you were interested in the messages that accompany the *GotFocus* and *LostFocus* events, then some things occur that are useful to know. The messages are WM_SetFocus and WM_KillFocus--and they travel as a pair. You get at least one pair of them when the

GotFocus event occurs *and* when the *LostFocus* event occurs. (Therein lies the weirdness!) You get *both* messages, regardless, because if one control is getting a WM_SetFocus message, then another control is getting a WM_KillFocus message.

In Windows SDK/C programming, we think in terms of *Focus*. *Focus* is one of the most important concepts in Windows. *Focus* is either (1) where you are or (2) where you are *trying* to go. Since Windows applications tend to let you go wherever you want, it is very important to know where you *are* before you go somewhere else, but you also need to know where you are *going*. It may not be immediately obvious, but a little light should have started blinking when you read my statement that WM_SetFocus and WM_KillFocus messages travel in *pairs*.

If every time you change *Focus* you get a WM_SetFocus and a WM_KillFocus message, and if you decide not to allow the change in *Focus,* then, since *Focus* had already started to change *prior* to your putting it back where it was, you are going to have to *set* the *Focus* explicitly to another place (specifically, back to where it *was*). The fact that you are *setting* the *Focus* in response to the user's trying to *change* the *Focus* seems to introduce another *pair* of WM_SetFocus and WM_KillFocus messages, an occurrence which appears to be (and is) somewhat--if not totally--*recursive*.

There are a few things that you do to avoid the *recursion*, most notably you use a special Windows SDK/C function that solves this problem (in most cases), but it is philosophically and conceptually a weird problem. Visual Basic does not handle GotFocus and LostFocus in exactly the same way that the comparable events are handled by a Windows SDK/C programmer. Therein lies a very subtle problem that may not really be a problem unless you are used to the way *Focus* is handled in Windows SDK/C programming.

In order to avoid some of the weirdness associated with the Windows SDK/C process of recognizing and processing *Focus-related* messages, Visual Basic limits the *scope* of *GotFocus* and *LostFocus* messages in such a way that (for me) these events are basically *useless*. Therefore, I do not use them. In fact, I *avoid* using them--and suggest that you do the same. What I do, instead, is (1) set the focus via the *SetFocus method* and (2) do not allow bad actions to occur.

In Windows SDK/C programming most of what you do is done by calling Windows SDK/C functions. Some of those functions do things like add strings to list boxes, get the contents of edit controls, set and clear certain data items, and so many other kinds of things that you do not want to know about them. In Visual Basic, a major effort was made to make this as *transparent* to you as possible, but some of the Windows SDK/C functions are so commonly used (and so necessary) that they *must* be available in Visual Basic. The Visual Basic designers decided to call them *methods (*probably because that was the only word they could think of that made any sense).

Method is as good a term as any. Because it is the name they gave it, then it *is* its name. Internally, when you use a *method*, Visual Basic is calling one or more Windows SDK/C functions to do something to a control. I suppose that, because Visual Basic uses a particular "method" to do things, the term *method* makes sense. For example, when you want to add an item to a list box you use the *AddItem method* which causes Visual Basic to add the string to the appropriate list box.

When you use a *method* just be aware that it is essentially an internal function or subroutine that consists of one or more Windows SDK/C functions and subroutines that do something useful and intuitively obvious for you. You probably get closest to Windows SDK/C programming when you use Visual Basic methods. Since the Visual Basic *methods* are (to a certain degree) generalizations of techniques that Windows SDK/C programmers use, it would not hurt you to learn Windows SDK/C programming techniques.

Also be aware that, in the effort to make Visual Basic as simple as possible, some Windows SDK/C techniques were *not* included in Visual Basic *methods*, even though they would have been useful. I would like to have a *method* in Visual Basic for emptying a list box. In Windows SDK/C, I can empty a list box with a single function, but in Visual Basic, it appears to take a lot of unnecessary work.

Except for using Windows SDK/C functions in Visual Basic, I have found no other practical way to empty a list box than to get a count of the number of items in the list box and then remove each item via the *RemoveItem* method, as demonstrated in the following code example:

nLBCount = Form1.Listbox.ListCount
If nLBCount > 0 then
**   For I = 1 to nLBCount Step 1**
**   Form1.Listbox.RemoveItem 0**
**   Next I**
End If

There are several things worth noting about this code example, which is also the first code example in this book. The primary thing to note is that if the number of items in the list box is relatively small (i.e., less than 100), then this algorithm is fast. Next, you will note that the first variable,

nLBCount, probably looks a little strange to you, if you are not a Windows SDK/C programmer, because it begins with a lowercase 'n'. Well, this is a Windows SDK/C convention that I use (and modify any time I feel like doing so).

It is called Hungarian notation, and it is a convention in which you preface the names of variables with one or more lowercase characters that tell you the data type of the variable. In this case the lowercase 'n' tells me that the variable is an integer. The more precise rule would be to use a lowercase 'i' but I prefer a lowercase 'n' and use it more frequently. Some of these prefixes are shown in the following table:

Prefix	Definition
b	Boolean
d	double
h	handle
hwnd	handle to a window
l	long
lpsz	long pointer to a string
sz	string
w	word

Why do I do this and why should you do it? Well, the reason is that it makes it very *easy* to determine the *type* of a variable when you have no more information than the *name* of the variable. It also gives anyone else who knows the notation the same information. Also, it does something that is very subtle. It gives you a way of *distinguishing* between local variables and global variables. This second feature is subtle because you have to know and do a few more things for it to work. In effect, you have to make and follow a few more rules.

In Visual Basic, variables have *scope* and their *scope* is related to how *global* or how *local* they are. The most *global* a variable can be is to be globally defined in your applications global definition file. These variables are *really global*. The next level down is to be *global* to a form or to a module. The lowest level is to be *local* to a particular function or subroutine (and this includes event procedures, which you will notice are subroutines).

My general rule is to avoid any redundancy in definitions whenever possible and practical. Since there are three *levels* of *scope* we might as well give them three names: (1) *global* refers to application *scope*, (2) *regional* refers to form scope or module *scope*, and (3) *local* refers to function or subroutine *scope*. This seems logical to me and makes the entire concept of *scope* easier to grasp.

Since variable *scope* is very important, it is something that would be useful to know by inspection. This suggests that it would be nice to be able to determine *scope* when the only information you have about a variable is its *name*. In this regard, I am proposing the following set of rules:

(1) If the *scope* is *global* then append a lowercase 'g' to the Hungarian prefix,

(2a) If the *scope* is *regional* then use the Hungarian prefix,

(2b) [*optional*] - If the *scope* is *regional* then append a lowercase 'f' or 'm' to the Hungarian prefix to indicate whether the variable is *regional* to a *form* or to a *module*, respectively.

(3) If the *scope* is *local* then append the Visual Basic data type character to the end of the variable name and use the Hungarian prefix only if it makes you happy.

For example, szgText is a *global* string variable,

szfText is a *form-regional* string variable, and szText$ is a *local* string variable. Please note that szText$ is *not* equivalent to szText. These are two different variables. If you use the Visual Basic data type character (**$, %, &, #, !, @**) as part of the variable name, then it *must* always be used to identify that particular variable. This is another good reason for using the global, regional, and local naming convention. If you follow this convention, you will not have any problems distinguishing variables.

There is one exception to this; it occurs when you have *not* previously defined a variable at the global or regional level but use that variable in a function or subroutine without appending the Visual Basic data type character. When you do this, the variable will assume the default data type of *single*. It is convenient at times to use this default, but it can cause problems; so I do not recommend it. It does not take much more effort to follow the convention. Also note that by including an **'Def***type***'** statement in your declarations, you can change the default data type (e.g., **'DefInt A-Z'** changes the default data type to *integer)*. You must, however, do this in each form and module to which you want it to apply (e.g., in each form, in each module, *and* in the global module if you want it to apply *everywhere*). I do not generally change defaults (and do not generally use them) and have had no problem with the fact that Visual Basic uses *single* as its default.

You will find that (although it requires some learning and adjustment) the benefits of using this naming convention for Visual Basic variables will prove to be useful. It makes you *think* about the ways in which you use variables and it adds a layer of *consistency* to your code that would probably be absent, otherwise. While it is convenient to invent variable names whenever and however you desire, if you are working on a project with other programmers it will save *everyone* a considerable amount of time and effort when both the *type* and the *scope* of variables can be determined from their names. After a while, it will become intuitive. Your designing and programming will improve as a consequence. It also makes code management and configuration much *easier*. *Hungarian notation* is defined in the Windows SDK/C documentation and in Charles Petzold's classic book on Windows programming, all of which can be ordered directly from Microsoft Press.

Some of you will observe the fact that, in using the Hungarian prefix 'sz' for Visual Basic strings, I am arbitrarily *presuming* that Visual Basic strings are actually C strings because the 'sz' means that the string is NULL terminated (that is generally *not* the case for a Visual Basic string). **However, please be informed that regardless of what you think (or what *anyone* else tells you) Visual Basic strings *are* C strings (for all practical purposes).**

If you do *not* treat Visual Basic strings with the same care and respect that you *must* give C strings, then at some time or another you will find yourself wasting a lot of time trying to solve all kinds of *unusual* problems when you do things that involve strings. Visual Basic strings are C strings *more often* than they are Visual Basic strings. It is *easier* to just *ignore* all of the Visual Basic string *nonsense* and look at it as if you *are* working with C strings because either you *are* or Visual Basic *is*.

I have verified that the following facts are true: (1) when you use the *AddItem* method to put a string into a Visual Basic list box, a Windows SDK/C function is called and (2) the Windows SDK/C function that is called does *not* care *diddly* about Visual Basic strings. To the Windows SDK/C function that loads a string into a list box, the string *is* a C string and follows the rules for C strings precisely.

This also occurs in the other standard controls. That is the way it is, and there are *no exceptions*!

You can do very little in Visual Basic without *indirectly* encountering a Windows SDK/C function that does something with or to a string. When that happens (*even if you do not know about it*), your Visual Basic string is subject to the *same* set of rules that apply to C strings. So, what you need to know about Visual Basic strings is that they are *unusual derivations* of C strings and do *not* follow all of the real rules.

One thing that seems especially *unusual* to me is that Visual Basic occasionally thinks it is *cute* to put a single blank character in front of strings. A friend of mine, who is an expert Basic programmer, told me that this bit of *cuteness* comes from early versions of Basic and is included in Visual Basic for compatibility reasons. Well, *cute* as it may be, it took me about three hours to discover it (and even *more* time find a way to avoid it). I now arbitrarily **LTrim$()** every string, and **LTrim$()** has become my *favorite* string function. Actually, this occurs when you use Str$ to convert a positive number to a string. The space is present because the conversion does not generate a "+" character. However, I still use **LTrim$()** rather regularly.

Another more subtle problem with Visual Basic strings is that the NULL character [or **Chr$(0)**], is a *valid* character in a Visual Basic string and does *not* signify the end of the Visual Basic string (as far as Visual Basic is usually concerned). However, when *anything* occurs that results in a Windows SDK/C function being called and there is a NULL character in your Visual Basic string, then that string ends at the *first* NULL character that the Windows SDK/C function encounters.

I scan my Visual Basic strings for *embedded* NULL characters prior to using *methods*, replace the *embedded* NULL characters with blanks, and then *explicitly* position a NULL character *exactly* where I want the Visual Basic string *really* to end via concatenating a **Chr$(0)**. This is a *lot* of work and requires that you really understand how to manipulate strings in both Visual Basic *and* Windows SDK/C. Needless to say, the **InStr()**, **Chr$()**, **Str$()**, **Mid$()**, **Left$()**, **LTrim$()**, and **RTrim$()** functions will become *very* well known to you when you use *strings* in Visual Basic. It is *not* really that much extra work; so do *not* let this bother you; just be aware of it. Look at the code samples relating to manipulating strings for examples of how and when to do the extra work.

In fairness to the Visual Basic designers, I must say that (1) they really had *no* alternative way to handle strings and (2) the way they did it was the *only* way it could be done *without* adding more *confusion* to the process. It gives me something to write about that is undocumented--so I am grateful for the opportunity.

Sooner or later, you *will* do something that results in an *embedded* NULL or a call to a Windows SDK/C function. From that point forward, you *are* working with C strings. It is *easier* just to do it the *correct* way from the *beginning*. You will find that C strings are really *simple* to use in C and are only a *little* more trouble to use in Visual Basic. In terms of additional work, I equate working with C strings in Visual Basic with having to use a Working Storage Section in COBOL, because there is really no alternative method and it does work. If you know how to touch-type or cut-and-paste, then it is easy medicine to take (and it a guarantees a healthy program).

I suspect that more of the C string manipulation functions and capabilities will creep into Visual Basic as it evolves. Actually, I would like to have an installation option or design mode option to use C strings instead of Visual Basic strings (at some time). I would prefer that Visual Basic start using C strings as its *default,* but I realize that it is not really possible for that to happen (for some time) because it would *confuse* all of the Basic programmers--many of whom have been fighting with NULL characters for a long time and are not nearly as confused as the C programmers who are trying to learn Basic.

However, I also *know* that some Basic programmers are going to be *confused anyway* when they find out that in *some* cases Visual Basic strings are *really* C strings. So I do not know which approach is *ultimately* more *confusing.* Considering that everyone, including me, will have considerable amounts of Visual Basic code by the time the next Visual Basic version is released, I *prefer* the *installation-option* and *application-option* methods for choosing whether to use C strings *all* of the time or only *some* of the time.

Actually, when you consider that a C string does nothing more than begin at a specific address and continue from that address until the first NULL character is encountered, there is *not* a lot of complexity involved (even though it took *me* a long time to understand C strings). A C string is a very simple thing (*provided* the NULL character is where it should be). A C string with a NULL character (which is a redundant statement because by *definition* a C string *is* NULL-terminated) is like your *mind.* A C string without a NULL terminator (which is a paradox) is like your *mind* on *drugs* (and is actually *not* a C string).

In fact, when you somehow create the condition where you have something that begins at a certain address and is supposed to be a C string but is *missing* the NULL terminator, then the effect on both Visual Basic and Windows is equivalent to introducing some *fantasy* into the behavior of your application. I suppose this would *not* be a big problem, except that the your Intel processor chip does not handle *fantasy instructions* very well.

Another thing about the code example that is useful to note is that I *explicitly* included the name of the *form* in the reference to the list box control. Why did I do that? Well, I did not start making every reference to a control be a complete, full reference, because I thought it was too much trouble. I put all of the code for an event in the event procedure, and quickly found myself doing an enormous amount of *repetitive* coding. Then, when I moved the code from the event procedures into modules, I got hundreds and hundreds of messages about the module code *not* knowing which controls I was using. This happened because the module does *not* know to which *form* controls belong and does *not* presume any default.

I strongly suggest that you *explicitly* include the *form* name in any references to anything that has a form name associated with it. This will save you time. There are some instances where you do *not* have to do this. Including the form name does not require much extra work when you pick relatively *short* form names. It will make your programming *much* easier.

I always explicitly include the loop variable in the *Next* statement that terminates the loop. I think this makes the code easier to read and gives a good clue as to which *Next* statement goes with a particular *For* statement. When I start a *For loop*, a *Select Case group*, or a *If group*, I always type the appropriate end statement immediately so I do *not* forget it. This is somewhat less important with *For loops* and *Select*

Case groups than with *If groups*, but it will save you some time trying to debug unusual problems caused by having a misplaced *Next*, *End Select*, or *End If* statement.

The final thing to note in the code sample is that the index value is 0 (i.e., *zero*) for the item being *removed* from the list box. This makes sense, if you *think* about it, because there is *always* going to be an item with index value of *zero*, as long as there is at least *one* item in the list box. It is a fairly common mistake to code this routine so that it removes the item identified by the loop index rather than item *zero*. This will work for the first half of the loop but will cause an error when more than half of the items that were originally in the list box have been removed. This is because the loop index is increasing while the number of items in the list box is decreasing as a result of items being removed.

This concludes the chapter on Events, Properties, and Methods (and whatever else came to mind). At this point, there is still *more* to be said about general application *design* and how to program Visual Basic applications.

Forms, Modules, and Controls

So far we have discussed nearly all of the components that go into building an application with Visual Basic, but more needs to be said about the proper use of forms, modules, and controls with respect to design and programming. If you are reading this book, your background in programming will fall into one of two major categories: (1) Windows SDK/C experience or (2) *no* Windows SDK/C experience. There are other categories, but they will generally relate to one of the two major categories.

Just because you do not have Windows SDK/C experience does not mean that you are automatically excluded from that category. If you have any kind of *transaction* processing experience, you already know how Windows works--even though you may not be aware that you do. As I stated earlier, Windows is a *transaction* processing system. If you understand how *transaction* processing works, you can design a Windows application without knowing anything about Windows SDK/C programming--provided you know that *objects* are *transactions*.

One of my first Windows contracts involved designing a generic way to code Windows applications. When I first began on the project, I did not know very much about Windows SDK/C programming. However, I was able to explain to the more experienced Windows SDK/C programmers some things that proved to be useful. How I was able to explain complex Windows design techniques to programmers who also were aware that I did not know how to use the Dialog Editor was a constant source of bewilderment for quite a few of my colleagues.

If you have *transaction* processing experience, then you are already an advanced Windows designer and programmer. The only thing missing is knowing specifically how to program a Windows application--and that is where Visual Basic makes a difference. It will not hurt you to learn Windows SDK/C programming. However, since it is more difficult to learn than Visual Basic, I recommend that you learn Windows SDK/C programming after you have learned Visual Basic programming. For now, Visual Basic is easy to learn, and it is a complete but simple language. If you need more complex capabilities, they are available (or soon will be) in the form of tool kits and Dynamic Link Libraries (DLL).

One thing which is very unique about PC programming in general (and Windows programming specifically) is that it is something you teach yourself. The best way to learn about Windows programming is to get the software you need to do Windows programming, start doing it, and read every book you can find about programming.

Most of the programmers I know have more books on programming than they can count or identify. I have been buying programming books at the rate of approximately 10 to 20 per month for the past three years and see no end to it. The fact that I have at least looked at all of these books means I have a good understanding of the current state of programming and I can find out how to do nearly anything I need to do without having to go to a library or bookstore (because I have my own library).

Things are changing so quickly in Windows programming that it is literally impossible to keep up with it all. However, you must do everything you can at least to try to keep current. I also collect Windows applications and actually spend more on applications than on books.

Providing valuable information about how to do things in Windows, books and applications are excellent sources for ideas. If you are going to develop Windows applications seriously, you need to understand the Windows market. The best way to do this is to buy nearly everything that runs in Windows (within reason).

The more software and hardware you have, the more you can do (and the more quickly you can do it). Some opportunities are explicitly linked to what you have (and what you can do with it) rather than to what you can do with what you do *not* have. Some people will say they cannot afford an HP LaserJet III, but I think that not having a laser printer costs you more in the long run than it saves you in the short term. If you are going to develop Windows applications, you need the fastest PC you can get (a 486 33-MHz PC is *slow*), and you need books, software, and a quiet place to work.

You need to contact Microsoft and join their Consultant Relations Program. You need to read the major Windows magazines (**BasicPro**, **Microsoft Systems Journal**, **Windows Magazine**, and **Windows Tech Journal**) and the major industry magazines (**InfoWorld**, **PC Magazine**, and **PC Week**). There are other good magazines, but these are the ones I find most useful regarding Windows.

Think about what you are doing and what Windows users want to do. I think the current trend in new Windows applications is directed at small but complete applications that do something useful but not particularly awesome. I call these types of applications *professional toys*. There is a big market for them for two reasons: (1) they are inexpensive and (2) they are entertaining and useful. I have been trying to think of a major Windows application for several years and have not thought of a practical one yet. But I have many ideas for *professional toys* (or *applets* as some people call them); so that is what I am concentrating on now.

Designing a Windows application that does nearly anything useful and somewhat complex will, at some point, become a complex task. Finding ways to simplify anything involved in a complex task is both useful and invaluable--especially if you are doing everything by yourself, which is really the only way to guarantee that it gets done. Diagramming and flowcharting is often helpful in the design process.

There are several very good Windows diagramming and flowcharting tools: **ABC Flowcharter** (Roykore, Inc.), **RFFlow Professional Flowcharting Version 2** (RFF ELECTRONICS), and **MetaDesign** (Meta Software Corporation). **System Architect** (Popkin Software and Systems, Inc.) is a CASE tool that can also be used for diagramming. These types of products are necessary for large projects but also prove helpful on small projects. It is so easy to develop complex applications in Visual Basic that anything helpful to you in maintaining a map of your application is valuable.

When you decide to start working on your new Windows application (the one you are developing in Visual Basic) you have to do some design work; one of the best ways to design an application is to begin with a blank form and then look at it and ask yourself, "What is missing?" This is the *fill-in the blanks* method of application design. It works very well for me because I usually have nearly no idea of what I am going to do even when I start doing it. Designing a Windows application is a creative process and is therefore something that you can do any way you please. The important thing is to begin. **The best place to begin is at the beginning.**

Now that you have your first form in front of you, and since it has nothing on it, you need to begin putting objects on the form. The objects you choose will be determined by what you want the form to do for you. In general, you have several types of available objects. If you have purchased additional tool kits, you have even more available objects with which to work. We will concentrate on the objects that come with Visual Basic because they are the basics and you can get quite a bit with just the basics.

Because you are beginning to design your application, it makes sense not to create any restrictions on what you can do. You should think in terms of *generic forms*. If you design *generic forms*, you can use them independently of any particular application you may create (and you will not be wasting any of your time). I generally approach designing an application from the viewpoint of designing *generic forms* and then combining them later when I start to *see* what I am doing. As I stated earlier, it really does not matter where nor how you begin, just that you begin and do not waste time.

So what objects are available? Well, you have **labels, text boxes, frame boxes, radio buttons, check boxes, push buttons, horizontal scroll bars, vertical scroll bars, timers, picture boxes,** and **combo boxes** (to name a few). You can also have *hybrid objects* that are nothing more than combinations of the *basic objects* previously identified. The primary difference between a *hybrid object* and a *basic object* is that a *hybrid object* requires *tight coupling* whereas **a *basic object* is already *tightly coupled* to itself**.

As previously defined, *coupling* refers to the way in which *objects* (i.e., forms, frames, and controls) are *connected*. There are two kinds of *coupling*: (1) *loose* and (2) *tight*. *Loose coupling* occurs when *objects* are independent. *Tight coupling* occurs when *objects* are *dependent*. *Hybrid objects* will *always* require some *tight coupling* because the *basic objects* that are used to *construct* the *hybrid objects* must work dependently--*not* independently. However, *hybrid objects* can be *loosely coupled* to other *objects*. The only way to make a *hybrid object* truly independent is to put it in a *separate* form. In this regard, **true independence is only possible at the form level** (and then *only* if some *generic* coding techniques are used).

An example of a *hybrid object* is something I call a **RowData** object. It consists of several labels arranged in rows, with a vertical scroll bar to the right of the rows, and a horizontal scroll bar below the rows. Its purpose is to be a *virtual list box* that recognizes the *Click* and *DoubleClick* events (something basic list boxes and combo boxes do *not* do very well). To make the **RowData** object portable, I build it on top of a frame box and thereby *partially encapsulate the visual objects*. I make it as *generic* as possible by limiting the lines of code in the event procedures for its components to an absolute minimum and by putting the main code into a module. There is are several examples of this *hybrid object* in the code samples.

So we now have two types of things to put onto the form: (1) *basic objects* and (2) *hybrid objects*. We can invent *hybrid objects* whenever the need arises if it saves us time (or seems like a fun thing to do). Constructing *hybrid objects* requires a general understanding of the *basic objects*, and the best ways to get it are to read some books on Windows programming and to read the Visual Basic manuals.

I could write an entire book on nothing more than *basic objects*, but you will have to learn about the *basic objects* yourself. This book is more philosophical (or conceptual) in nature and is intended to be a enhancement to the *already* available Visual Basic documentation rather than a replacement for it.

The Visual Basic manuals are *exceptionally* good sources of information. Read *every* word in them, and memorize all of the information contained in them. When the entire documentation for a language as powerful as Visual Basic consists of two half-inch manuals, then you know that somebody did a good job of presenting the material. The classic C manual is about half an inch thick, and it does an excellent job, too.

What I am trying to do in this chapter is convey the concept of *form design*. The process is basically one of looking at a blank form, *seeing* in your mind what the form needs to be, and then making it be what you *see*. In a basic sense, you really have four things with which to work (because I am excluding pictures): (1) *text boxes*, (2) *labels*, (3) *list boxes and combo boxes*, and (4) *buttons*.

Scroll bars are somewhat advanced and really belong to the set of objects you will need when you build hybrid controls. List boxes and combo boxes are really *all* list boxes (in various permutations), and their purpose is to maintain lists. In this regard, lists are one of the building blocks of forms. If you need to conserve space, use a drop down list box. To add items to list boxes via data entry, use a combo box. To present read-only lists, use a list box or a drop down list box.

Use buttons (1) for selecting one or more choices from a group of choices and (2) for causing something to happen. You can also use list boxes for causing something to happen when there are many *choices* of what should happen. Use text boxes to get data from the user. Use labels to identify objects on the form and to display read-only data to the user.

If you have Excel or Word For Windows, look at them and pay particular attention to the basic forms they use. Both of these applications have a tool bar, a status bar, a menu bar, and a work area. You can design a similar form in Visual Basic. It would be useful for you to think about how you would do it. Since I am using Word For Windows (and can see it now), I will describe how to design the Word For Windows form that I am now using.

Before I begin, though, let me say a few words about what I am doing. One of the best ways to learn is by example. I have already told you that, in my opinion, Microsoft products certainly set a standard for *excellence*. Anytime I am in doubt regarding the proper way to do something in Windows, I look to either Excel or Word For Windows for guidance. In using the general format of Word For Windows in this example, I am showing you how to approximate *some* of the *look* of an excellent Windows application.

I am doing this purely for educational purposes. My using Word For Windows as a teaching example in a book on Visual Basic is not intended to infringe on Microsoft's copyrights and trademarks. In actual practice, it would be extremely difficult (if not impossible) to duplicate Word For Windows exactly if your primary development language was Visual Basic. With some carefully selected add-on tool kits, you could do a good job insofar as *look* was concerned, but behavior is a different story. At some point, you would have to build one or more Windows SDK/C DLLs to handle the intricate behavior. With all of this in mind, let us continue studying Word For Windows.

The title of a form is a *property* in Visual Basic, and all you have to do to use it is give it a text string as a value.

If it needs to change (or if you want to change it) then just give it a new value. The menu bar is a typical Windows menu bar and is built in Visual Basic with the Menu Design Window (a somewhat sophisticated menu bar *generator* that is very easy to use). The next bar is a tool bar and consists of two labels, two combo boxes and nine push buttons. Nothing particularly amazing in terms of form design, but quite amazing in terms of usefulness. The next bar is another tool bar and consists of one label, one combo box, and 14 push buttons. Again, nothing too complicated.

Next is a 3-D ruler and typewriter tab/margin *metaphor*. It can be duplicated with a complex set of labels. But that is not practical in Visual Basic due to the 255 controls per form limit. If you want to have a 3-D ruler and a typewriter tab/margin *metaphor*, then you can do some Windows SDK/C programming or use an add-on tool kit. You can also think of another *metaphor* that is more appropriate to the capabilities of Visual Basic.

The next thing down is the work area. It is very complicated; so we will skip it for now (even though it looks as if it could be a multiline text box). We could use a multiline text box, but multiline text boxes have too many limitations for them to be useful as word processors. This is one of those times when you either have to invent a new metaphor or learn Windows SDK/C programming.

However, we have the **RowData** *hybrid object* and it might do what we want to do (but it would need to be modified to do everything we want to do). The **RowData** *hybrid object* is good for displaying data but cannot be directly used for data input because *labels* cannot be used for input. However, it seems like there should be a way to work around that limitation; so I am giving the matter some thought.

To the right, there is a vertical scroll bar with three picture boxes. At the bottom of the screen is a horizontal scroll bar, and below it is a status bar which consists of seven labels and some 3-D shading. You can easily duplicate the status bar with a product called **ButtonTool** (OutRider Systems). It cannot be easily built with Visual Basic objects because it would take too many controls (this form is already approaching the limits of being *too* complicated).

However, there is a way to work around the problem of having too many controls on a single form. There is a better way to design this form than the way we are doing it now. Instead of using a single form, we can use *several* forms. We can use *several* forms to build the Word For Windows interface. Because there are some *mechanical* problems with doing what we would like to do, we will take a big clue from Visual Basic, itself, regarding how to proceed. The problem with using several forms is mostly one of what happens when any *one* of the forms gets *Focus*.

If a form is *partially* on top of (or beneath) another form and it gets *Focus,* then it gets moved to the top. That would change the appearance of our application when we use several forms and is, therefore, a problem. It is most likely to be a problem for the form containing the menu bar and the toolbars. However, we can work around the problem by combining the menu bar and the tool bars into one form, by making the work area become a separate form, and by making the status bars become another form. This separates the forms nicely and also increases the number of controls with which we can work but still be within the practical limit of the number of allowable controls on any single form. In effect that is the approach Visual Basic takes in its presentation, and it is a good example to follow.

In fact, one of the *new* things about Visual Basic is that it is *not* a full screen application unless you want it to be. The basic interface for Visual Basic is a bar (an *application bar*) across the top of the screen. All of the other components are *loosely coupled* forms that can be made visible or hidden on demand. I think that this was done with some *intent* and that possibly part of Visual Basic was written in Visual Basic (or could have been if it was not). Notwithstanding that possibility, I strongly suspect that Visual Basic was written in Windows SDK/C and would be very surprised if it was not. However, we are working in Visual Basic; so we can adjust our design to work within the capabilities of Visual Basic, and that is what we will do.

Thus in copying the design for Word For Windows with Visual Basic forms and objects, we now have several forms, and there are several objects on each of the forms. The first thing to note at this point is that we have designed the forms, we have placed the appropriate objects on them, and everything looks as it should, but we have done absolutely *no* programming. The objects are there because (1) we know we *need* to provide a way to perform actions and (2) the purpose of the objects is to give the user a way to *request* that specific actions be performed at appropriate times. This is both simple *and* complex, but the level of complexity can only be *understated* at this point in the design process.

We do know that all we are going to be concerned with in terms of the push buttons is the *Click* event because that is all the user can do with our push buttons. In fact, it is *all* you can do with a push button (and that is the reason I like push buttons so much). Push buttons are *simple*, but they can be used to trigger complex processes. We do not care about any other events for the push buttons at this time. The labels are just labels, and the most we will want to do with them is change their captions (when it is convenient and necessary). The combo boxes will need some programming, depending primarily on whether the user selects existing items or uses them as data entry devices for creating new items. Again, just a few events are needed.

Therefore, I am proposing to you that we can *clone* the majority of the Word For Windows application interface in Visual Basic with no more than a *few* events and no more than a *few* objects, although some of the objects will really need to be *hybrid objects* that we create using *basic objects*. I think this is a very powerful capability that Visual Basic is making possible. Just the fact that we can design the forms, add objects to them, and run the application without doing *any* coding is *remarkable* (even though the application will not do very much without any coding). At least everything will work in terms of push buttons going up and down, adding items to the combo boxes, using the scroll bars, and displaying information in the labels.

The next step in the process is to identify where we need to add code to make our *cloned* Word For Windows really do something. At this point we are moving into the detailed design and programming phase of a Visual Basic application; that means we need to understand exactly what is going to happen in the application and how to make it happen easily. In effect we are going to *loosely couple* the *forms* and *objects*. We may need to *tightly couple* a few *controls,* but remember that we want to avoid *tight coupling*, whenever possible.

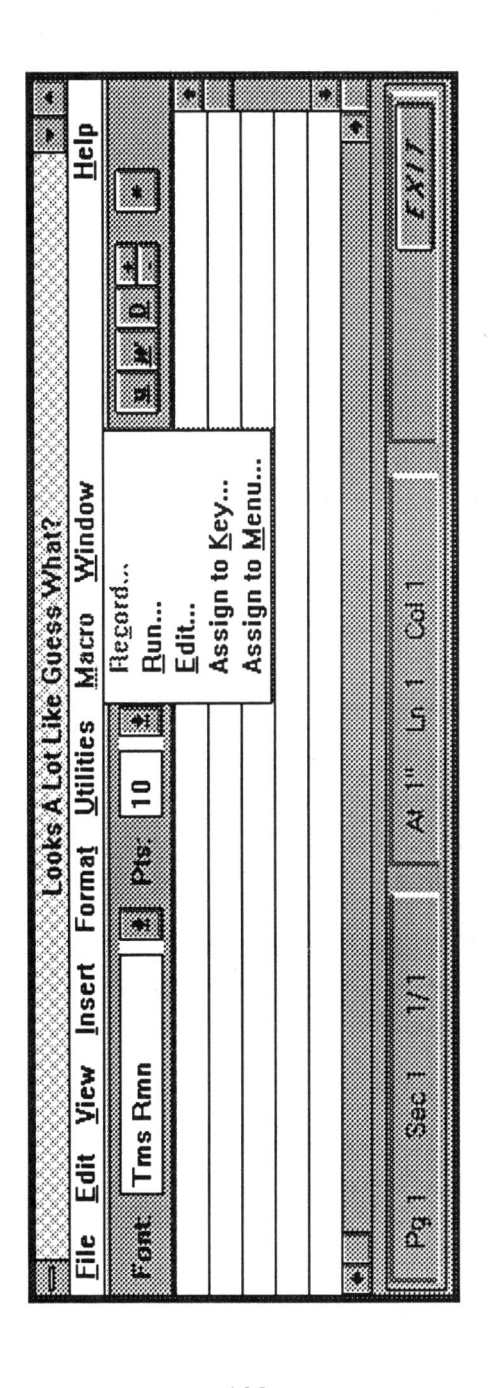

Looks A Lot Like Guess What?

| File | Edit | View | Insert | Format | Utilities | Macro | Window | Help |

Font: Tms Rmn   Pts: 10

Record...
Run...
Edit...
Assign to Key...
Assign to Menu...

EXIT

Pg 1   Sec 1   1/1   At 1" Ln 1 Col 1

It would not hurt you to go through the actual process of cloning Word For Windows in terms of constructing forms and putting objects on them. When you become proficient in adding objects to forms, then it should take you no more than a few hours to construct a set of forms that *looks* a lot like Word For Windows.

In fact, I think that you should do it; so I will make a copy of the screen I *cloned*, identify each part of it, and show you how to *clone* it visually. Making the *clone* do *real* work is a big project; so we will *not* do that in this book. I am calling my *clone* of Word For Windows the **Looks A Lot Like Guess What?** application and am including it in the sample code. Constructing the forms is quick, but building the menu bar is a slow process. You can use the **Looks A Lot Like Guess What?** forms as a starting place for building your application (it is much easier to modify code, or *clone* it, than to begin with *nothing*).

We will examine some code samples which do some of the major functions a real Word For Windows *clone* needs to do so you can get an idea of how easy it is to generate working code in Visual Basic. For now, just note that I think you should be able *visually* to prototype the basic Word For Windows screen in Visual Basic in a few hours. If you limited the capabilities of a working model to a complete, but simple, subset of the *real* Word For Windows, then you could probably complete it in a few months by yourself (maybe even quicker).

A good way to learn how to design applications in Visual Basic is to begin by *cloning* other applications. Any time the application you are *cloning* does something very complex, then just skip that part. Stick to the simple things, but get complex when you are building *your* application. For example, a word processor could just have one font and one point size and still be useful. You can do whatever you want to do to make things simple when you are beginning your application. If it is really important to add complex features, then add them (but realize that it will take *more* time).

I would not spend any time inventing a Windows spreadsheet, page layout program, word processor, shell, icon editor, drawing program, graphics program, or anything else for which there are already a large number of existing choices. Spend your time inventing something that does *not* exist (there is considerably *less* competition). It is easier to duplicate or *clone* something than to create something totally new. That is the reason most software developers *clone* rather than invent. *Cloning* is a useful way to learn how to use Visual Basic, but is generally a waste of time unless you are making a significant improvement in the application you are *cloning*.

A few comments about *cloning* will prove to be useful at this point. When I use the term *cloning*, I am referring to the technique of using code that you have already written. This can also include code that someone else has written but which you have purchased. *Cloning* can also be copying. There are many, many programming books and a great majority of them include code examples. Most of these books have companion diskettes. In general, the authors of these books provide code examples *intentionally* and *want* you to *use* them in your applications. This is one of the reasons programmers buy books. I *want* you to *use* the code examples in this book in your application if it will help you (and some of the code examples *will* help you).

If we look at spreadsheet applications, it becomes somewhat *obvious* that someone must have actually invented the first one, but who that person was is not easy to determine. It was definitely not Lotus, Microsoft, Apple,

Borland, Computer Associates, IBM, or any other company that comes to mind. I have seen some reference to VisiCalc being the first spreadsheet but do not know if it was. It is entirely possible that someone had a spreadsheet on a mainframe back in the 1950s. In all likelihood, the spreadsheet was probably invented by an industrious Italian in the Fourteenth Century--or by a Chinese clerk in 2,000 B.C. (The Chinese invented spaghetti--so why not give them credit for spreadsheets?)

In any event, it does not really matter *who* invented the spreadsheet, insofar as Windows applications are concerned. If you want to design a new spreadsheet, then do it. If you do, I would suggest that you get a copies of *all* Windows spreadsheets and study them. Most importantly, I suggest that you make your new Windows spreadsheet *different* from all the other Windows spreadsheets. Improve them, but feel free to *clone* at will (within legal bounds). When you do *clone* something, make it different and better.

Do *not* copy exactly. You will be wasting your time if you do. Actually, I do *not* really suggest that you should waste *any* time designing another Windows spreadsheet. (Excel is nearly *perfect*; so why try to top it?). Spend your time doing something useful. Invent something I do not have, something I do not know about, but something I really need. Invent a new Windows application so useful it makes me much more productive (and happier).

There are literally thousands (if not millions) of these Windows applications. The interesting thing about them is that only *you* (and a few other like-minded individuals) know about *one* of them. Your Windows application will probably never come to market *unless* you design and program it. This is the way new ideas work. Visual Basic makes it possible for you to design and program a Windows application *a cappella*.

I need to say a few words about *modules* since they are one of the subjects of this chapter. I am only introducing *modules* at this point and will do most of the detailed *module* discussion in the code samples because it will make more sense when tied to code than as a philosophical discussion.

The main purpose of *modules* in Visual Basic is one of a *repository* for code. I have already told you that you should *not* put very much code in event procedures. However, since you will have to have a lot of code if your application is going to do anything significant, the only remaining place to put your code is in modules, and that is *why* you use them. **The *key* to *module* code is to make it *generic*.** This means that module code is *more* like traditional code, except that it will often contain references to objects (but *not* always).

If you are doing things with files, tables, and lists, then you can have functions and subroutines that have nothing to do with objects but, instead, perform operations *only* on data structures. Most of these types of functions and subroutines should already be familiar to you, and they are no different in Visual Basic than in any other language. In terms of *style*, I follow a few conventions regarding *forms* and *modules* and suggest that you do the same.

For each *form*, I have a *module* with the same name. For example, if I have a *form* called FORM1.FRM, then I have a *module* called FORM1.BAS. The form code (which is arbitrarily limited to event procedures) goes in the *form* (and this is the only place it can go). The other code goes in the corresponding *module*. The *non-object-related* functions and subroutines can go in the associated module (if that makes sense) but can go in another module if they are more *application generic* than *form generic*. The most important thing to know about *module* coding is how to *choose* the proper *scope* for variables.

A *generic form,* which you should know by now is a form that is *not* particularly *tightly coupled* to any other form (and therefore operates as an independent entity), will require at least one global variable that will be used to give it whatever information it needs to make itself *specific*. Other variables should primarily be *regional* and should be placed in the corresponding module. Local variables go in the functions and subroutines that use them. Remember that code is always available and does *not* cost much in terms of system resources. Windows can usually discard and load code almost anytime it wants to do so.

Variables are subject to some *constraints*, but the major consideration for *affect* on system resources is the forms themselves, specifically, the visual component of the forms. You do *not* want to have many *hidden* forms and probably should have *none*. Remember that if a form does *not* need to be visible, then *unload* it. You will need to do some additional coding (and will need to use more *global* and *regional* variables to make this work), but the *benefit* of doing this is an application that runs *efficiently* in Windows. But note that I am not necessarily saying that the application will be fast on anything *less* than a 386 33-MHz machine.

One of the prices you pay for power in Visual Basic is application *speed*. The more bells and whistles you add to your Visual Basic applications, the slower they will run. This does not mean that Visual Basic produces slow applications, but that the power of Visual Basic can lead you to design forms that are infinitely *more* complex than they *need* to be. Very complex forms in Visual Basic will be slower than similar forms in Windows SDK/C. You need to pay special attention to keeping things *simple* but *complete*.

In writing this book, I am not following very many traditional rules and am more interested in describing a *real* way to *use* Visual Basic to build Windows applications than in providing an introduction to Visual Basic or *cloning* the documentation that comes with Visual Basic. If you can program and are willing to spend a weekend with Visual Basic, you should be able to begin doing *real* work by Monday morning.

At this point in the book, a few things should be clear to you:
(1) Forms should be *generic*.
(2) There are not many controls from which to choose.
(3) You can invent *hybrid controls*.
(4) You can use frame boxes to group--or *encapsulate*-- the visual components of controls.
(5) A screen can be *composed* of several forms.
(6) You do *not* need at least 90 percent of the events that forms and controls recognize.
(7) You should *never* put *non*-event code in a form.
(8) You should follow my convention for naming variables with respect to *global*, *regional*, and *local* usage.
(9) You should *avoid* tight coupling--unless it is necessary.
(10) Loose coupling is *useful*, does not require much extra effort, and is the *key* to connecting *generic forms*.
(11) Form and control properties are useful for changing the *runtime* appearance and behavior of your application.
(12) Every *form* should have a corresponding *module*.

(13) Visual Basic strings are weird--but not so weird that you cannot use them.
(14) It would be nice if code could be *encapsulated* within frame boxes.
(15) Event procedures should be fewer than 20 lines--in *nearly* all cases.
(16) You can have *invisible* controls.
(17) You MUST *unload* forms which are *not* visible.
(18) You must *not* have a large number of visible forms.
(19) You *cannot* have a large number of controls on a single form without confusing Visual Basic.
(20) *Cloning* is an acceptable--and useful--programming technique.
(21) Professional toys--or *applets*--are easy to create and (probably) to sell.
(22) Nothing is really *easy*.
(23) Nothing is really *difficult*.
(24) You will eventually create an application with so many forms that it will have to be *split* into separate applications controlled by another application which is nothing more than a *menu*.

A few of these things are *obvious* (I hope), but the majority of them are *not* very obvious unless you have spent a lot of time designing and programming with Visual Basic *and* Windows SDK/C. To date, I have seen *nothing* in print that gives any *real guidelines* for when to use *modules* in Visual Basic. I think it is because few people have really written any big or complex Visual Basic applications. I have and can tell you from experience that you had better learn the *difference* between *event* procedures and *non-event* procedures (and when to use each type).

It is intuitively easy to put code in forms, but it is not a good thing to do if you are really doing *serious* Visual Basic programming. I was not born knowing this and, consequently, had to learn it the hard way. After discovering how much work is required to take code out of a form (where it did not really belong) and put it into a module (where it really did belong), I quickly learned the *purpose* of modules. In the process, I also discovered that the Visual Basic designers have created something that is much more than they imagined. Visual Basic has incredible *depth*.

Modules have a special capability that I recently discovered through doing some experimentation as a result of some conversations in the MSBASIC Forum in CompuServe about limitations on the number of lines of constant definitions, variable definitions, and DLL/VBX declarations that would fit into the Global module. A friend asked me to help him find a way to get all of the Windows API declarations and definitions into the Global module. Having had no particular need to do this, and presuming that it was possible, I approached the problem from the perspective of it being a matter of finding a text editor capable of copying and inserting large amounts of text rather than from the perspective of there being any limitation to the size of the Global module.

As it developed, there were some problems with doing the actual text copying and inserting, but using **Brief** (**Solutions**ystems) quickly solved them. However, after inserting the entire Windows API declarations and definitions into the Global module and trying to use it in a project, the real problem appeared: the Global module was too big and Visual Basic was unable to load anything else (it did load the Global module, however). This came as a small shock and I proceeded to investigate both the cause of the problem and its solution (knowing that there *must* be a solution).

Until now, my understanding of DLL/VBX declarations included the belief that they should always go in the Global module. Having discovered that only a limited number of such declarations would actually fit into the Global module, and not finding much additional help in the Visual Basic documentation, I got involved in a series of discussions in the MSBASIC Forum (Visual Basic Section) about the problem. Several of the experts suggested that DLL/VBX declarations could go into regular modules (i.e., the modules other than the single Global module) and that the functions and subroutines in each module would have access to the DLL/VBX declarations in their respective modules. In addition, all forms would have access to the DLL/VBX declarations in all modules. However, there was some uncertainty regarding whether the functions and subroutines in one module would know about DLL/VBX declarations made in another module and this led me to perform some experiments.

Programming experiments are interesting to perform and are an excellent way to determine hidden rules. Having done system software testing and installation many years ago, I had no problem devising a simple set of experiments that would resolve the questions I had about non-global modules, forms, and DLL/VBX declaration scope. The important result of my experiments was the discovery that a DLL/VBX function or subroutine is available for use everywhere provided it is declared in some module (global or otherwise). This appears to be a minor violation of the scope of non-global modules, but is nonetheless very convenient.

The ability of a function contained in one module to call a DLL/VBX function that is declared *not* in the same module but in a *different* module has started me on a new line of thought regarding the ideal programming structure for a large application. I did another quick experiment and verified my suspicion that a function contained in one module could call another function contained in a *different* module. This means that the *boundaries* between modules are *transparent* when it comes to functions and subroutines. I already knew that forms had access to all functions and subroutines contained in all modules, but was somewhat surprised to discover that this is also true of modules. When you include the form name in references to the event procedures contained in forms, then modules also have access them.

The net result of this is that with proper declaration and use of complete name referencing, you can call any module function, any module subroutine, and any form event (Note: event procedures are always *subroutines*.) from anywhere--forms and modules--in Visual Basic, with the two exceptions that (1) a module *cannot* call a DLL/VBX function or subroutine that is declared only in a *form*, and (2) functions and non-event subroutines contained in a form can only be accessed *within* their form [i.e., (2a) a module cannot access a function or non-event subroutine contained in a form and (2b) a form cannot access a function or non-event subroutine contained in another form]. This means that it is even more important to pay attention to *variable scope*. It also means that code structuring in Visual Basic is very flexible, provided you are careful with the *visibility* of variables. I still favor the practice of having a *specific* module associated with each form, but am pleased to have discovered that you can also have *general* purpose modules that contain functions and subroutines that are intended for use by all forms and modules. This is a clear structure for your Visual Basic application code. I consider it to be an impressive example of the *depth*, subtle *capabilities*, and *power* built into Visual Basic by its designers and programmers.

In fact, the *depth*, subtle *capabilities*, and *power* of Visual Basic are still being discovered. I continue to learn new ways in which to combine forms and controls (and expect to go on doing so). The ability to do things *quickly* in Visual Basic provides the opportunity for you to invent new techniques *nearly* as quickly as you can think. This makes it possible to do things with Windows *objects* that were always possible but *never* practical and were therefore *not* even considered.

My current fascination in Windows design is a group of high-level objects I call *symbolic calculators*. The now common Windows *tool bar* is an example of a *symbolic calculator*. I am working on a fairly complex *symbolic calculator* that does mathematics. I am including part of it in this book as one of the code samples. I see no end to the usefulness of *symbolic calculators* in Windows applications. I think this is something worth investigating for two reasons: (1) it is *not* very difficult to use a push button when you understand what it does and (2) if the push button does something *useful* for you, then what it does will probably make *sense* to you.

I have absolutely no *conceptual* difficulty in understanding what the Bold push button in Word For Windows does. I find it both convenient and easy to use. It took a minute or so to learn how to use it, but it was *not* a difficult process (and it certainly makes using a word processor much easier). In truth, all of the push buttons on the Word For Windows toolbars are easy to use and *become* intuitive (even if their purpose is not so obvious at the beginning).

This relates, in part, to one general principle of Windows which is that at some point you must learn how to use a *sophisticated* Windows application. Once you learn it, you have learned the general behavior of nearly *all* Windows applications. As a result of this, I do *not* concern myself with the question of whether a typical Windows application user will understand any particular interface. If you understand one Windows application interface, you understand them all because they all have the same *interface*.

I think I am beginning to experience some of the frustration that the people doing Research and Development at Microsoft must feel. There are so many possibilities for doing more and more complex--but simple--things in Windows than are quickly possible. However, by putting on the *thinking hat*, there are always ways to make *leaps* in technology. I expect this to happen in the next few years.

I can imagine a scenario in which Excel has an *embedded* expert system that enables it to take a set of data and automatically run a standard set of statistical operations and reports. I can imagine that I can cause this to happen by doing nothing more than supplying a data set. At the same time, via Object Linking and Embedding (OLE), Word For Windows will prepare a set of documents, with supporting graphs, and all of this will happen almost instantly and without any *thought* on my part.

I can also imagine another set of applications that will make it easy for me to ask, "What if..." questions about the data. But I know *none* of this will be possible without a considerably higher level set of programming tools for Windows. The nearest thing to it at the present time is Visual Basic. But while Visual Basic is *conceptually* in the right area, it is not anywhere near it in terms of high-level programming.

For example, DDE and OLE are really cool, but no single person can do anything with them because they are so complex to the extreme. You have to have a staff of programmers and each of those programmers has to be expert in Windows SDK/C programming to be useful. Even then, the scope of their tasks is such that at least one of them has to be a genius to provide any *practical* direction for the others. I think what is missing here is something I discovered in **Mapper**, an early 4GL language developed by Unisys

Mapper is a very simple language (much in the way that Visual Basic is a very simple language). Mapper and Visual Basic are similar in another aspect: I know how to use both of them at the expert level. The key to Mapper is that it produces a *result* (a term that I have used frequently in this book). The *result* is what you have at any particular point in time when you work in Mapper.

Always having a *result* is not very monumental except that Mapper is designed in such a way that it is a language whose *purpose* is to modify one or more *results*. Again, nothing major about that, except that once you learn the concept and *change* your way of *thinking* about the way you program then you realize it is perfectly acceptable for the *result* to be in an undesirable form at various steps in the program. In fact, the *purpose* of a Mapper program is to take an undesirable *result* and make it desirable. Conceptually, Mapper programming is like successive filtering or refining. You begin with a crude *result* and transform it into a useful *result*. It is very much like the process used for making plastic out of oil.

The analogy of Windows programming being like making plastic is useful to explore because it makes a few things clearer. There are a number of major steps in the production of plastic from crude oil, but some of them are of absolutely no philosophical nor practical interest to the company making consumer plastic products. That is important to us because we are interested in building Windows applications, not in running an oil refinery. I equate the internals of DDE and OLE to the *internals* of an oil refinery. Someone needs to develop the process, but I do not want to have to know about it in order to use it.

I want to add an *intelligent* control to my Visual Basic application, and I want it to be born knowing *everything* about DDE and OLE so that I do not have to hurt my head *thinking* about it. That is currently something missing in DDE and OLE, even though Visual Basic does have some very powerful DDE capabilities (and will soon have some very powerful OLE capabilities). The reason for its practical absence is not that it is particularly difficult but rather that nobody has grasped the *concept* of using *results*--although some progress in that area is being made.

In effect, what I am suggesting is that there needs to be a complete, but *generic*, definition of what constitutes a *result* in a Windows application. For some types of things there are good and mostly complete definitions for results in Windows. A good example of this is a Device Independent Bitmap (DIB). Nearly everything you would ever want to know about a bitmap is included in the DIB specification and in the actual DIB file. A DIB file is a complete *result* and as such is something anyone can use in a program--provided the person knows the DIB rules.

Another good example of a completely defined *result* is a Tagged Image Format File (TIFF). It also includes nearly everything you would ever want to know about a bitmap in its specification and in the actual TIFF file. A TIFF file is also a complete *result* and as such is something that anyone can use in a program--provided the person knows the TIFF rules. The TIFF specifications include even more information about bitmaps than the DIB specifications.

To a certain degree, OLE is intended to produce something similar to a DIB or a TIFF (more like a TIFF) and

I suppose it does, but the entire process (especially when you include DDE) is so *complex* that it cannot be easily comprehended (or used quickly) by individual programmers. You have to have a DDE and OLE department, and this is something that I find irritating. I look forward to more *leaps* in programming and hope that Visual Basic will be used as a guide for how to proceed in the development of a very simple way to do complex things in Windows application design and programming. In all fairness, I must say that Microsoft is making significant progress in the development of a coherent and well-defined OLE specification and implementation. OLE is anything but simple when it only involves a few applications, but making it universally available for easy use by *all* Windows applications is not only a critically important capability for Windows but also a monumental task for Microsoft that requires both clear *thinking* and quite a few *geniuses*.

Regarding formats, specifications, and *results*, let me state emphatically that I would really like to have a single (but complete) definition of a *result* for use in Windows. I think if large corporations would devote more time to defining a universal *result* than to *continually* inventing more and more unusual, special purpose *result*s, then some significant progress in Windows programming could be made. I really do not need hundreds and hundreds of slightly (or tremendously) different variations of file formats. One is sufficient, if it does everything I need to do.

I do not complain too loudly, because all of the different formats (for everything imaginable) create an opportunity for special tools that convert from one format to another. However, I would still like to see a *generic result* definition for Windows and may have to invent it if nobody else does. Without an intelligent, *generic result*, Windows application software design and programming will evolve itself into a dimension from which it can never return.

I very seriously doubt whether there is any single person who is an expert in DDE, OLE, POSTSCRIPT, True Type, HPPCL, DIB, TIFF, PCX, dBASE, X-Base, Paradox, SQL Server, Windows SDK, C, C++, Visual Basic, and a few other things, including MULTIMEDIA. It is nearly too much for a single human being to comprehend and still have enough time to do *meaningful* work. And, yet, this is *some* of what you have to understand to be able to do anything really useful in a Windows application. There must be a simpler way to do all of this (and there is). The problem is identifying it (or solving the puzzle).

I suppose that at this point we have really *jumped* a long way from Forms, Modules, and Controls, but the purpose of these *jumps* has been to make you think about what you are really *doing* when you use Visual Basic. You are designing and programming a Windows application (obviously), but you are also *conceptually* building a very sophisticated *process*. You must *not* look at it in the same way that you look at it in more traditional programming systems. If you do *not* look at it in terms of *objects*, *actions*, and *results*, then you will miss the forest for the trees.

Regarding forests and trees, there is something else that needs to be discussed, the concept of what is *practical* and what is *impractical* at this time. Many people have the *preconceived* notion it is impractical to use large data files, global variables, and anything that is easy but traditionally inefficient. I think this is a *cute* way to look at the world but also think it is very *naive*.

Intel is already talking about a 586 processor; it will not be very long before other types of even more powerful processors will be capable of running Windows. Memory is cheap and readily available. Hard disks are relatively cheap and becoming smaller, faster, and more capable of storing enormous amounts of data. It will not be long before Compact Disks (CDs) become affordable and can not only read but also write many times.

I am not very concerned about whether there is enough hardware capability, except that it needs to be *less* expensive. My concern is that we are reaching or have *already* reached a point at which the hardware has *exceeded* the capabilities of the software. That is why Visual Basic is so important and why Visual Basic can become even *more* important.

My concern about hardware *exceeding* the capabilities of software will probably sound confusing when you consider that I think a 486 33-MHz PC is *slow*. However, what I am saying is that there is *not* much *delay* involved in bringing new *hardware* to market and that considerable *effort* is being made to design new hardware. In contrast, there is a significant delay in new *software's* coming to market; therefore it *appears* that considerably less effort is dedicated to designing new software. I also know developing software is not a quick process but believe that to be the case because of limitations in programming languages rather than because of limitations in programmers.

The fact that it is 1991 and I am relearning Basic in order to be able to use what is probably the most *advanced* Windows programming language in *existence* is somewhat amazing to me. If I had a quarter for every For Loop (in one form or another) I have coded in the past 15 years, I would be rich. Is there not some way to move programming from the world of *words* into the world of *symbols*?

Windows is an excellent environment for *symbolic programming*. I expect that Visual Basic will *evolve* into a *symbolic programming* language at some point. Instead of thinking in terms of an Application Programming Interface (API), I would prefer that Microsoft think in terms of an Application Programming Generator (APG). Visual Basic is a remarkable (but small) step in this direction. It is, however, the biggest *practical* step that *anyone* has taken at this time. Until something even newer becomes available, you have to approach Windows application development as a Windows SDK/C and Visual Basic programmer, rather than as a symbolic programmer.

As a Windows SDK/C programmer, you must think in terms of *controls* as your basic *objects*. In Visual Basic, you need to learn to think in terms of using *forms* as your basic *objects*--but to do so you need to be able to design and program *generic forms*. Using *generic forms* requires that you understand *controls* and *results*. It also means that you have to be able to use controls and results *efficiently* in terms of *time* rather than in terms of hardware.

I program for people who have 486 33-MHz machines with attached *disk farms* and more *memory* than could ever be used. This is *not* the average machine at present, but I do not care because 486 33-MHz machines are relatively inexpensive today. They will become even less expensive in the next year. The 486 33-MHz *clones* are leading the way in lowering prices, and they work just as well (and just as *reliably*) as the leading machines. Actually, some of them *are* leading machines (as a direct result of *quality* manufacturing and very *aggressive* pricing).

We have done quite a bit of *jumping* from topic to topic at this point; although the *jumping* was somewhat random, there are some *connections*: (1) forms and controls are used in *jumping* from one activity to another *within* a Windows application and (2) modules are a good *place* to put code that is relatively *jump-independent*. Since *jumping* is not only something that I do when *thinking*, but also the way people *use* Windows applications, it is a good idea to investigate *jumping* as it relates to Windows.

The key to *jumping* is to *jump somewhere*. The key to *controlling* where you *jump* is *Focus*, because what you really do when you *jump* is *change* your *Focus*. *Focus* is very important in Windows SDK/C and Visual Basic programming and *must* be *understood* before you can really design and program a Windows application.

Hocus Pocus: Who's Got *Focus*?

While there is no such thing as magic, things can appear to occur magically. In general, when something appears magical it does so because it is unexpected and incomprehensible. In other words, when something happens that you do not expect or do not understand, your brain tries to explain it to you; if you are relatively foolish (and prone to mental laziness), you will not put on your *thinking hat* and may reach the incorrect conclusion that you have experienced something magical.

Someone said that as technology evolves in both capability and complexity it appears more and more magical to people who do not understand it. I think this is a correct observation, but I do not want you to get the impression that I think people who believe in magic are inherently foolish (they are foolish, but not inherently foolish). If you are *inherently* foolish, then you probably should believe in magic and may have no other choice. However, if you are just *plain* foolish then there is hope. You can learn.

But this chapter is not about magic, it is about *Focus*. *Focus* is very important in Windows and may be the most subtle and difficult concept in Windows programming to recognize as well as understand. In very simple words, *Focus* is where you *are*. It is not very difficult (most of the time) to know where you *are*, but it can become confusing if you do not know the **Rules of *Focus*, Unannotated**:
(1) Know where you are.
(2) Remember where you are.
(3) Determine where you can go from where you are.
(4) Control where you can go from where you are.

(5) Be able to get back to where you were when you find yourself someplace where you do not want to be.
(6) Know what you need to do when you are where you are.
(7) Finish what you need to do when you are where you are before going someplace else.

In other words, if you are programming in Windows, then you must know (1) where you are, (2) what you are doing, (3) where you are going, and (4) what you are going to do when you get there. This probably seems very obvious (and in a traditional programming environment probably would be), but Windows is *not* a traditional programming environment. As I mentioned earlier, Windows applications are somewhat random in terms of *explicitly* controlling what their users can do at any given time, and therein lies the importance of *Focus*. When you cannot *explicitly* control what happens, then you must *implicitly* control what happens.

This will eventually evolve into a semantic discussion (and serve no useful purpose);so in the interest of getting to the point, or maintaining *Focus*, we need to concentrate on learning what *Focus* is. To begin learning about *Focus*, it is useful to identify those things that can attempt to change *Focus*: (1) the keyboard, (2) the mouse, and (3) the user. Most, if not all, attempted changes in *Focus* are a direct result of item (3) and are initiated with either item (1) or item (2).

Windows, itself, is involved in this process and is (to a certain degree) a willing accomplice in doing things that we (as programmers and controllers) would rather prevent. If an object is visible and enabled, then Windows will *not* usually prevent it from getting *Focus*. Modal dialog boxes are an exception to this rule. In fact, one of the functions of modal dialog boxes is to *restrict* the transfer of *Focus*.

Being visible and enabled are the two general requirements for being *eligible* to receive *Focus*. If an object is *not* visible, then it cannot get *Focus*. If an object is *not* enabled, then it cannot get *Focus*. These two rules are the foundation for controlling *Focus* in your Visual Basic application. If you want to control *Focus*, then you *must* control (1) which objects are visible and (2) which objects are enabled. You must also be a *Focus Dictator*. In other words, an object can only be visible or enabled with your *permission*.

Objects do not become visible or enabled because they decide it would be a neat thing for them to do. Objects become visible, invisible, enabled, or disabled because *you* program them to do so. There is no other way for this to happen. If it happens and you think to yourself, "I did not program this!" then you are absolutely correct. It happened because you forgot to control it and because both Windows and Visual Basic really do not care about it.

In previous chapters, I have referred to a small *dilemma* regarding flowcharting a Windows application (i.e., "All roads lead everywhere!"). In Windows, objects are like cities, and you can travel with no restrictions other than the restrictions that you or someone else create via programming. This makes Windows application design very interesting because you have to learn a new way of *thinking* about the ways in which a user will *interact* with your Windows application.

I find it useful to look at Windows applications from both sides of the *Glass Wall* rather than from one side only, but this requires a *Looking Glass*, some imagination, and a little help from Rod Serling: "Picture, if you will..." two rooms separated by a *Glass Wall*. Imagine a third room that borders both rooms and is, itself, separated from them by a *Mirror* or *Looking Glass*. You are in the third room, and you can *observe* what happens in the other two rooms. The *Glass Wall* (not the *Mirror*) is made of a special kind of glass that is capable of *transforming* portions of itself into *objects*: text boxes, labels, buttons, scroll bars, list boxes, combo boxes, and so on.

One of the first two rooms is the *User Room*, and the other room is the *Focus Room*. By touching objects on the *Glass Wall*, someone in the *User Room* can cause useful things to happen but *cannot* change the *Glass Wall* directly. When an object on the *User Room* side of the *Glass Wall* is touched, it starts glowing on the *Focus Room* side of the *Glass Wall* and a *Message* is sent to the person in the *Focus Room*.

The *Message* sent to the person in the *Focus Room* includes all of the information known about the object that is now glowing. Some of the information may be *cryptic* and probably requires some *interpretation*. There is a *Machine* in the *Focus Room*. Its *purpose* is to perform actions when requested to do so by the person in the *Focus Room*. The *Machine* is only capable of responding to formal requests contained on the *Official Request(s) to Do Something* form (available in triplicate from the *Office of the King*).

The primary functions of the person in the *Focus Room* are twofold: (1) to control the current state of the *Glass Wall* and (2) to generate and deliver *Request(s) to Do Something* to the *Machine*. This is *Windows From the Other Side of the Looking Glass*, and it will either further confuse you or make a few things clearer. In any event, and with some consideration given to not turning this book into an *allegory*, it should be clear to you that whoever controls the *Glass Wall* controls the *Machine*.

So, how do you control the *Glass Wall*? Well, you learn the rules followed by the *Glass Wall*, as described in *The Official Rules of the Glass Wall* (available from the *Office of the King*), and you use the rules to tell the *Glass Wall* to do things, via *Official Request(s) For the Glass Wall to Do Something* (available from the *Office of the King*). Note that the *Glass Wall* does *not* really do much.

In fact, the *Glass Wall* only does three things: (1) it *transforms*: (a) portions of itself into objects or (b) objects into portions of itself; (2) it *makes* an object glow on the *Focus Room* side when the object is touched on the *User Room* side; and (3) it *sends* a *Message* to the *Focus Room* side (as fully described in the *Official Guide to Interpretation of Glass Wall Messages* [available from the *Office of the King*]) when an object is touched on the User Side.

In this *allegory*, the person on the *Focus Room* side is the *Keeper of the Focus and Controller of the Glass Wall*, but you are the *Programmer* (the *Programmer* who works behind the *Looking Glass*), although you are really *more* of a C*ontroller* than a *Programmer*. In other words, *you* control *both* sides of the *Glass Wall* from *behind* the *Looking Glass*. You have *direct* control of the K*eeper of the Focus and Controller of the Glass Wall* and you have *direct* control of the *Machine*. You only have *indirect* control of the person on the *User Room* side.

I have intentionally separated the *Programmer* from the *Keeper of the Focus and Controller of the Glass Wall* and put them into two separate rooms for a *good* reason. In Windows SDK/C and Visual Basic programming, it is important to emphasize the *design* and *control* aspects of programming rather than to view the process as one of programming only. In a very real sense, the programming tasks are *less* important then the designing tasks. **The *less* time you spend *designing* forms, the *more* time you will spend *programming* forms.**

When you use Visual Basic as your application development language, the relationship between design and code is particularly important. There is an easy way to do things. *Design* is the key to optimizing your development effort. When you really understand the fact that Visual Basic automatically *generates* a considerable amount of code for you and when you learn to take advantage of this fact, you will find you do *not* have to do so much programming as in the past to get things done. Look at Visual Basic programming from the perspective of someone who is controlling an *event processor* rather than from the traditional perspective of a programmer. **Let Visual Basic be the programmer and let yourself be the *controller* of the programmer.**

In other words, the *Keeper of the Focus and Controller of the Glass Wall* is a *subordinate* programmer who can do useful work for you but can do so *only* if provided with proper guidelines and policies. And the proper guidelines and policies that the *Keeper of the Focus and Controller of the Glass Wall* must have are generally described in the *Rules of Focus, Unannotated Version* (as found in this book).

When you *annotate* the *Rules of Focus*, then the *Keeper of the Focus and Controller of the Machine* has a complete *set* of information with which to operate. The *Annotations to the Rules of Focus* are contained in the *event procedures* and in the *non-event procedures* of your Visual Basic application. I think you can begin to appreciate the difficulty inherent to attempting to flowchart all of this--it is *not* a simple process.

You may be wondering why it is necessary to spend all of this time on a Windows *allegory*? Well, it is necessary because understanding the importance of the *Keeper of the Focus and Controller of the Glass Wall* is the real key to understanding how to design and program Windows applications. It is something that *nobody* will tell you directly because everyone thinks it is a *Secret* (and, due to popular belief, it *is* a *Secret*). In fact, it is so much of a *Secret* that even when you begin to understand it you do not know about it.

Once you understand the *Secret of the Keeper of the Focus and Controller of the Glass Wall* (available from the *Office of the Court Jester*), then you are well on your way to understanding Windows application programming (which includes Visual Basic programming). The amazing thing about Visual Basic, with respect to the *Secret*, is that Visual Basic is really nothing more than a *combination* of (1) the *Official Language for the Keeper of the Focus and Controller of the Glass Wall,* (2) the *Official Language for Generating Annotations to the Rules of Focus,* and (3) the *Official Somewhat High-Level Language for Generating Request(s) For the Machine to Do Something* (most of which are available from the *Office of the King*).

I discovered this somewhat *indirectly* as a result of the screen saver application that turns your Windows screen into a *Wall of Bricks* which *disassembles* itself by making its bricks fall out one-at-a-time (leaving black *space* where the bricks once were). The first time I saw this, I was a little shocked and somewhat distressed because I had *always* considered that the computer and the programs which control it were located directly *behind* the screen. I suppose this is really foolish, but it was as good a place as any, *metaphorically*, for me to locate things. I now look at the screen from a different perspective--*sideways*.

Instead of being on the outside *looking-in*, I am on the outside *looking-across*. I get to *see* more this way and can *jump-in* on either side if I need to get a different *perspective*. At some time, it will *occur* to me that the computer and the programs that control it are *really* located in the *Box With All of the Lights* that sits next to the monitor. But in the meantime, I am *metaphorically* content. Since Windows is a *metaphor*, I suppose that is good.

Learning the Graphical User Interface (GUI) portion of Windows application programming is really nothing more than learning the *Secret of the Keeper of the Focus and Controller of the Machine*. If you are coming from the DOS world (or from some other world), you probably already know enough about the *Machine*. It is really the same *Machine* no matter which environment you are considering. Separating the GUI portion of Windows from the *Machine* is very helpful when trying to *understand* Windows application design and programming. In fact, Windows application design and programming will make *little* sense to you until you *know* the *Secret*.

However, knowing the *Secret of the Keeper of the Focus and Controller of the Machine* and being able to look at things, *metaphorically*, from *Behind the Looking Glass* is not enough. You also have to know the *Rules* (not just one rule but *all* of them). Knowing all of the *Rules* is important because, when you know all of the Rules, you will *realize* that there are *many* ways (both *metaphorically* and *realistically*) to program Windows applications. You can *cause* things to happen: (1) *indirectly* as the *Keeper of the Focus and Controller of the Machine*, (2) *directly* as the *Programmer of the Machine*, and (3) *directly* by *indirectly* making the *Keeper of the Focus and Controller of the Machine* think that the person in the *User Room* has touched the *Glass Wall*.

Of the three ways of causing things to happen, I like the third way best because it is *abstruse* but simple. In Visual Basic, most controls that do something have a design or runtime property called *Value*; and (1) by setting the *Value* to True (i.e., negative one in Visual Basic) if the *Value* property is only available at runtime or (2) by setting the *Value* to one of a valid range of values if the *Value* property is also available in *design mode*, you can *emulate* the *transfer* of *focus* from some other control to the control whose *Value* property you set. In effect, you can *push* a button *for* the user. If the push button is invisible but enabled, then the user does *not* even know about it.

Pushing *invisible* buttons and doing things with *invisible* list boxes is another area in which experience in Windows SDK/C programming is invaluable (but *not* necessary). Some *inventive* person discovered (1) list boxes are useful for maintaining lists and (2) the fact that a list box is *invisible* does *not* make in *unusable*. In fact, invisible list boxes make *excellent* linked list managers (but more so in Windows SDK/C than in Visual Basic). If you need to maintain a list of *nearly* anything for use in internal programming, then why go to all of the trouble involved in coding linked lists? Just put a list box on the form and make it *permanently* invisible. If space is at a premium on your form, then make the list box *small*. The *size* of the *invisible* list box has absolutely *no* effect on its functionality.

You can add items, remove items, and locate items in a list box. That is basically what you want and need to do with a linked list. In Windows SDK/C programming, removing all items from a list box and locating a particular item in a list box are single functions. This makes it *easier* to use *invisible* list boxes. But it is *not* that much more work to remove all items in a list box or to locate a particular item in Visual Basic. I suspect that these features will be added to Visual Basic at some time because they are so fundamental and so easy to do that it would be foolish not to add them to Visual Basic. I am still trying to deduce why these obviously useful and, I think, easy to program functions were not included in Visual Basic. However, you can directly use the Windows SDK/C list box functions on Visual Basic list boxes (detailed technical information on this is available in the Microsoft Knowledge Base in CompuServe--an excellent source of an enormous amount of very useful information about using Windows SDK/C techniques in your Visual Basic programs).

At this point, I have introduced (maybe not for the first time) the technique of using *invisible* objects in Windows application programming. These objects are *not* totally invisible. They are *invisible* to the *Keeper of the Focus and Controller of the Machine* because if they are *invisible* then the user cannot see them and if the user cannot *see* them, then the *Glass Wall* has *not* transformed portions of itself into them. Since that is the case, they *cannot* receive *Focus* (i.e., the person on the *User Room* side cannot touch them). Nevertheless, they *are* visible to you because you *know* they are there. In other words, you have some *extra* tools in your room *Behind the Looking Glass*. One of the most useful tools you have is the *Master Glass Wall*, and it is *like* the *Glass Wall* except that it contains all objects (visible *and* invisible).

With the *Master Glass Wall* you can *really* control Windows applications. In fact, when you can *draw* all of the *objects* that *appear* on the *Master Glass Wall*, then you have *designed* your Windows application. Remember that *forms* are *objects*. In other words, the *Master Glass Wall* is like a *Map* of your Windows application. Forms are like countries;

controls are like cities; and both countries and cities are connected by roads. Traveling from one country or city to another country or city can involve either *loose coupling* or *tight coupling*. If going from one place to another requires that you go to an *intermediate* place along the way, then the two places are *tightly coupled*. Otherwise, the two places are either *loosely coupled* or *not coupled* at all.

Another *allegory* I find useful is to *think* of a Windows application as being a *City With a Somewhat Complex Freeway System*. The various businesses located within the *City* can be used to perform useful work. You are the *Controller of the City*, and your workers are the businesses. You do not have a telephone and must, therefore, communicate via delivery service. The delivery service delivers *Messages* to and from the businesses via delivery vehicles that travel on the *Somewhat Complex Freeway System*. You have a real-time *Map* of the *City* and use it to dispatch and monitor *Message* deliveries.

If you then take the *Somewhat Complex Freeway System* and transform it into a *Long , Straight Road* (a set of such roads), then you have a *Queue* from which *Messages* can be retrieved. As each delivery vehicle passes a business, the business gets the opportunity to determine whether the delivery vehicle contains a *Message* addressing it or some other business (a business in which it is *interested*). In this extension to the *allegory*, all *Messages* originate from your office; so anytime one of the businesses wants to send a *Message* it sends it to you for either immediate or delayed *dispatching*.

This is a good way to *visualize* what happens inside of Windows and inside Windows applications. Replace the *City* with your *application*; replace the businesses with your objects (*forms* and *controls*); replace the *Somewhat Complex*

Freeway System with the *variables* connecting your objects to one another. Then display it on the *Master Glass Wall* and you have a good idea of how a real-time *Simulation of a Windows Application* would look from *Behind the Looking Glass*.

However, be aware that, when you make these replacements, you are *not* seeing *everything* that happens in Windows. You are *only* looking at a *portion* of the whole. You are really looking at a *City Within a City*. More properly, you are *transforming* a single business into a *City*. If you do *not* understand this, then put on your *thinking hat* and contemplate it for awhile.

Regardless of whether you understand the *City Within a City Allegory*, some of the first things you observe are that (1) there is a lot of *traffic* and (2) it is difficult for you to follow everything that is happening because it is so *apparently* random and continuous. Well, that is not exactly the case because you *know* the *Secret of the Keeper of the Focus and Controller of the Machine*. In effect, you *know* how to *Stop The World*, or at least you *know* some useful *points* at which the *World* can be conveniently *Stopped* for purposes of making it *possible* to understand and program the *way* in which the *World* operates. This is the *real* key to *Focus*.

In effect, *Focus* is the *only* thing you can use to make any *sense* out of Windows application programming. If an object does *not* have *Focus*, then it is *not* currently of much interest to you. Only *one* object can have *Focus* at any *single* time. Therefore, understanding and controlling *Focus* in a Windows application gives you a way to turn a very complex process into a simple, *single-step* process.

When you flowchart a Windows application, what you really want to show in your flowchart is the *path* followed (or left behind) as *Focus* moves from one object to another. While this is *not* very difficult to state, it *is* difficult to visualize and flowchart. It is more like being a *Hilbert Space Air Traffic Controller* than anything else (except possibly playing *Hilbert Space Chess*). You can flowchart a single screen with respect to *Focus* and then visualize that (1) *each* single screen flowchart is a *set* of *symbols* contained on a *Transparent Geometric Plane* and (2) the screens are arranged vertically like *Glass Pancakes*.

When *Focus* transfers from one *Plane* to another, you draw a *Curved Line* between the two *Planes* (connecting the particular objects on each *Plane* from and to which *Focus* is transferred). This is probably a good way to flowchart Windows applications but does *not* lend itself very well to representation in *two-space*.

It is somewhat like living in a world of many cities (all called Rome) and making the statement that, "All roads lead to Rome." It does *not* tell you a much, except the following: (1) you are always where you *were*, where you *are*, and where you are going *to be* and (2) all you have to do to get back to where you *were*, to be where you *are*, or to go where you are going *to be* is follow the road. Windows applications are very *gestalt* in that they are *more* than the sum of their parts. While you must understand and program the parts, if you do *not* understand the whole then you will *not* get much useful work done.

Think about this. Contemplate the concept of designing your Windows application not as a process of designing code modules but as a process of designing forms containing all of the objects necessary for doing whatever you want your Windows application to do. At this level of design, it is not important that the objects actually do *anything*, just that they are *present*. Essentially, you are designing a *prototype* for your Windows application with Visual Basic. Because Visual Basic does a considerable amount of *defacto* programming, your prototype *will* actually do something and is *not* really very far from doing *exactly* what you want it to do.

Good Windows application design requires you to design the *whole* application first rather than to design *parts* of the application. However, the *whole* design does *not* have to be detailed--just identified. You can *defer* some of the process of designing the *whole* application by using *generic forms*. This is because *generic forms* are *independent*. In other words, until it becomes *clear* to you what the *whole* application is going to do, you can design and code *generic forms* with the intention of using them in an application that is *not* as yet clearly defined. If you use this method of Windows application design, you need to pay particular attention to providing *flexibility* in your *generic forms*. After all, you do *not* know how they will *ultimately* be used.

These are some new concepts--especially if you have not done very much Windows programming; so do not be disturbed if you do not understand everything. However, if you think everything we have discussed in the preceding chapters is completely obvious and rather simplistic, then I suggest that you spend some extra time contemplating these concepts. You will probably *not* find any significant discussion of the concepts of designing Windows applications in any other books even though the *design* of a Windows application is *more* important than the actual *programming*.

Visual Basic does four significant things for you with respect to designing a Windows application: (1) it provides a very quick way to prototype your ideas; (2) it does nearly all of the GUI *work* for you; (3) it virtually eliminates GUI from the list of tasks that require explicit coding; and (4) it greatly reduces the complexity and amount of programming required in a Windows application. But in doing all of this work for you, it also makes you pay for it in terms of requiring that you really *understand* how to design a Windows application. It is a small price to pay, however, because the more you understand about design, the more you understand how to make Visual Basic do most of the coding.

With a little help from a strong background in Windows SDK/C and mainframe transaction system design, I find I am able to do nearly everything I can think of doing in Visual Basic by using a very small *subset* of the Visual Basic properties, events, and methods. Doing something complex is really *simple* in Visual Basic if you know how to do it the *easy* way. Learning this is neither easy *nor* difficult, but it requires that you *understand* objects and how to *use* them.

Visual Basic is really a *language of objects*, specifically, *GUI objects*. The really *cool* thing about Visual Basic objects is that they *are* born knowing what to do. All you have to do is *refine* (or *define*) their *behavior*. In other words, when you put a Visual Basic object onto a form, the object *knows* what it does, and it *knows* how to do it. If it does *exactly* what you want it to do, you do *not* have to do *any* additional programming. If you want it to do something in addition to what it already does, you can *change* its *behavior* via *programming*.

You will discover that Visual Basic objects *already* do approximately 90 percent of what you want them to do. When you discover this and understand it, you will *realize* why *design* is *more* important in Visual Basic than *programming*. This is the case in Visual Basic because you are working with *objects* that are *already* programmed.

When I state that Visual Basic objects are *already* programmed, I *really* mean it. Visual Basic objects are not just *already* programmed a little--they are *already* programmed a *lot*. Really to appreciate the *extent* to which Visual Basic objects are *already* programmed, you have to have a considerable amount of experience in Windows SDK/C programming. The more I learn about Visual Basic, the more I continue to be *amazed* at how much of the traditional GUI work it does.

Thinking in *metaphors* is very important in Windows and visualizing objects, via *allegory*, is a useful way to *expand* your *imagination*. With Visual Basic and Windows, you are *only* limited by your *imagination*. If you cannot *see* a screen in your mind, then you need to learn how. Visual Basic will *help* you do it because it is a *language of visual objects*. The programming is really *trivial* and can be easily mastered, but it will take you some *time* to master the art of designing with *visual objects*. It will take some time, but it is not really difficult, just different.

At this point in the book, I have said most of what I want to say about Windows application design concepts. However, before jumping into code examples, I need to clarify some of the *Rules of Visual Basic*. The next chapter is a good place to do it.

Strings, Structures, and Other Strange Things

In previous chapters, I made reference to certain irregularities in the behavior and definition of Visual Basic strings (and a few other things). There *is* a *real* set of rules. It will save you a considerable amount of time if you know and understand them. The primary areas in which Visual Basic deviates in practice from its formal set of rules involve (1) strings, (2) structures, (3) pointers, (4) functions and subroutines contained in a Dynamic Link Library (DLL), and (5) behaviors of certain methods and properties. The great majority of the *real* rules I am giving you are either undocumented or difficult to discover.

In fact, without some Windows SDK/C programming experience, the *real* rules will not make any sense to you. You could *mistakenly* get the impression that Visual Basic does not work correctly in some situations. Strings are a good place to start because you must use them and because they do *not* follow the set of rules you know. In Visual Basic, there are three types of strings: (1) *variable* length strings, (2) *fixed* length strings, and (3) *literal* strings.

Variable length strings are defined via **As String** or $ and do *not* have *any* length until you put something into them. Variable length strings will *adjust* their length (by either expanding or contracting) to contain whatever you put into them. This is a useful capability, and it is very important.

Fixed length strings are defined via **As String** * <value>, and have a length *exactly* equal to the number of positions specified by <value>. If you follow my rules for including *scope* information in the names of variables, then you will *not* have any *local* fixed length strings. If you really need *local* fixed length strings, you can replace the **'g'** with an **'l'** in the naming convention, but I do *not* recommend it. By properly using *global* and *regional* fixed length strings, you should *not* need any *local* fixed length strings. You *cannot* define a fixed length string by using the **'$'** postfix, but you *can* give a variable length string a fixed length (or at least a *definite* size) by *assigning* it some value [e.g., via **Space$()**, or **String$()**]. If you need a *local* fixed length string, you *must* use **Dim <varname> As String * <value>** . If you do this, then be sure to use the **'l'** in place of the **'g'** in the name.

The third type of string is the *literal* string. A *literal* string is one or more characters enclosed in double-quotes (e.g., "this is a literal string"). The Visual Basic documentation does *not* list this as a third type of string, but it is *neither* a *variable* length string *nor* a *fixed* length string; so I consider it to be a third type of string. **Never use a *literal* string as a parameter to a DLL function or subroutine!**

With all three types of Visual Basics strings, an examination of the documentation will lead you to believe that the valid character set for strings is the ANSI character set (decimal values 0 through 255). This is true insofar as Visual Basic is concerned, but there is a major exception. The C NULL character, or **Chr$(0)**, is *not* really a valid Visual Basic string character. This will require some further explanation. The C NULL character, or **Chr$(0)**, is the *key* to understanding how Visual Basic strings *really* work.

Although I am relying entirely on intuition, inference, and deduction, I am relatively certain that Visual Basic is *not* written in Visual Basic. Rather, Visual Basic is written (at least in part) in Windows SDK/C (or some equivalent thereof). Therefore, I know (or suspect) that, regardless of what Visual Basic thinks it is doing when it performs string manipulation, at some point *all* string manipulation in Visual Basic *follows* the string manipulation *rules* of Windows SDK/C. This means that the NULL character *must* be treated *exactly* the same way in a Visual Basic string as it is treated in a C string.

In C, a string begins at some address, continues for none or more non-NULL characters, and is terminated by a single NULL character. Note that I *do* mean *none* or more non-NULL characters *because* a string can be *empty*. However, even an *empty* C string *must* have the NULL terminator or it is *not* a string. This does not mean that a NULL character is an *empty* string, just that a string *must* be NULL terminated or it is *not* a string.

If you have not done much Windows SDK/C programming, the distinction between a NULL character and an empty string will probably be unclear. However, it is important to understand the *difference* between *characters* and *strings*. In C, the *address* of *data* is very *important* and the *address* of *data* is (to a certain degree) the *key* to understanding the *difference* between a *single character* and a *string*.

In C, when you *define* a *variable* as being a single *character*, its *length* is *determined* and will *never* vary. When you *define* a *variable* as being a *string* you also *define* its *length*, but its *length* can *vary*. You also use a different set of functions for working with strings. The C string manipulation functions are *aware* of the NULL character terminator rule. The primary (if not only) *difference* between the definition of a character and a string is *length*:

```
char    cInitial;      // defines a character variable...
char    szName [21];   // defines a string variable...
```

A character variable can contain *any* value that can fit into a single *byte* (and the NULL character is included in the *set* of *values* that can fit into a single *byte*). In other words, NULL is a *valid* value for a *character* variable. If you want to use a string to hold a single character, then you normally define the string variable as having *two* positions, (e.g., **char szCharStr [2]**). The reason for having *two* positions is that *one* of them is *required* for the NULL terminator.

An *empty* string is a string that has its NULL terminator in the *first* position. Note that the *first* position of a string variable called szCharStr is szCharStr[0] because nearly everything in C begins at ZERO not ONE. A character variable that contains the NULL character is *just* a character variable, and it is *not* equivalent to an empty string. These two data items are *not* equivalent because *one* of them, the *empty* string variable, contains *nothing* while the other one, the character variable, contains a single NULL character. In other words, a single NULL *character* is not *nothing*; it is *something*.

C programmers *know* the rules followed by strings and do a few *extra* things to make strings (and their programs) work smoothly. The primary thing C programmers do is *always* make sure the NULL is *where* it is *supposed* to be. They do this because if the NULL is *not* where it is supposed to be or is *missing* entirely, some bizarre things happen, not the least of which is a locked machine followed by a *three-finger salute*. This is the way it works, and it is neither a hassle nor a wonderful thing. It just *is*. You *cannot* argue with it, and you *cannot* change it. If you want to use a C string, then you follow the rules. No big deal.

Since Visual Basic does *not* recognize the NULL terminator (for all practical purposes), a problem exists. You can use Visual Basic strings that contain *embedded* NULL characters, and everything will work exactly as you think it should (up to a point). Everything *stops* working as you think it should *precisely* at the moment when either you or Visual Basic attempts to do something with the string that results in manipulation of the string *by* a Windows SDK/C function. When the Visual Basic string is used as a parameter to a Windows SDK/C function, the string is subject to a *different* set of rules: the *Rules of C Strings*.

Before proceeding, let me define what I mean by *embedded* NULL characters. Since the NULL character is a valid character in a Visual Basic string, there can be *more* than one NULL character in a Visual Basic string. In a C string, there is *only* one NULL character, and it is the NULL character that terminates the string. **Any NULL characters contained within a Visual Basic string are *embedded* NULL characters**. Consider the following statements:

tmp$ = "This " + Chr$(0) + " is "
tmp$ = tmp$ + Chr$(0) + " a VB string!"

In this example, **tmp$** will contain two *embedded* NULL characters after the statements are executed. The two *embedded* NULL characters are valid (insofar as Visual Basic is concerned), and do *not* terminate the string in any way. However, when interpreted according to the *Rules of C Strings*, the *actual* string is terminated with the *first* NULL character. The *actual* content of the string is **"This "**. In other words, insofar as Windows SDK/C is concerned, the *remainder* of the Visual Basic string following the *first* **Chr$(0)** does *not* exist although it *is* in *memory*.

If you are a Windows SDK/C programmer then you are probably screaming at this point, "...but that is not entirely true!" You are correct because you can access the entire string in most cases (if you are *brave*), depending on the way in which Visual Basic sends the data to the Windows SDK/C function. In effect, Visual Basic sends the Windows SDK/C function a LPSTR (a long pointer to a string), and is really *passing* the *address* of the Visual Basic *string* to the Windows SDK/C function *by value*.

In fact, **all parameters are passed to Windows SDK/C functions *by value*.** *Nothing* is passed *by reference* to a Windows SDK/C function or subroutine. This may *contradict* popular *belief*, but it *is*, nevertheless, *true*. Many programmers refer to using addresses in parameters as passing data by *reference*. Nonetheless, using addresses in parameters results in sending the address *by value* even though the address is *then* used *by* the *receiving* function to *reference* data *in* the *sending* function (or anywhere else). In Visual Basic, when you use a fixed length string variable as a parameter, the *address* of the variable is passed *by value* to the Windows SDK/C function. Because Visual Basic is providing an *address* to the Windows SDK/C, and because Windows SDK/C is *very* powerful, there are many ways to access data.

For example the C function **memcpy** will let you copy data beginning at one *address* to another *address* regardless of the *presence* or *absence* of NULL characters. However, you *cannot* safely *presume* that every Windows SDK/C programmer will use **memcpy** in preference to **strcpy** for doing operations on strings. In my experience as a Windows SDK/C programmer, I find that it is much more probable that a Windows SDK function will use the ***strxxx*** suite of functions than use the ***memxxx*** suite of functions when manipulating strings.

This is certainly the case for the Windows SDK/C functions that load list boxes, labels, edit boxes, combo boxes, and just about everything else. What this means to you as a Visual Basic programmer is that while Visual Basic will let you use *embedded* NULL characters some of the time, the Windows SDK/C functions that Visual Basic *must* use internally will *never* let you use *embedded* NULL characters.

In effect, there are *two* sets of rules: (1) the *Rules of Visual Basic Strings* and (2) the *Rules of C Strings*. In the event of a *disagreement* between the *two* sets of rules, the Windows SDK/C will *always* win. So in my interpretation of the world, there is really only *one* kind of string in Visual Basic, and it is the C string--*not* the Visual Basic string.

The easiest way *always* to be correct is to treat *every* Visual Basic string as though it is a Windows SDK/C string because at some time or another it *will* be. If you have never worked with C strings, it may *appear* to be a lot of extra work to do the things you have to do to guarantee that Visual Basic strings are *also* C strings. The extra work involved is much *less* than the work involved in diagnosing the cause of a UAE or missing data.

What do you have to do to make everything *work* the way it should? Well, it is somewhat involved because of the differences in the way variable length strings and fixed length strings operate. I have tried several different methods but have settled on a single method that *always* works. It is not an extra effort because I use it so frequently. It is like using the *arrow* keys or the *mouse* in a text editor. It is *not* additional work; it is the way it *must* be done. Using C strings in Visual Basic is like *burping* after *chugging* a Coca-Cola. It is impossible to avoid. If you are going to program in Visual Basic and *chug* Coca-Colas, then you are going to use C strings, and you are going to *burp*.

I begin building a fixed length string by using a variable length string. Note that I said I *build* strings. I build strings piece by piece, and I begin with an *empty* string (i.e., a string of length *zero*). After I copy the contents of a *literal* string into a variable length string, I explicitly NULL terminate the string with a Chr$(0), as demonstrated in the following example:

tmp$ = LTrim$("this is a literal string")
tmp$ = tmp$ + Chr$(0)

At this point, **tmp$** contains a string that is valid in *both* Visual Basic and Windows SDK/C. It contains *exactly* what I want it to contain, so there are *no* surprises. You will note that I used the **LTrim$()** function to trim leading blanks from the literal. This is *not* really necessary in this particular case, but I do it anyway because sometimes it *is* necessary. Specifically, it is necessary when using the **Str$()** function (and no telling when else). I quit *trying* to discover when Visual Basic thinks it is useful to add a single blank character to the beginning of a string. Because I *never* find it useful to have blanks *mysteriously* appear at the *beginning* of my strings, I now use **LTrim$()** on nearly everything, even though it is unnecessary most of the time.

At this point, **tmp$** contains the correct information, but it has a definite problem regarding using it as a parameter to a Windows SDK/C function. It is a variable length string variable, and that is *not* good. In fact, it is *very* bad: **Never use a literal or a variable length string as a parameter to a Windows SDK/C function.** Always use fixed length string variables as parameters to Windows SDK/C functions. Make the length sufficiently *large* so that the fixed length string variables can *entirely* contain *any* string that the Windows SDK/C function decides to *copy* to the fixed length string variable. Failure to do this will nearly *always* result in a UAE.

Continuing with the example, I copy the variable length string to a fixed length string:

(in your GLOBAL.BAS):
Global szgFixedLenStr As String * 100

(in your Code):
szgFixedLenStr = LTrim$(tmp$)

Now everything is as it should be and you know how to build a string. Note that you may *not* want to use the **LTrim$()** in *all* cases because you will often *want* to preserve *leading* spaces. The same is true of **RTrim$()**, if you *want* to preserve *trailing* spaces. **Left$()** is another useful function and can be used to get the *first* part of a string. **Mid$()** can be used to get *portions* of strings. **InStr()** can be used to *test* for *embedded* NULL characters. Look at the sample code for specific examples of when and how to use these Visual Basic string manipulation functions.

When you declare a DLL function or subroutine in your GLOBAL.BAS file as having a parameter that is passed **ByVal** and is **As String**, this tells Visual Basic (1) to append a NULL character at the end of the string and (2) to do some internal work that results in its being able to send the DLL function or subroutine the *address* of the resulting string. Some programmers refer to this latter process as passing the string by reference, but what actually occurs is that the address of the string is passed by value (as previously explained). This makes it possible for the DLL function or subroutine to *refer* to the string knowing nothing more than its *address*.

The *appending* of a NULL character by Visual Basic is useful but is done more to maintain *order* than to make things work as you *think* they should. If you want to send a

10 character string to a DLL function or subroutine and send it via a fixed length string of length 100, then Visual Basic will append the NULL character at position 101 (*not* at position 11) because position 101 is the *end* of the fixed length string variable. However, you *really* want a NULL character at position 11, but the *only* way to get one there is for you to *put* it there yourself.

In other words, there are *special* cases; so I prefer doing everything *explicitly* rather than remembering all of the special cases. If you put the NULL character *exactly* where it belongs, then it is *correct*. Otherwise, it *may* be correct, but then it may *not* be correct, too. It just *depends* on how everybody votes, and that is entirely too *indeterminate* for me.

The rule about Visual Basic appending a NULL character to strings used as parameters for DLL functions and subroutines in which the parameters are declared to be **ByVal** and **As String** is always in effect, *except* when you are passing *user-defined* data types. In Windows SDK/C, it is common practice to use data constructs called *structures*. *Structures* are composed of *items*. The *items* within a *structure* can be of nearly *any* type: *integer*, *long*, *double*, *and string* (but *not* of *currency*, in usual practice) . To define a *structure* in Visual Basic, you use the **Type ... End Type** construct.

You do *not* pass a *user-defined* type variable **ByVal**. Instead, you pass it **ByRef** and, as a result of this, Visual Basic does *not* append any NULL characters for you. This means that if you have a string item in your *user-defined* type, then *you* must *supply* the required NULL character terminator (in all cases) or it is *very* likely that you will get a UAE. You can generally avoid having to pass *user-defined* types to DLL functions and subroutines as long as you generally avoid using any Windows SDK/C functions and subroutines (including the regular Windows functions and any other DLL products). However, you will find that if you generally avoid using any Windows SDK/C or other DLL products, then (1) you are dramatically limiting what you can do and (2) this is just *not* practical in the *real* world.

Consider the following example showing the use of a Visual Basic user-defined type:

```
(in GLOBAL.BAS):
Type SpecialStruct
   sztFirstName As String * 10
   sztLastName As String * 20
   ntAccountNumber As Integer
   dtPurchaseAmount As Double
End Type

Global gSpecArray (1 to 10) As SpecialStruct
Global ngRetVal As Integer

Declare Function Generic_Funct Lib \
    "GENERIC.DLL" (gSpecArray As SpecialStruct) \
        As Integer

(in your Code):
' initialize the structure array...
tmp1$ = Space$(9) + Chr$(0)
tmp2$ = Space$(19) + Chr$(0)
For I = 1 To 10 Step 1
   gSpecArray(I).sztFirstName = tmp1$
   gSpecArray(I).sztLastName = tmp2$
   gSpecArray(I).ntAccountNumber = 0
   gSpecArray(I).dtPurchaseAmount = 0
Next I
' now...load something into ROW 1...
```

```
        tmp$ = "Plato"
        tmp$ = tmp$ + Chr$(0)
        gSpecArray(1).sztFirstName = LTrim$(tmp$)

        tmp$ = "Twitty"
        tmp$ = tmp$ + Chr$(0)
        gSpecArray(1).sztLastName = LTrim$(tmp$)

        gSpecArray(1).ntAccountNumber = 2001

        gSpecArray(1).dtPurchaseAmount = 259.95
        ' now...call the function...
        ngRetVal = Generic_Funct (gSpecArray)
```

  Several things are worth noting in this example. **SpecialStruct** is the *user-defined* type, and it contains several data types: string, integer, and double. **gSpecArray** is defined as a *structure array* of type **SpecialStruct**, and it has 10 rows, occurrences, or members. Note that the NULL character, or **Chr$(0)**, string terminator is *explicitly* appended to each of the string items. And, note that the entire *structure* is passed **ByRef**--even though the term **ByRef** is not mentioned because it is the *default*. In other words, this *structure array* is passed as a simple *numeric array*.

  Note that I explicitly *initialized* the entire structure array. I did this because I am sending the entire structure array to the DLL function and do not want to send any garbage. Visual Basic will absolutely *not* put a string of blanks terminated with a NULL character in each of the string items. If you do not *explicitly* provide the NULL terminators for the string items, then some bizarre things could happen.

  Note that I included the **'Struct'** in the name of the structure and that I included **'Array'** in the name of the array. I think that this helps make the variable type and its use more obvious. Also, I used a lowercase 't' in the prefix of the structure items. This is done to indicate that these variables are defined in a **Type...End Type** statement. Using the 't' in the item name is a little awkward so I am trying to find a good place for it [before the array name seems like a good place because it identifies the array as being a *user-defined type* array (e.g., **tgSpecArray**)].

Of course, maybe nothing bizarre will actually occur when you do not explicitly provide NULL terminators for structure string items (it all depends on how the DLL function is coded), but it is likely that the DLL function will try to read the entire array at some point and if any NULL terminator is missing then you will get a UAE (or something similarly disastrous). I guarantee it will happen at least some of the time if *you* do not guarantee that the NULL terminators are present.

However, it is not really much extra work to put the NULL terminators where they belong. The amount of processing required on a 386 33-MHz PC for doing this is so *minimal* as to be nearly unnoticeable. Just do it, and *know* that because you did it the *correct* way, your code will work as you *intend* it to work. All things considered, this is a very, very small price to pay for being able to access *any* Windows SDK/C DLL. The power that this makes available to you is enormous.

If you are planning on using Windows SDK/C functions and subroutines, just remember that, when the function or subroutine requires that you provide a *structure*, you define that *structure* by using the Visual Basic **Type...End Type** construct. You can get the complete set of definitions and declarations for all of the Windows SDK functions, subroutines, types, constants, and variables from Microsoft and from the MSBASIC forum in CompuServe. You can get the documentation for the Windows SDK from Microsoft Press or your local technical book store. The cost of doing this is very small compared to purchasing the Windows SDK/C.

Now, when you look at Visual Basic and think it is a good language but lacking in depth, remember that it does *not* take much effort to extend the capabilities of Visual Basic to include *direct* access to the complete Windows SDK function and subroutine libraries. Very *powerful* indeed!

However, there are a few things you cannot do unless you have either the Windows SDK/C (or some derivative thereof). The primary thing you cannot do is build a DLL. If you want to make your own Visual Basic custom controls, you *need* a language and supporting processors which can build a Dynamic Link Library (DLL). You also *need* the Visual Basic Control Development Kit (CDK). The Visual Basic CDK is available from Microsoft. If you do not want to use the traditional Windows SDK/C for building your DLL, then you should consider using Microsoft's new QuickC For Windows. However, I do not find it easier to use QuickC For Windows for building a DLL; so I prefer to use the Windows SDK/C. If you are going to construct a DLL, then you are going to have to learn Windows SDK/C programming, and there is no better way to do it than with the Windows SDK/C. QuickC For Windows will *not* make building a DLL any easier, but it works and has excellent Windows Help files.

If you are using Visual Basic professionally, then your tools should include at least the following, in my opinion:
- (1) Visual Basic
- (2) Visual Basic Control Development Kit (CDK)
- (3) Windows SDK/C
- (4) Windows Help Compiler (included in Windows SDK/C)

(5) Word For Windows V2.X or higher.
This set of tools give access to everything that is available to Windows SDK/C programmers. The retail cost of these tools is approximately $1,500.00, which is reasonable in my opinion (the actual cost is lower), considering the amount of work you can do with them.

There are also quite a few Visual Basic tool kits available that greatly extend the capabilities of Visual Basic but do not require you to build your own Dynamic Link Libraries and Visual Basic Custom Controls. I mention some of these tool kits in various places in this book.

I have not said much about *pointers*, yet, but will say a little about them now: I avoid using *pointers* whenever and wherever possible. In general you will only be interested in long pointers of one kind or another. The primary kinds of long pointers that will appear from time to time are the following: (1) lpsz (i.e., LPSTR, a long pointer to a string), and (2) lptr or lp<var> (i.e., a long pointer to *something*). Regardless of what the long pointer actually points to, it is still a long pointer. Long pointers *map* directly to long integers in Visual Basic. The difficult part of working with long pointers is knowing *where* to get them and *what* to do with them *when* you get them. This is where having access to the Windows SDK functions and subroutines is mandatory.

Knowing what to do with long pointers also requires that you understand Windows SDK/C programming--and this is why I recommend that you get a copy of Windows SDK/C. I am not going to say much more about long pointers because you can generally *avoid* using them and still be able to do *nearly* everything you want to do. However, if you are interested in this, then get some books on Windows SDK/C and read them. Actually, *study* them, because they are *not* easy subjects to master.

I do not use very many *methods* in Visual Basic, but the ones I use most frequently are connected with list boxes. The *AddItem* and *RemoveItem* methods are used to add and delete items in list boxes. The important thing to note about the *AddItem method* is that if you specify that the list box is to be sorted (which is done by setting the *Sort property* to TRUE) but then provide a *specific* value for the list box item *index* when using the *AddItem method*, then the *specified* index value will be used *instead* of the *computed* sort index value. Once you understand that this is the rule, it is obvious, but it is *not* very obvious otherwise.

Properties generally work as you think they should. However, when you are working with a *control array* the value of the *Index property* can be automatically assigned a value that is *not* what you want it to be. I think what happens is that there is a counter and that, at some point, it loses track of what you are doing. Knowing this occurs, I always check (and correct) the values of *control array* indexes as a regular step in form design. If you decide to change an index value, then be aware that you *cannot* change an index value to the value of another index. This means that you may have to *temporarily* change other index values to be able to *adjust* a particular index value. This is not much trouble, but is useful to know. *Control arrays* are very *powerful*, and you must learn how to use them.

In general, you should make an effort *not* to use as many Visual Basic methods and properties as possible because when you *do* use one of them you are working. You want to avoid having to work as *often* as possible. The more unnecessary work you can avoid the *better*. The key to Visual Basic is learning how to make Visual Basic *do* as much *work* for you as is *possible*. In other words, learn to use Visual Basic as a *not-programming* language and take advantage of the fact that Visual Basic provides *smart objects*. I will have more to say about using s*mart objects* in the next chapter.

Smart Objects

In the early days of computing (when there were only mainframes), programs were generally divided into two categories: (1) batch and (2) transaction. Batch programs were used to perform complex calculations, generate reports, and a few other useful things. Transaction programs were used to control and process interactive data accesses. But in the early days of computing the only interactive display device was the one used by the computer operator. There were neither programmer nor user display devices: GUI did not exist.

In an attempt to be historically correct, I should point out the fact that I am talking about *my* early days of computing. Computers have nearly always had some kind of visual display device, even though it was somewhat primitive. It was, and continues to be, called the display panel and is nothing more than a series of light bulbs that correspond to registers and their words, bytes and bits. It is fascinating to watch the display panel, and I have worked with a few people who could tell *and* program what the computer was doing by watching the display panel. I never learned how to program a computer from the display panel, but I did discover how to tune mainframe databases by feeling disk drive vibrations. Nevertheless, from 1975 until 1979, nearly all of the programming I (and quite a few other people) did was done via computer cards.

If you were a batch programmer, your primary input device was the card reader, and your primary output devices were the card punch and the printer. Later, if you were a transaction programmer, your input and output device was the computer terminal. Computer terminals were basically nothing more than a video display (a Cathode Ray Tube or CRT) and a keyboard. CRTs were generally called *dumb terminals* because they could not do anything by themselves. Everything the CRT did was controlled by the mainframe transaction program.

Transaction programs have nearly always consisted of two general parts: (1) display processing and (2) calculation processing. Early transactions were run via small card decks because there were no accessible display devices. The calculation part of transaction programs has *not* changed very much over the years--it is still what it always *was*. But display processing has changed *dramatically* in the sense that it has become more and more complex since it first became available. In fact, display processing has become a major task. This is especially true in Windows because of the enormous capabilities of its Graphical User Interface (GUI).

When I first began working on computers (as a student at the University of Houston) there were only cards and card punch (or keypunch) machines. There was no computer terminal for an undergraduate student. In those days, programming consisted of flowcharting an application, writing the code, punching the cards, inputting the cards via a card reader, and getting a printed output report. All things considered, it was an amazingly *slow* process.

A two thousand line program would require at least that many computer cards. If you made a mistake, you had to punch a new card and resubmit the entire card deck. If you (or the computer operator) dropped the card deck, you could spend several *hours* putting the cards back in proper order. There were plenty of tricks for working with card decks, including drawing a diagonal line across the top of the card deck and putting sequence numbers on the cards (only useful if you had access to a card sorter).

One useful benefit of having to use cards and keypunch machines was learning to visualize the process of interactive programming because at that time anything interactive was pure fantasy. At some point, I learned to visualize what I was doing and could use the keypunch just like an interactive terminal, except that the display was *inside* my head. I suspect that I would have learned how to do this without cards and the keypunch but do not know what *form* the visualization would have taken. In the early days, nearly everything--card reader, printer, disk drives, tape drives, and mainframe--was someplace *else* (with really good air conditioning). So if you wanted to *see* the *big picture*, then the only *place* to *see* it was in your *mind*.

Until I could *see* it, programming did not really make any sense to me . When you learn to think *visually*, everything involved in programming will be much *easier*. This is especially true in Windows application design and programming. If you cannot *see* an object and the code that controls it, you should spend a lot of time *drawing* flowcharts because that is the *best* way to learn how to *see* programs.

Designing and programming a Windows application is very similar to designing and programming a set of mainframe transactions, but there is a major *difference*. The visual (or display processing) component of a Windows application is much more *complex* than the visual component of a mainframe transaction. In fact, nearly half (or more) of a Windows application is involved *exclusively* with *GUI work*. The *GUI work* is what makes Windows SDK/C programming such a *slow* task. Most of the work you do in Windows SDK/C programming is involved with GUI tasks and has nothing to do with what I call *real* work.

My concept of *real* work is a direct result of learning to program in a batch environment. *Real* work is not associated with displaying information on a computer terminal. *Real* work is performing a calculation. Making a list box function correctly as a GUI object is not *real* work, but *generating* the *data* that goes *into* the list box is *real* work. When you divide Windows application design and programming into *real* work and *GUI* work, you will *see* that you are *not* doing much *real* work when you use the Windows SDK/C. However, that is *not* the case with Visual Basic.

Visual Basic is decidedly *different* from Windows SDK/C in terms of *real* work and *GUI work*. The reason for this difference is that Visual Basic has *smart objects*. The GUI portion of a Windows application is its *visual* component and is really nothing more than a *set* of *visual* objects. In Windows SDK/C programming, the visual objects do not have much *intelligence*--they are *dumb objects*. If you want an object to do something in Windows SDK/C, you have to tell it, *explicitly*, everything (or nearly everything) that it is supposed to do. In Windows SDK/C, visual objects are *not* born knowing very much.

In Visual Basic, visual objects *are* born knowing nearly everything they have to do. Visual Basic's objects are *smart objects*. In fact, Visual Basic objects are *smarter* than nearly everyone *imagines*. One of the amazing things about Visual Basic is that its *smart objects* do most of the GUI work for you. However, they will *only* do most of the work if you *know* how to *use* them correctly. It would be nice if all you needed to know was that *smart objects* are easy to use, but there is more to it than that. Learning about *smart objects* and learning how to design and program with *smart objects* is made somewhat more difficult by the inclusion in Visual Basic of an enormous amount of *smart object* capabilities (most of which you will nearly never need to use).

I am not suggesting that Visual Basic *smart objects* are too smart, just that you do *not* need to use most of their capabilities. For example, I rarely use anything other than the *Click*, *Change*, and *KeyPress* events. These events do just about *everything* that I need to do. I could use *every* event, but if I did I would be wasting time and effort and would not really be getting any more *useful* work done. I think it is wonderful that there is are *GotFocus* and *LostFocus* events, but I do *not* need them most of the time(and they do *not* do exactly what I would want them to do if I actually did need them). I do *not* use them most of the time because, in my opinion, they only do *part* of the work that they should *really* do.

You are probably wondering how I can do anything useful when I only use the *Click*, *Change*, and *KeyPress* events (noting that I rarely use the *KeyPress* event). I can do nearly everything I need to do *because* I have *learned* how to design and program with *smart objects* that only respond to *Click*, *Change*, and *KeyPress* events. For me, these are the *only* events. In some cases, I use *other* events (but only if there is no way to *avoid* it). In other words, I just *ignore* the great majority of Visual Basic events. They are *available* when I *need* them, but I usually do *not* need them.

The same thing is true of Visual Basic properties, except that you will use more of the properties (primarily when you are adding objects to a form). Most of the properties can be set as you build your forms and then *never* changed. The properties that will generally be used at runtime are *Visible*, *Enabled*, *Text*, *Caption*, *BackColor*, *ForeColor*, *Value*, *Min*, *Max*, *ListCount*, *ListIndex*, *List*, *MultiLine*, *BorderStyle* and *Index*. The other properties are useful, but I generally do not use them.

The primary methods that I use are *AddItem*, *RemoveItem*, *Show*, and *SetFocus*. I do not use the *Hide* method and strongly suggest that you do not use it--use the *Unload* function instead. If you *Hide* forms, your application will use up *all* of Windows Free System Resources (at some point) and will mysteriously disappear. It does *not* require much extra work to avoid using the *Hide* method. You *must* do it at some point; so you may as well start doing it the correct way *now*, instead of later.

Since I learned Windows application design and programming as a Windows SDK/C programmer, I was already familiar with Windows events, properties, and methods when I began learning how to use Visual Basic. It took me a little while to decide which *subset* of events, properties, and methods I wanted to use (or needed to use), but when I did pick a subset it was as *small* as possible. From my perspective, less is better.

Because doing anything with Windows SDK/C is a big task, I had already learned how to do as little as possible. Learning Visual Basic and applying my Windows SDK/C knowledge made it possible for me further to refine the art of *Doing As Little As Possible* (DALAP). Please note that *Doing As Little As Possible* is just a variation of *Keep It Simple* (KIS). Both of these methods are variations of *Working Smart* (WS). If you do not *Work Smart* in Windows application design and programming, you will *not* be able to do much work. You will waste *nearly* all of your time and effort.

This chapter is devoted to *smart objects* but is really just another way to teach you how to program in Visual Basic. You have probably noted, at this point, that I have devoted much of this book to describing and explaining a particular *style* for designing and programming Windows applications with Visual Basic. I am doing this because it is the single most *important* aspect of Visual Basic programming and because it is *not* very easy to explain. It is really more like a *system* that has *style*, than just a *style*.

The Visual Basic documentation contains nearly everything you need to know about specific programming statements--but it provides very few clues regarding which *style* you should use. You have to discover--or invent--an appropriate *style* to use in Visual Basic. One purpose of this book is to define an appropriate *style* for Visual Basic programming. The concept of *smart objects* is one of the keys to the *style* I use.

What is a *smart object*? Well, a s*mart object* is a Visual Basic object. Visual Basic objects are *forms* and *controls,* and they are *smart*. The unique *characteristic* of a *smart object* is that it is born knowing (1) *what* it is, (2) *what* it does, (3) *when* to do it, and (4) *how* to do it. In other words, a *smart object* is *already* programmed. Because it is *already* programmed, you do *not* have to do any (or at least very much) programming to *use* it.

What am I talking about? Well, look at a push button in terms of *style*, *smart objects*, and the art of *Doing As Little As Possible*. What does a push button *really* do in terms of GUI? Not much! A push button not only does *very* little, but it also comes *already* programmed to do it. Remember that, at this point, we are talking about the GUI portion of a Windows application. A push button does *everything* it needs to do in terms of GUI. The fact that it does *everything* it needs to do means you do *not* have to do any more *GUI work* to use it.

When you add a push button to your form you do so because you want the push button to do something. In other words, you want the push button to do some *real* work. **The *key* to Visual Basic is to *separate* the *GUI work* from the *real work*.** The entire purpose for adding a push button to your form is to have something you can *use* to enable the user of your application to *notify* you when you *need* to do some *real* work. Except for the somewhat subtle purpose of giving the user a visual *clue* when it is appropriate to do things, that is *all* a push button does, and that is all it should be used to do.

As a programmer, you use the *Click* event of the push button as the *trigger* for the *real* work you need to do. In other words, (1) Visual Basic provides the push button (in the form of a *smart object* that is born knowing what to do for GUI purposes), (2) you only use the push button as a *visual mechanism* for being notified when the user of your application wants you to do some *real* work, (3) you use the *Click* event of the push button ***only*** to *initiate* the *real* work, and (4) the *real* work is performed in a *non*-event procedure that is contained in a *module*.

There is a story about a physicist and a mathematician that contains an interesting observation about the technique of *Working Smart*. In this story, there is a room. In the room, there is a table, a box of matches, some wood, and a wood stove. A pan of water sits on the table. A physicist and a mathematician are each given the problem of showing how to boil the water.

The physicist begins his solution to the problem by putting some wood into the wood stove and starting a fire with the matches. The physicist then gets the pan of water from the table and puts it on the wood stove; and (after a few minutes) the water boils. The problem is solved. Now it is the mathematician's turn.

The mathematician begins his solution to the problem by putting some wood into the wood stove and starting a fire with the matches. The mathematician then gets the pan of water from the table and puts it on the wood stove; and (after a few minutes) the water boils. The problem is solved.

Then, the physicist and the mathematician are given a *new* problem to solve. Once again, there is a room. In the room, there is a table, a box of matches, some wood, and a wood stove. A pan of water sits on the *floor*. The problem is to show how to boil the water.

The physicist begins his solution to the problem by putting some wood into the wood stove and starting a fire with the matches. The physicist then gets the pan of water from the *floor* and . puts it on the wood stove; and (after a few minutes) the water boils. The problem is solved. Now it is the mathematician's turn.

The mathematician gets the pan of water from the *floor* and *puts* it *onto* the *table*. In reducing this *new* problem to a problem that has *already* been solved, the mathematician thereby solves the problem. That is essence of *Working Smart*.

The original story (upon which this version is based) was told to me by one of my mathematics professors. Because (1) I really like this story, (2) I know that this professor has always wanted to have a theory named in his honor, and (3) I am not very good at mathematical theory, I have, nevertheless, invented a theory that I call **Sinkhorn's Dilemma**: **Every paradox has at least one nontrivial solution.** In essence, what this theory states is that, *somewhere* (possibly in *Another World*), there *is* a mathematical system in which paradoxes do *not* exist.

In Visual Basic, objects already *know* what to do when they are on the table. All *you* have to do to make *them* do most of the work is (1) know *when* and *how* to get them *onto* the table and (2) *put* them *onto* the table. In terms of *real* work, there is very little difference between Windows and a mainframe batch program. At some point, you must do *some* computing. Nearly all programmers know how to make a computer do *some* computing. For doing *real* work, there are not really many different choices--just flavors.

For example, there are *not* very many different ways to add two numbers. The exact method for performing addition will (of course) vary from language to language. There will also be some variation in terms of the type of numbers that are being added (e.g., integer, real, complex, decimal, binary, hexadecimal, and so forth). But there are just *not* that many *different* ways to do addition. Addition is something that I consider to be *real* work.

Addition is *real* work because it is a task that is virtually *independent* in terms of batch and transaction processing. In other words, addition does not have (nor require) a visual component. So, given the problem of adding two numbers, the solution is basically the same for mainframe batch and transaction programs *and* for Windows applications. The *differences* do *not* appear until you consider how to *present* the *result* of the addition. In a mainframe batch program, you would probably print the *result* in a report. In a mainframe transaction program or in a Windows application, you would probably display the *result* on the screen (although you could print the *result*).

The important thing to observe is that the work involved in printing or displaying the *result* of the addition is often more complex than the addition itself. I generally view printing as a less complex task than displaying, but that is not always the case. However, it would be very convenient, especially in a Windows application, if displaying a *result* were easy. Displaying *results* is not easy in Windows SDK/C, but it *can* be in Visual Basic because Visual Basic has *smart objects*.

In effect, what I am telling you is that it does *not* matter whether you are working on a mainframe batch program, a mainframe transaction program, or a Windows program when it comes to doing *real* work. At some point, you *must* perform a *computation* to produce a *result*. You have to do it, and there is no way to avoid having to do it. It is just something you do because it *must* be done. But it does matter, considerably, whether you are working on a mainframe transaction program or on a Windows program when it comes to the work involved in controlling and programming the *visual* representation of *real* work.

I am suggesting that the *better* way to approach the GUI portion of a Windows application is *not* to have anything to do with it (or, at least, as *little* as possible). Take care of the *real* work, and then give the *results* to a *smart object*. Let the *smart object* take care of the *GUI* work. When you do this in Visual Basic, the *distinction* between event procedures and *non*-event procedures becomes very *important*.

Nearly everything you put into an event procedure does no *real* work. Therefore, you want to do as little coding in an event procedure as possible. Doing absolutely *nothing* is the best you can do. Visual Basic event procedures are your interface between the *real* work (that you absolutely *must* do) and the GUI work (that you want to *avoid* whenever possible).

You cannot totally isolate yourself from *smart objects* and the GUI component of a Windows application (because you have to *know* how everything works in order to be able to use it effectively), but you can certainly let Visual Basic *smart objects* do the great majority of the *GUI* work for you. You can also take advantage of another capability of Visual Basic *smart objects*. Visual Basic *smart objects* can do *real* work.

For example, a list box that is not visible has no visual or GUI component (obviously), but it nevertheless provides nearly all of the functions and capabilities of a sophisticated (but *invisible*) list manager. This is a fact that is *not* obvious until you notice it. An edit box is an *already* programmed data entry object. The fact that Visual Basic *smart objects* can do *real* work is something you can use beneficially if you adjust the design of your Windows application in such a way as to make the *smart objects* do as much work (both *real* and *GUI*) as possible. One way to do this is to enforce the rule that you **always know exactly what is happening**. The best way to do this is to control *Focus* (something I have already discussed).

In other words, you can look at a Visual Basic form (and the controls on it) as a *State Machine* of sorts. You are nearly always in the *domain* of a *smart object*; so you need to capitalize on that fact. The key to using Visual Basic forms and controls as a *State Machine* is to enforce the rule that you **never go from one *state* to another unless the *state* you are leaving is determined (or *known*)**. Since this is getting very close to the real *key* to designing with *smart objects*, let me make this clearer.

In a very real sense, **you do work in Windows only in response to messages**. Windows is a *transaction processor*, and so is your application. Messages are usually generated as a result of the user's doing something (e.g., moving the mouse or pressing a key). An application can send itself (or other applications) messages, but it is easier to understand the process if you look at messages as being things which Windows *delivers* to your application when Windows determines that you *may* need to do some work (*real* or otherwise). Because this is the way it works, you can generally make the statement that **when you have processed *all* of your outstanding messages, you are in a *known* (or determined) state and have *finished* all of your work.**

In other words, since you do *not* have to do anything *unless* you have outstanding messages, one very good way to *avoid* having to do *any* work is to keep your application in a *state* in which *all* messages have been *processed* (i.e., in a state where you do *not* have any *unprocessed* [outstanding] messages). This is important because attaining this particular type of *state* is one of the goals of Windows design and programming. It is both the most trivial and the most complex thing to do. It is also completely foreign to traditional mainframe (or DOS) programming.

Another way of looking at it is to observe that **as a programmer you are constantly striving to do *nothing* in a Windows application.** I suppose this is obvious, but it is *not* so obvious as it *appears*. You really do *not* want to do *nothing*. You just want continually to reach points (or *states*) where you do not have to do anything. You do not have to program for those times when you are doing *nothing* in Windows. **Since doing *nothing* is usually very easy, you want to do *nothing* as often as possible. The only thing that *interferes* with your being able to do *nothing* is messages.** We already know that most of the messages are generated by the user's doing something with or to a GUI object.

In other words, you begin your Windows application in a known *state* (i.e., one in which you do not have to do anything) and then continually move your Windows application from one known *state* to another in response to messages. **If you do not have any messages you do not do anything (i.e., you do *nothing*).** When you get a message, the message tells you what to do and you do it (if it is something you *want* to do). *Focus* becomes important (essentially critical), in this process because *Focus* **is the** *mechanism* **you use to** *restrict* **messages.**

Note that, when I refer to *messages* in Windows, I am using Windows SDK/C terminology. In Visual Basic, you do not use the term *messages* very frequently. Instead, you use the term *events*. When Visual Basic receives a Windows *message*, it (1) examines the *message*, (2) determines its type, and (3) calls the *event* procedure used to process that type of *message*. If you have *not* added any code to the particular *event* procedure, then *only* the *default processing* for the *event* will be done. But if you *have* added code to the particular *event*, then your code will be performed (in addition to the *default* Visual Basic code for the event).

For example, in Windows SDK/C, *clicking* on a push button generates a WM_COMMAND *message*. In Visual Basic, this same *message* is translated into a call to your push button's *Click* event. So, in Visual Basic *events* are roughly equivalent to *messages* (for all practical purposes). You can, therefore, continue reading with the *understanding* that the *messages* you get in Visual Basic are requests (or commands) to perform *event* procedures.

You do not necessarily want to prevent (or restrict) *all* messages, but you do want to prevent *frivolous* messages. *Frivolous* messages require *make-work* and are, therefore, *undesirable*. Instead of attempting to deal with hundreds and hundreds of *frivolous* conditions (or *states*), you want to control everything that happens in such a way that *frivolity* is *limited* to a minimum.

For example, if you have a text box which is used to input a date, then it makes sense to verify (or validate) the value in the text box to determine whether it is a good date *before* changing *Focus* to another control (or *state*). If it is illogical (or *frivolous*) for a push button to be enabled and visible (i.e., available for use), then *explicitly* make that push button *unavailable*. **Do *not* create conditions in which the user can do illogical things.** Keep such conditions to a minimum.

Note that I am telling you *not* to *create* conditions in which the user can do illogical (or *frivolous*) things. Remember that, in Visual Basic, you begin your Windows application with a single blank form. Your user can do nearly *nothing* with a blank form. Each time *you* add an object (or control) to the form, *you* add new capabilities to the form. The users of your application do *not* invent ways to do frivolous things--*you* do. If the users of your application can do something *frivolous*, they can only do it because *you* made it possible and because you *created* the condition and then *empowered* it. That is a very important *concept* for you to understand.

If it is *illogical* to do something in your Windows application, then do not do it! The users of your application will not always *know* when doing something would be illogical--but *you* will. I would find it very unusual for a user to complain when an application does not let him do *silly* things, but this may happen when a user does not know that doing something is *silly*. **I do not think you will get many requests from your customers to add *errors* to your application.** Nobody is going to call you and say, "This application is really working very well, but could you add some code to make it randomly format my hard drive? I get much more work done now that I am using your application, and, well, I miss the frustration and inconvenience of being able to waste my time doing *silly* things."

Preventing users from doing illogical (or *silly*) things is neither restrictive nor wasteful. If performing a particular action would cause an error, then it makes absolutely no sense (to me) to allow the user to initiate that action. In other words, why in the world would you want to invent *more* ways of doing *unnecessary* work in Windows when there is already *too* much work for you to do!

If you make it possible for your Windows application to do *silly* things, you will (1) have to code special procedures to check for *silliness* and (2) have to take appropriate action whenever *silliness* is detected. What a tremendous waste of your valuable time! What a tremendous waste of your user's valuable time! If it does *not* make any sense to do something, then you should not only *not* do it, but also *not* allow it. In doing this, you are *not* limiting freedom of action. You are limiting the ability to do *frivolous* things. In effect, you are creating and *enforcing* a *state* in which you do *not* allow *frivolous* activity.

This requires some thought; so now is a good time for you to put on your *thinking hat*. In general, messages come from *smart objects*. Since messages usually require some amount of *real* work, you would *prefer* to have control over both the *type* and the *source* of messages. This means that you need to control the *behavior* of *smart objects* with respect to message generation. Let the *smart objects* do as much work for you as possible, but do *not* let them create *frivolous* work. *Smart objects* do *not* always *know* whether they are generating meaningful messages or *frivolous* messages. In general, they do not really care one way or the other. So, you have to give them some *guidance*. The best ways to *guide* them are (1) to enable or disable them and (2) to make them visible or invisible.

In other words, if a *smart object* cannot do anything *meaningful* in the current *state* of your application, then disable the *smart object* or make it invisible. Do *not* let it do something it should not do! If the *smart object* can do something *meaningful* in the current *state* of your application, then enable the *smart object* or make it visible. But in some cases, you may *not* actually *know* whether a *smart object* is doing something meaningful or *frivolous* until the user *attempts* to transfer *Focus* to another *smart object*.

In Windows SDK/C programming, you can use two messages that are roughly equivalent to the Visual Basic *GotFocus* and *LostFocus* events (or messages) to test for meaningful and *frivolous* activity. I do not usually do this in Visual Basic because there are some things that *GotFocus* and *LostFocus* miss. The better way to handle transfer of *Focus* is to create (via design) a set of conditions in which it is nearly impossible for the user to do *frivolous* things.

If, as a result of *explicit* control, everything the user does is intelligent (or at least not incorrect), then your application will nearly always be in a known *state* in which (1) there are no unprocessed messages and (2) only meaningful *smart objects* are available for use. When that is the case, you do not have to concern yourself with transfer of *Focus* from one *smart object* to another *smart object* because you have already solved *and* eliminated the problem by not allowing *anything* to happen that could introduce *any* incorrect actions as a consequence of change in *Focus*.

The best way to understand this is to view a Windows application as an *entity* that responds to action, rather than as an *entity* that initiates action. If there are no requests (or messages) for action, then you do not need to do anything (*including program*). If the *smart objects* that are currently available for use can only trigger valid requests (or messages) to do meaningful work, then you have *no* need to *restrict* their behavior, because they are *well-behaved*.

The more *well-behaved* your Windows application is, the less *GUI* work you have to do. You must do a certain amount of *real* work because there is no way to avoid it. However, *GUI* work can usually be avoided and should be avoided whenever possible. The *real* work must be done. It is the *minimum* amount of work that your application must do. Nearly everything you do in addition to that minimum amount of *real* work is *make-work*. *Make-work* is a total waste of time and effort. A considerable amount of *GUI* work is really *make-work*, and it is unnecessary.

In other words, by doing a little extra design work to *fine-tune* the *behavior* of Visual Basic *smart objects*, you can virtually *eliminate* most of the *GUI* work and thereby limit your work to doing *meaningful* tasks and *real* work. That does not mean you will *never* have to do anything *complex*. Instead, it means you can *reduce* the amount of programming required in a Windows application by designing *well-behaved* forms. You *must* do the *real* work, but there is nothing wrong with letting (or making) Visual Basic *smart objects* do most of the other types of work.

In a traditional mainframe batch program you *explicitly* control exactly what happens on a *step-by-step* basis. In my style of Visual Basic programming, you give the user a choice of actions (each one valid) and then do *nothing* until the user selects one of the actions. When the user selects an action (via a *smart object*), you then know *exactly* what to do and you do it. More importantly, you begin *and* complete the action and, consequently, move from one known *state* in which you are doing *nothing* to another known *state* in which you are, again, doing *nothing*.

In my *style* of Visual Basic programming, you only do *something* so that you can get to a point at which you do *nothing*. This is really nothing more than *transaction processing* at the *smart object* level. It is probably an unusual way to look at the process of designing and programming a Windows application, but it works for me. However, you will *not* see much mention of doing *nothing* in new product announcements.

Nobody is going to announce that the new version of their application, "does absolutely *nothing* nearly 90 percent of the time." And you will not read many testimonials to the effect that, "With *Fribble Software's* new *Silly Windows Application*, my ability to do absolutely *nothing* has improved dramatically. I never realized that I could do *nothing* so easily, and the price is right, too! If, like me, you need to do absolutely *nothing*, then *Silly Windows Application* is the product to get. "

Yet, as a Visual Basic application designer and programmer, one of your *goals* is to keep your application in a *state* in which *you* are required to do absolutely *nothing*. Think about it for a few minutes. Doing absolutely *nothing* is probably one of the *easiest* things to do in Windows, but it is also one of the most *difficult* things to do.

When you look at a Windows application from the Visual Basic *perspective* of doing absolutely *nothing*, then you will *see* that, by carefully selecting *smart objects* and linking them to *real* work, you can really *minimize* the amount of programming that you must do. In other words, use Visual Basic *smart objects* as *visual program steps*. Transform your Windows application into a Türing Machine that (1) begins in a known *state*, (2) does something, and then (3) moves to the *next* known *state*. Use Visual Basic *smart objects* as a mechanism that lets the user tell you (1) when to do something, (2) what to do, and (3) when to move to the *next* known *state*.

When you look at it this way, you will *see* that designing and programming a Windows application with Visual Basic is really *easy* because Visual Basic *smart objects* can (and will) do most of the *GUI* work (and some of the *real* work) for you. This is what is so *amazing* about Visual Basic. It really *transforms* designing and programming a Windows application into an *easy* task.

Begin with a blank form, add one Visual Basic *smart object*, and empower it. Then add another Visual Basic *smart object* and empower it. If necessary, connect it (preferably via *loose coupling)* to the other Visual Basic *smart object*. Continue this process of (1) adding, (2) empowering, and (3) connecting Visual Basic *smart objects* until your application is *complete*. *Adding* and *empowering* are easy, but *connecting* is often a somewhat complex task.

However, (1) by limiting event procedures to no more than 20 lines and (2) by putting most of your code into *non-*event procedures residing in modules, the task of connecting Visual Basic *smart objects* becomes *less* complex. Always maintaining a current *result* makes this process even *easier*, but it *requires* you to do some additional coding to *separate* the current *result* from the Visual Basic *smart objects*. The key to *everything* is to maintain and enforce *independence*. The more *independent* your Visual Basic *smart objects* and current *results* are, the *less* work you have to do.

It is also very important to learn how to program with *generic* functions and subroutines in Visual Basic. If you have a Computer Science background, you will know this (even though you may not use it). Nonetheless, it is very important to design and program with *generic* functions and subroutines in Visual Basic because Windows applications tend to do a lot of *repetitive* work. This is also important because you will probably want to write *more* than *one* Windows application.

There are generally three sources for functions and subroutines in Visual Basic: (1) Visual Basic, (2) Visual Basic Add-On Libraries and Tool Kits, and (3) yourself. **QuickPak Professional For Windows** and **VBTools** are two very good general purpose libraries and tool kits for Visual Basic. **PowerLibW** (ETN Corporation) is a useful X-Base DBMS and function library for Visual Basic. **PowerShoW** (ETN Corporation) is an excellent Image Management System library for Visual Basic. **ChartBuilder** (Pinnacle Publishing, Inc.) is a attractive custom control used to add dynamic charting capabilities to your Visual Basic applications. **ButtonTool** and **EditTool** (OutRider Systems) are useful, special purpose tool kits. **3-D Widgets** (Sheridan Software Systems, Inc.) adds impressive-looking controls and menu buttons to your Visual Basic tool kit. **DataLIB** (DatTel Communication Systems) is a quick and easy to use Dynamic Link Library (DLL) that provides sophisticated data import/export capabilities to your Visual Basic applications.

In fact, there are so many add-on libraries and tool kits for Visual Basic that I am having a difficult time keeping track of them. I expect their numbers to grow significantly in the next year. Even Microsoft has announced that it is developing a Visual Basic add-on tool kit! Visual Basic is an ideal language for tool kits and libraries, especially if they are easy to use and provide *generic* functions. In a very real sense, you can view designing and programming a Windows application with Visual Basic as a process of connecting *smart objects* with *generic* functions and subroutines. You are probably using Visual Basic because you do *not* want to do much programming or because you want to do as much work as possible in the shortest amount of time (or both). I encourage you to use as many add-on libraries and tool kits as possible, provided they make your work easier and faster.

But you can also write your own *generic* functions and subroutines and will often have *no* other choice. When you start to code a process or task, ask yourself whether it is possible you may want to do the same thing (or something very similar) at a later time. If the answer is yes (or even maybe), then make it a *generic* function or subroutine. More importantly, make it *generic*. I extend this concept to the *form* level and suggest that you begin building a library of *generic* forms. While I am not taking any credit for inventing the term *generic form*, I do take some credit for being among the first group of people to direct *attention* to *generic forms*.

The real credit for *generic forms* must go to Microsoft and the designers of Visual Basic, because they are the ones who decided to provide *encapsulation* at the form level. As I stated earlier, I would also like to see *complete encapsulation* at the frame box level but do not expect it to occur until later releases of Visual Basic. However, I do expect to begin to see add-on libraries of *generic forms* and may even write one myself. I am including a few such *generic forms* in this book so that you can see examples of what I call *generic forms*.

Smart objects are not just Visual Basic controls. They can *also* be Visual Basic *forms*, especially if the *forms* are *generic*. Visual Basic is really an Object-Oriented Programming System (OOPS) *disguised* as a *simple* language for writing Windows applications. The amazing, but subtle, power of Visual Basic is its *ability* to function as a very high level (VHL) OOPS language. In fact, that is *really* what

Visual Basic is: a VHL OOPS language for Windows. The fact that Visual Basic is easy to learn and use makes it even *better*.

Generic Form Design: The Calculator

Up to this point in the book, I have discussed designing and programming a Windows application in Visual Basic from a *conceptual* perspective. There were a few code examples relating to using strings and structures, but that was about all. Everything I have discussed so far has been in preparation for doing what we are going to do now: design and program a generic form. Specifically, I am going to show you how to design and program a medium complexity, scientific calculator using Visual Basic.

In deciding to use a scientific calculator as the first example of a *generic* form, I have done some research on the subject of calculators in Windows and have observed a few things in the process. One observation is that most of the calculators do *not* use push buttons. I do not really understand why there is anything inherently troublesome about using push buttons on a calculator, but nobody seems to use push buttons on calculators in Windows (with a few exceptions).

One such exception is **MacroCalc** (Anderson Consulting & Software). It is a very nice and very sophisticated, calculator application. Anderson Consulting & Software is also responsible for **Tiffany Plus** (a very good Windows screen capture program). **MacroCalc** uses push buttons. That makes me feel better, even though the calculator I am using to demonstrate *generic* form design is not so sophisticated as **MacroCalc**. I like push buttons, and I think everybody should use them as much as possible.

Push buttons are easy to use in Visual Basic and are an ideal choice for *some* of the *objects* that need to appear on a calculator form. Another continual source of amazement for me is that in most Windows calculators, there is only an immediate register (and possibly a memory register). It is not that much more trouble to add a few extra registers to a calculator, but nobody seems to do it.

When I began designing this calculator, I had not seen **MacroCalc**. Later, I saw some literature on it included in a copy of **Tiffany Plus** that I bought for doing screen captures. There are a few similarities, but they are result of logical *thinking* rather than *cloning*. I did not *clone* **MacroCalc**, but certainly could if I wanted to do so. I used my **Sharp Scientific Calculator Model EL-509H** as a model for the calculator in this chapter. However, I decided that the **EL-509H** had too many buttons and could be simplified without sacrificing any functionality.

Another thing I observed in my research on scientific calculators is that they tend to become very elaborate with respect to both quantities of buttons and complexity of functions. Some of the Hewlett-Packard scientific calculators are so complex that learning how to use them is nearly equivalent to learning everything one must learn to get an advanced degree in engineering or physics (mathematicians generally view calculators with considerable contempt). There is some merit to the mathematician's view of calculators because if you do not use a calculator, then you either (1) tend to reach a lot of incorrect conclusions or (2) learn to do mental arithmetic very well.

If you want to learn mathematics, do not use a calculator. Using a calculator to improve your mathematical ability is like using those paint-by-the-numbers art kits to improve your painting ability: both entirely miss the point. The most difficult thing to do in learning to paint is getting the energy (and courage) to go to an art supply store and purchase oil paint (lasts longer), brushes, solvent, linseed oil, and canvas. Everyone is born knowing how to paint abstract pictures and think symbolically. The last thing most mathematicians want is to be forced to do arithmetic (which is about all a calculator can do).

Several of my mathematics professors had (and enforced) the rule that calculators were not allowed in their classes. Encountering this rule in an advanced Probability and Statistics course and having to *justify* my use of a calculator led me to memorize the value of the transcendental number *e* to 50 decimal places. My ability to very quickly recite the value of *e* to 50 decimal places so amused the professor that he allowed me to use my calculator in class, and it laid the foundation for one of those profoundly funny things that can only happen once.

I spent a considerable amount of time in the computer lab and, like most other senior Computer Science majors, enjoyed giving advice to anyone needing it (whether they really needed any advice or not). One afternoon, I happened to be standing next to the drop-off window for submitting card decks and could not help overhearing a conversation between a student and the computer operator in which the computer operator was (rather unsuccessfully) attempting to explain *e* to the student.

The student was from another country and (1) had a limited grasp of English, (2) did not appear to understand anything the computer operator was telling him, and (3) kept repeating the question, "But what is *e*?" Well, this was a golden opportunity in the making, so I interrupted the conversation and asked if I could be of any assistance. The student repeated his question, "What is *e*?"

I replied, "*e* is 2.7 1828 1828 45 90 45 235 360 28 747 135 2662 49 775 724 709 369 996..., *approximately*," and was pleasantly awarded with a few seconds of total silence in the computer lab followed by a few minutes of nearly pandemonian laughter. This was exactly the answer the student wanted to hear, even though the response to it was an obvious surprise. The look on his face, his laughter, and the "Thank you for helping me," that followed made me feel I had actually learned *something* in all of the years I had been in college.

Nevertheless, there are times when having and using a calculator is both necessary and useful. A calculator is also something ideally suited to demonstrating how to design and program a *generic* form in Visual Basic. This is because the work performed by a calculator is representative of a large percentage of the work done in a typical Windows application screen.

The first thing to do in designing a calculator is to identify the major design requirements. In other words, (1) what does the calculator do, (2) how does it look, and (3) how does it do what it does? In using the **EL-509H** as a prototype for this calculator, I have already determined that the calculator is not going to be very big. It is going to be a little calculator and, therefore, will not require a full screen. I have also identified (as a design criterion) the fact that I do not want *many* push buttons on the calculator. Having too many push buttons would make the calculator too difficult to use.

Knowing that the calculator does not have many push buttons introduces another design criterion. If the calculator is going to be simple but do complex things, there needs to be some way of presenting its complex capabilities other than via push buttons. In a real calculator this would present a *dilemma*, but in a Windows calculator this is not a problem because Windows has list boxes. Therefore, by using a list box, the calculator can still perform complex operations and *not* have many push buttons. However, since the calculator is going to be a little calculator, there should be some way to keep it small. I am, therefore, using a *dropdown* list box to conserve *space*.

Using a *dropdown* list box is a nice solution to the problem of providing access to an *extensive* list of functions but is limited (in a certain sense) in its *apparent* inability to function as a selection mechanism for a *nonhomogeneous* (or *dissimilar*) set of functions. However, this is *not* really a problem because (1) I am using Visual Basic *smart objects* and (2) I know a few facts that may surprise you. Primarily, I know that a list box does *not* necessarily have to do what everyone *thinks* it should do.

This is useful to know because it will increase your understanding of the flexibility of Visual Basic *smart objects*. Normally, a list box is used (1) to contain a list and (2) to select one or more of the items contained in the list. However, there is *no* rule saying the contents of a list box cannot change *dynamically* (even *dramatically*). I can unload a list box just as easily as I can load it. I can change both the *contents* and the *function* of a list box just as easily.

What I am proposing (as an *advanced* exercise) is to *modify* the *behavior* (or *mechanics*) of this particular list box in such a way that it becomes a *multilevel* list box in terms of its *response* to selecting an item. This is not an *unfamiliar* behavior and is most obviously demonstrated by the typical file selection list box. In the file selection list box, you can jump from one directory level to another by clicking (or selecting) appropriate items. When jump points are selected, the contents of the list box *dynamically* change. In this regard, the file selection list box is similar to a simple *hypertext* system (and functions in a similar manner).

Ellipses and directory names are *anchors* (a *hypertext* term for something from or to which you can *jump*), and the *anchors* are either (1) always *present* or (2) *derivable*.

There is absolutely no reason why a single list box cannot function in exactly the same way as a *set* of single list boxes. In fact, this is a good technique when *space* is critical. In other words, while I would like to have several list boxes (I do not even know how many at this point), I do not have enough *space* for all of them. But that is not a problem because I can make *one* list box do what *several* list boxes do. All I have to do is add some *intelligence* to the *single* list box.

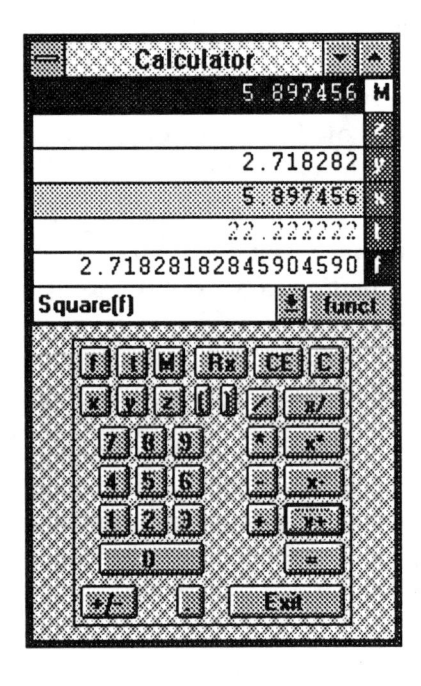

For example, if all I want to display in the list box at the highest level is a list of general function categories (e.g., trigonometric, geometric, rational, integer, complex, Boolean, and so forth), then I can certainly do so. I can also add some code to the selection event that will replace the contents of the list box (*dynamically*) with a set of second-level choices whenever a first-level choice is selected. In other words, when the user selects the trigonometric category, the list box will *dynamically* change itself into a list of trigonometric subcategories. If necessary, I can continue this process of *dynamically* adding more detail until the level of most detail is finally reached.

For example, the first level of trigonometric could include *regular*, *arc*, and *hyperbolic*. Then at the next lower level, *regular* could be expanded to show *sine*, *cosine*, *tangent*, *cotangent*, *secant* and *cosecant*. *Hyperbolic* could be expanded to show *hyperbolic sine*, *hyperbolic cosine*, and so forth. In practice, this could become a very complex *hypertext* system for selecting *specific* functions for use in the calculator.

If we were designing and programming a *library calculator*, then the single *dropdown* list box could become (and function very adequately as) a *metaphor* for the Dewey Decimal System card files at the Library of Congress. In other words, I could make a single list box behave just like a *catalog* for the Library of Congress. Of course, I would need a database and a few other things, but I could make all of it fit into a little *dropdown* list box and still have *nearly* the entire screen available for use to do other work. I suppose that if I carried this to its logical extreme, I could create a single screen *metaphor* for the Library of Congress, complete with a book *metaphor* that would display the text for the book that was currently selected. I could even invent a *metaphor* for a librarian to assist in locating particular books.

However, I am working on a scientific calculator (not on a desktop Library of Congress); so just accept the fact that I only need one *dropdown* list box on the calculator. In fact, I could even begin the calculator with nothing more than a list box. In that case the list box would contain a list of available calculators. In other words, you would begin with a list box and pick the type of calculator with which you wanted to work; then the calculator would appear. There is actually no reason why that capability cannot be included in this calculator as one of the first level choices in the list of first-level functions.

In that case there would be a default calculator that could be changed into another type of calculator by simply selecting one of the many other types of calculators from the single *dropdown* list box. This is such a good idea that I will leave it for you to implement as an *exercise*. If you extend this concept to its extreme, I suppose you could have a calculator that is a *metaphor* for all calculators and create a *universal calculator* that is capable of *transforming* itself into *any* type of calculator imaginable, including a calculator that can design and program calculators.

I think I have established the fact that I can do a considerable amount of complex *state* transformation with a single list box and will therefore move onto the next design criterion (leaving you to ponder the outer limits of such *transformations*). At this point, there are some push buttons on the calculator and a single, *super-dooper* list box. I also need a way to display the results of the calculations this calculator is going to perform. Labels are an excellent choice for displaying information.

I have already decided I want to have several registers and have settled on six as a good number. This gives me a useful set of registers:
- (1) **f**: the current register,
- (2) **t**: the temporary register,
- (3) **x**: a secondary register,
- (4) **y**: a secondary register,
- (5) **z**: a secondary register,
- (6) **M**: the memory register.

I also know that, because I have six registers, I will probably need to have a way to select each one of them at appropriate times. Since I am using label controls for these registers, I can use the fact that a label control is *already* programmed to recognize the *Click* event as a mechanism for selecting a register. I can change the colors (via *BackColor* and *ForeColor*) of the label control as a *visual* indicator that a particular register has been selected. Incidentally, this is very easy to do.

It occurred to me that it would be nice if I could easily *reset* a particular register; so I need a way to do that but do *not* want to use a push button because I am using *color* to indicate register selection. Therefore, I will add a second label for each register and will use it to *reset* its corresponding register (this is also easy to do). It is very easy to use *color* in Visual Basic. *Color* is an excellent way to provide *visual* clues but cannot be the only mechanism provided because all monitors are not color monitors. In the very near future, *sound* can be used as an *aural* identification *mechanism*.

At this point, the calculator is generally designed, except for identifying the exact function of each of the push buttons. The first set of push buttons will serve as numeric keys. There will be a set of push buttons for simple arithmetic calculations, and there will be a set of push buttons for register-selectable arithmetic calculations. This last set of push buttons is an interesting way to do *more with less*.

In a normal calculator, there will usually be a set of buttons for doing things with the memory register (e.g., recall memory (RM), add to memory (M+), subtract from memory (M-), and so forth). Well, it occurred to me that (considering the fact that I had six registers), it would be nice to have a set of push buttons for doing arithmetic calculations with the current register and *any* of the other registers. The problems with this *idea* were that (1) it would require an additional 20 or so push buttons and (2) it would make the calculator look rather complex.

However (after putting on the *thinking hat*), it occurred to me that I could use the *same* set of traditional memory buttons for *more* than just memory arithmetic *if* I did two important things: (1) changed the *Caption* of the push buttons and (2) changed the *behavior* of the push buttons depending upon which register they were *affecting*. As it developed, this, also, is not very difficult to do. I just (1) tied (via *tight coupling)* the *Click* of a register label to changing the *Caption* of the memory buttons and (2) tied the actions performed by the memory buttons to their *Captions*. This was so easy to do that it is just *slick*!

The next group of push buttons are used to copy directly the contents of one register into the current register. I also added push buttons for (1) changing the sign of the current register, (2) inserting a decimal point in the current register, (3) using parentheses, (4) clearing the current register, (5) clearing all registers, (6) performing a list box function, and (7) exiting the calculator. Then I decided this was a *sufficient* number of push buttons for the calculator and, therefore, stopped adding more push buttons.

The visual results of the design are shown in the screen capture of the calculator (page 186 or thereabout). You will note that the calculator has a simple, *uncluttered* appearance, even though it is capable of performing complex calculations and could be capable of *transforming* itself in several interesting and unique ways. By adding a few more push buttons, but making them initially invisible, it would be *possible* for the calculator to *transform* itself into a complex number system calculator. In other words, with a few more push buttons and some modification in the *behavior* of the arithmetic operators, this calculator could compute and display the square root of negative one. It could also *transform* itself into a hexadecimal calculator.

This brings up another interesting concept related to *transformation*. If a calculator can *transform* itself into another calculator, then there is really no reason why *any* form cannot *transform* itself into any other form, provided that a *generic* mechanism for such *transformation* exists. In other words, it is both possible and feasible to design a single *generic form* that can be *transformed* into many different types of *specific forms* at runtime. This is certainly an interesting *idea* to contemplate.

After several years of designing and programming Windows SDK/C screens, I have observed that a typical Windows application screen has (1) a few list boxes (seldom more than five), (2) a few push buttons (seldom more than 10), (3) a few radio buttons or check boxes (again, seldom more than 10), (4) a few labels (maybe ten or so), (5) a few edit boxes (again, maybe ten or so) and that is about all, with the possible exception of (6) a scroll bar or two. There is certainly no reason why you cannot design one or more such *generic* screens and use them repeatedly in place of many *specific* screens.

The primary thing you would have to do is design and code these screens in such a way that (1) the *Captions* of the push buttons could change dynamically, (2) the radio button and check box *Captions* could change dynamically, (3) the list box *contents* could change dynamically, (4) the label *Captions* could change dynamically, (5) the edit box *contents* and *behavior* could change dynamically, and (6) the scroll bar *settings* could change dynamically. In short, each of the six standard controls would be represented and would be available on the *generic form*. The *behavior* and *appearance* of each of the six standard controls would be *dynamically* changeable at runtime.

Visual Basic not only makes this possible, but it also facilitates it by introducing the *control array*. A *control array* is something that is unique to Visual Basic, but is something that is *inherent* to Windows. A *control array* takes advantage of the fact that each of the six standard Windows controls (edit, static, list box, combo box, button, and scroll bar) are really Window *classes*. A Visual Basic *control array* is a physical manifestation of a Window class. Once you have defined the first occurrence (or *instance)* of the *control array*, you can create and destroy additional *instances* of the *control array* as necessary. You can also position and size each *instance* of the *control array* at runtime. The only thing you cannot do is destroy the *first instance* of the *control array*. A *control array* can be created but not destroyed (in contrast to *matter*).

This last bit of information concerning Visual Basic *control arrays* provides a very important *clue* regarding the ways in which a *control array* is used. Knowing that there are only six standard Windows controls and that you can make a *control array* for each one of them leads me to the conclusion you can make a single *generic form* beginning with *nothing* on it except six *control arrays*, each of which currently has only one *instance*. In other words, you design a *form* that has one push button, one list box, one combo box, one edit box, one label box, and one scroll bar, but you make each of these *controls* be *control arrays* (instead of *single controls*). You also make them initially *invisible* and *park* them in the upper left corner of the *form*.

Now, you have the ultimate (more or less) *generic form*. If you need a form with 10 push buttons, you just *dynamically* create nine more *instances* of your push button *control array*. You can do the same thing anytime you need other controls. You can just *dynamically* create them. This is a very powerful capability, but it is only powerful if you can attach some very *specific code* to the controls.

Attaching *specific code* (or event procedures) to controls that are *dynamically* created and destroyed requires some designing. You certainly cannot put the code in any of the *particular* instances because it would be destroyed when you destroyed the *particular* instance. However, this is not a problem because the Visual Basic designers had the foresight (or insight) not to *allow* this to be done. In fact, there are *no* event procedures for any *instance* other than the *first instance* of a *control array*. This moves the problem (of coding an event procedure, *in advance*, for a control that does *not* yet exist) into the area of *non*-event procedure coding (where it is easier to provide a *generic* solution). In other words, you make the event procedures of the *control array* become *generic* by having them do *nothing* more than call a *specific* (but *generic), non*-event procedure.

This is a very *abstruse* thing to want to do, and it is not immediately obvious *why* you would want to do it. But the fact that it can be done in Visual Basic is a good indicator of the power provided in Visual Basic. You are really going to have to *think* about this for awhile before it makes sense, but when it does you will see that you can make Visual Basic do some very interesting things for you. In fact, I am going to have to do some serious thinking about the implications of this observation. An *aside* will help make this clearer.

Back in my early years as a mainframe programmer, I became involved (purely by coincidence) in systems programming on a Univac 1100 Series computer and discovered a very interesting language called the **Symbolic Stream Generator** (SSG). Mainframe system programming involved doing a considerable amount of work with batch jobs, and the particular work done in a batch job would vary from day to day (even from hour to hour). Some bright programmer decided it would be nice to have a language that could generate particular batch jobs (or *streams* of instructions) based on variable input data. This is basically what SSG does. In other words, SSG is a high level language used to generate programs. In actual practice, SSG is used to generate particular *sets* of programs and to supply variable data as appropriate.

Being somewhat prone to carrying everything to its logical extreme, I spent a considerable amount of time trying to discover a way to make an SSG program generate *itself*. After quite a bit of experimenting and research, I finally found a way to use SSG to generate SSG programs that in turn could generate other SSG programs (and so on and so on). In the process of doing this, I discovered that if this was possible with SSG, then it should be possible with *any* other language that was *complete*. Since this is such a useful capability, I then decided that it was an enormous waste of time to use anything except *complete* languages.

Consequently, the first thing I do when I learn a new language is determine whether the language is *complete* (i.e., can *generate* itself) or *incomplete*. Windows SDK/C is *complete*, Actor is *complete*, Borland C++ is *complete*, and Visual Basic is *complete*, but all with some *restrictions* (primary of which is an inherent limitation in their *ability* to be run on a processor that can really handle *recursive, asynchronous tasks*). I will probably get a few comments about this statement, but believe it to be correct at least in the context in which it is made.

Nevertheless, due to the *recursive* capabilities of the Univac (now manufactured by Unisys, as a result of the merger of Burroughs and Sperry) and SSG , I can write an SSG program that dynamically generates and executes a *recursive* compile, link, and execute series. This *recursive* capability can create some interesting problems in a *multiprocessing* operating system, but it is *powerful* when used *correctly*. I *know* that the Windows NT designers are going to have *fun* with this problem. However, I hope that they do *not* solve the problem by *not* allowing it to occur. (That would be a very *big* mistake!) A *multitasking, multiprocessing* operating system that cannot correctly handle *recursive asynchronous processes* is a big joke in my opinion.

Now, *recursion* is something that is somewhat inherent to software but is *more* inherent to hardware--at least in a certain sense. Univac is the all-time *champion* multiprocessor (with the possible exception of Cray). But computers continue to evolve, and it will not be very long before Windows enters the realm of multiprocessing (something I look forward to with a certain amount of *humorous* expectation). I suppose this will also require a brief explanation.

Coming from a mainframe background, I am continually *amused* when someone who has only worked on a PC begins telling me about some new capability of the PC and why this new capability of the PC makes it *vastly* superior to a mainframe computer. With the *dramatic* exception of the Windows Graphical User Interface (GUI), there is nearly *nothing* being done in Windows that has not been done for years (and years and years) on mainframes, especially *multiprocessing*.

The *humorous* part comes from knowing what is in store for quite a few PC programmers when Windows NT is released. If you want to have *fun* with computers, then try doing *asynchronous multiprocessing*. Mainframe experience will prove to be quite *useful* when Windows NT moves into the realm of *multiprocessing*. I know that *multiprocessing* considerations are (or at least should be) driving the Windows NT designers *bonkers*. But I have great confidence in Microsoft. Microsoft C is solid as a rock, and I expect Windows NT to follow suit. When it comes to systems software, Microsoft takes care of business, but I am also learning to appreciate the applications side of Microsoft as well.

In fact, Visual Basic is a product of the applications side of Microsoft, *not* the systems side. Visual Basic would never come from the systems side; it is too *easy* to use. I am therefore learning to view the applications side of Microsoft with new respect. Something important is happening in Microsoft, and it is happening in the applications side.

I think someone has decided (*correctly*) that people like intelligent push buttons. I think it is great to have powerful languages, but I would really rather *not* have to program at the instruction level. I want to do my computer software design and programming *symbolically*, and the applications people at Microsoft know this. Visual Basic, Excel, Word For Windows, PowerPoint, Project, Money, and all of the other Microsoft applications are *evolving* toward increased *intelligence*. I want to be able to do what I need to do by pushing *intelligent* buttons on the tool bar, not by writing macros. Look at the new Word For Windows and you will be amazed at what you can do. I have not seen the new Excel, but I expect it also to be amazing.

I was training a group of clients, recently, in Windows SDK/C and Visual Basic CDK design and programming and thought that this would be a good time to introduce them (and myself) to QuickC For Windows. First, we programmed "Hello World" in Windows SDK/C. Next, we programmed "Hello World" in QuickC For Windows. Doing "Hello World" in Windows SDK/C and QuickC For Windows took about eight hours--two afternoon sessions, including explaining what each function was doing. Then we programmed "Hello World" in Visual Basic, and it took about TEN SECONDS. It would have taken *less* time, but we were using an IBM PS/2 Model 70 (which is a *slow* machine in my opinion). My clients found it enormously *funny* that it took approximately 3,000 lines of code in QuickC For Windows to program "Hello World"! (We also had a push button and a separate dialog box, so this required additional code.)

I also thought it was *funny* but was impressed with the *caliber* of code that QuickC For Windows generated (actually, QuickCaseW did the code generation). I was even more *impressed* with the use of *color* in the code editor, and so were my clients. QuickC For Windows is really neat, and it is a powerhouse, but it is *not* so quick as Visual Basic for designing and coding a Windows application. It is useful for learning Windows SDK/C programming but is not a replacement for Windows SDK/C when it comes to building a Dynamic Link Library (DLL). However, you cannot beat the price, and I must *emphasize* the fact that it *generates* very good code. QuickC For Windows Help is *excellent* (nearly an *on-line* reference for the Windows SDK/C).

The difference between Visual Basic and QuickC For Windows demonstrates the difference in the philosophy of Microsoft's applications and systems groups. The systems people are always going to be interested in minute *detail* while the applications people have learned that people generally would rather work at as *high* a level as possible. The minute *detail* must *exist* (it is the *foundation* upon which you build your house), but there is no reason why you cannot have *air conditioning* without having to *know* how and why an *air conditioner* works.

I like QuickC For Windows, but I know that I would like it even more if the applications group added an *extra* layer of *smarts* to it. In fact, I think everyone is *not-so-patiently* waiting for Visual C. It cannot be that difficult a thing to do considering that Visual Basic *already* exists. For that matter, most of the C language could be added to Visual Basic (possibly as an option), and if this were done I would have absolutely no problem paying two or three times the current retail price for Visual Basic to get the C language *and* functions (with Windows SDK/C speed) built-in. Actually, if you are very good at Windows SDK/C programming, you can build a DLL to do this. I am seriously considering doing just that as one of the subjects of another book--something along the line of **Using Windows SDK/C and Visual Basic CDK to Build a DLL/VBX for Visual Basic** or **VB = mc^3: The Art of Visual Basic CDK Programming with Windows SDK/C and QuickC For Windows**. [I like the second title.]

You are probably *wondering* at this point how all of this relates to *generic forms* and *control arrays* (and possibly which *planet* I am from). Well, it relates to them in the sense that Visual Basic has some built-in *smarts* which are partially *derived* from mainframe languages (more correctly, from basic computer science) but are more generally derived from the work of some *bright* people at Microsoft (and possibly a

Think Day or two). In other words, Visual Basic has a few *subtle* capabilities that move it into a new *dimension* with respect to its capability for *transformation*. In fact, this is almost *reverse* OOPS--or SPOO (Systems Programming Oriented-Objects) and almost makes as much sense backwards as forwards.

If you *think* about this for a few minutes (or days), I think you will *see* that you could almost write an entire Windows application using Visual Basic with no more than a single *generic* screen (or at most a few *generic* screens, if you needed to have a few modal or modeless screens all of which were visible). This is something I find extremely *intriguing* and worthy of further *investigation*. How much extra work is involved in using a single *generic form*? Is it difficult *dynamically* to create and destroy *objects*? Is it difficult *dynamically* to position and size *objects*? If it is relatively *easy* to do all of these things, then I suggest that it is relatively easy to use a single *generic form* (maybe *not* simple, but not so complex as to be difficult). In fact, it should be a *useful* and practical thing to do, but *not* necessarily *trivial* in terms of design and programming.

When you begin to talk about writing programs that dynamically *transform* themselves or *generate* variable appearance based upon specific conditions, you are entering an area that requires a solid understanding of what you are doing *conceptually*. This is the case because you have to program (or create) the actual implementation. In the case of Visual Basic, you are building (or *transforming*) a *regular* Windows application into an *expert* Windows application.

In other words, you are removing the actual coding (of a Windows application with Visual Basic) just a few more *dimensions* away from where it would *normally* be done. When you first begin programming with Visual Basic, you create a new form, add controls to the form, and then put all of your code into event procedures for those controls. Next, I suggest that you can take *most* of the code out of the event procedures and put it into *non*-event procedures. You are now working in a different *dimension*.

Then I suggest that you can (1) create one *generic form*, (2) put one *control array* for each *type* of *control* onto this *generic form*, (3) code the event procedures for each *control array* in such a way that they contain *absolutely* no *specific code*, and then (4) move *all* of the *specific code* (effectively) into *non*-event procedures *located* entirely in *modules*. Now you are doing nearly *all* of *GUI work* and all of the *real work* in *non*-event procedures.

The interesting thing about doing nearly all of the work in *non*-event procedures is that you do *not* really need to use Visual Basic in *design mode* to do this. The *module* files (i.e., the "*.BAS" files) can be edited with a traditional DOS program editor (e.g., Brief), provided you are *proficient* in the language. If you can do this in DOS with a program editor like Brief, then you can write a C program to do the work for you. If you can write a C program to do the work for you, then you can write a Windows SDK/C program to do the work for you. If you can write a Windows SDK/C program to do the work for you, then you can write a Visual Basic program to do the work for you. If you can do that, then you can write a Visual Basic program that will write a Visual Basic program. And if you can do that, then you can do a *lot* of work. Then, you are *really* programming in another *dimension*.

But before you reach the point at which you can *really* do a lot of work (more or less automatically), you have to *know* Visual Basic *inside and out*. This will involve some work, but not that much work and certainly not much more work than the work you will need to do in order to learn how to use Visual Basic in more traditional ways.

Another aspect of *generic programming* (one of my favorite topics) is creating a *generic scripting language* that is used to dynamically control *generic forms*. Windows applications are especially *well-suited* for this type of construction because of their OOPS (or SPOO) characteristics. Once you have created a few *generic forms* (actually there is only *one generic form* because all other *generic forms* are just variations of *one generic form)*, then you can control this *one generic form* with a *generic scripting language*.

There *is* a way to make a Visual Basic *generic form* do nearly anything you want it to do, but discovering the way to do it will involve (1) *adjusting* the way you *think* about Visual Basic design and programming (*conceptually*) and (2) *learning* nearly *everything* you can about *how* Visual Basic works. In other words, you must know the *real* rules.

As usual, I have jumped around considerably (possibly more so in this chapter). I do this *partly* because it is the way I think and *partly* because I am trying to teach you how to *think* in more than one *dimension* when you *think* about Windows application design and programming with Visual Basic. Both Windows and Visual Basic are *multidimensional* and (in a very literal sense) represent a considerable amount of *uncharted* territory. Occasionally, I discover something in Windows that appears to be a significant event. Visual Basic is one such thing. The 3D Tool Cube in **TbxShield** (The Stirling Group) and the icon cube in **Icon Pak Developer's Kit** (Software Workshop, Inc.) are other such things.

There is something fascinating about the concept of using a cube (or *any* three dimensional object for that matter) as a control or switching *metaphor* in Windows. I continually contemplate this because it appears to represent something *fundamental* in the evolution of Windows, an evolution toward multiple *dimensions*. I have not settled on a definite answer, but think this is in some way connected to Windows NT and, particularly, to *multiprocessing*.

This concept is really related to an innovation from IBM that became a feature of its typewriters: the typewriter ball (I guess that is what it is called). It is a metal ball, approximately one inch in diameter, and it contains all of the characters the typewriter uses. Instead of having individual keys for each character, there is one typewriter ball. Different characters are typed by rotating the typewriter ball.

I use the concept of a three dimensional control *metaphor* to represent a *metaphor* of programming with a *symbolic* typewriter ball and can *see* such a system as being capable of typing, or programming, with symbols. In effect, this would *transform* your traditional, data entry keyboard into a *programming* keyboard. Instead of typing, or *spelling*, programming statements, you would type *symbols* and each *symbol* would be a *function* or *subprogram* that performed some operation on a *result*.

A system of this type would require a considerable amount of *learning* (probably comparable to learning shorthand and computer science), but would certainly be a *leap* in programming technology. With the extra power gained from *multiprocessing* and the Windows Graphical User Interface (and possibly several monitors), such a *symbolic* programming language is not very far from becoming a *reality*. We are already programming (and *thinking*) with *objects*. I *see* no reason why we cannot *visually* (or *symbolically*) program with *objects*, too. In fact, I think that approximately 20 *expert* Windows SDK/C designers and programmers could produce such a language in one year, if they had some *direction* and 20 *thinking hats*.

That may be a somewhat optimistic estimate of the amount of time and effort required to produce such a leap in software programming technology but it is not overly optimistic. Some company is going to create a programming language that uses visual symbols as its primary programming constructs. It will occur sooner rather than later and it will trigger one of the most significant leaps in knowledge to occur in this century.

I know this will happen soon because I am looking at its precursor (in the form of the Word For Windows V2.0 toolbar) at this moment. The more I think about it, the more trivial it becomes. In fact, with a few of the more specialized Visual Basic Add-On Tool Kits, you should be able to design and code a Visual Basic application that will enable you to write Visual Basic applications in such a way that selecting Visual Basic functions and subroutines and inserting them into your code can be done almost entirely via symbolic buttons.

In other words, I see no reason whatsoever why there cannot be a Visual Basic Function Box that looks and works like the Visual Basic Tool Box. There is absolutely no reason why I cannot add a **Mid$()** function to my Visual Basic code by clicking on a **Mid$()** *button* contained in a Visual Basic Function Box. Adding this capability to Visual Basic will require some design and programming, but it is certainly nothing *monumental* in terms of effort. Microsoft already has the technology to do this, and it is a standard feature of Word For Windows V2.0 (i.e., assigning macros to the tool bar). This is one of the areas in which I am looking forward to some pleasant surprises from Microsoft!

Code Examples

There are three major code examples in this book: (1) a medium complexity scientific calculator, (2) an ASCII text file viewer, and (3) a very complex SQL Select Statement generator. The code for these sample forms appears in its entirety, except for the *FileOpen* and *FileSaveAs* forms used in the SQL Select Statement generator. The Companion Disk for the book contains all of the code and forms.

I selected these code examples because each one of them demonstrates some interesting techniques that are unique to programming in Visual Basic. The hybrid object, called *RowData*, that is used in both the text file viewer and the SQL Select Statement generator is particularly useful. It will also function as a virtual list box and requires only minor modification to do so. Color and bitmaps are becoming very popular among Visual Basic developers, especially bitmaps. By using bitmaps as backgrounds for your screens or main menu, you can make your application *look* very impressive.

Because some of the code examples were written before I invented all of my *special rules* for Visual Basic programming, you will note that it appears as though I do not follow my own advice. To a certain extent, this is the case but it does not mean I do not wish that I had discovered the rules earlier. If I have discovered nothing else in the past ten months, it is that Visual Basic is not a toy. If someone tells you he thinks that Visual Basic does not do very much, then he does not know very much about Visual Basic. I have been able to do nearly everything I could imagine with Visual Basic, and I suggest that you will be able to do this, too. You can do some *amazing* things with Visual Basic!

The Generic Calculator

Sub NumPB_Click (Index As Integer)

```
' reset F-Register...if it needs to be reset...
If ((ngResetFReg < 1) Or (ngLastErrValue > 0)) Then
    ngLastErrValue = 0
    ngResetFReg = 1
    ngResetDecPoint = 0      ' clear DECIMAL POINT ENTERED indicator...
    szgFRegTxt = "0"
Else
    szgFRegTxt = LTrim$(RTrim$(f.Caption))
End If

' reset F-Register...if last operator was EQUALS...
If ngLastOperatorIdx < 0 Then
    ngLastOperatorIdx = 0
    szgFRegTxt = "0"
End If

tmp$ = szgFRegTxt + LTrim$(RTrim$(Str$(Index)))

' remove any leading ZEROS...except leave one if value entered is ZERO...
nDone% = 0
Do While nDone% = 0
    nStart% = InStr(1, tmp$, "0")
    If nStart% = 1 Then
        nLength% = Len(tmp$) - 1
        If nLength% > 0 Then
```

```
            cpy$ = Mid$(tmp$, 2, nLength%)
            tmp$ = LTrim$(RTrim$(cpy$))
        Else
            nDone% = 1
        End If
    Else
        nDone% = 1
    End If
Loop

' put formatted NEW value into the F-Register...
szgRJustTxt = Space$(22)
If (Len(tmp$) <= 22) Then
    RSet szgRJustTxt = tmp$
Else
    RSet szgRJustTxt = Left$(tmp$, 22)
End If
f.Caption = szgRJustTxt
End Sub

Sub cePB_Click ()
szgRJustTxt = Space$(22)
RSet szgRJustTxt = "0"
f.Caption = Left$(szgRJustTxt, 22)
ngResetDecPoint = 0
ngSign = 1
```

```
    ngLastOperatorIdx = 0
End Sub

Sub DecPtPB_Click ()
If ngResetDecPoint < 1 Then
    szgFRegTxt = LTrim$(RTrim$(f.Caption))
    If (Len(szgFRegTxt) > 20) Then
        MsgBox2002
        ngResetDecPoint = 1     ' set DECIMAL POINT ENTERED indicator…
        ngResetFReg = 0         ' clear F-Register RESET indicator…
        Exit Sub
    End If
    nVal% = Val(szgFRegTxt)
    If nVal% = 0 Then
        tmp$ = "."
    Else
        tmp$ = szgFRegTxt + "."
    End If
    szgRJustTxt = Space$(22)
    RSet szgRJustTxt = Left$(tmp$, 22)
    f.Caption = szgRJustTxt
    ngResetDecPoint = 1
    ngResetFReg = 1
End If
End Sub
```

```
Sub Form_Load ()
ngCurrMType = 6    ' i.e., 'M'
ngResetDecPoint = 0
ngSign = 1
ngLastOperatorIdx = 0
ngResetFReg = 0
szgRJustTxt = Space$(16)
RSet szgRJustTxt = "0"
f.Caption = Left$(szgRJustTxt, 16)
t.Caption = Left$(szgRJustTxt, 16)
x.Caption = Left$(szgRJustTxt, 16)
y.Caption = Left$(szgRJustTxt, 16)
z.Caption = Left$(szgRJustTxt, 16)
m.Caption = Left$(szgRJustTxt, 16)
nLBCount = LBfun.ListCount
If (nLBCount > 0) Then
    For I = 0 To nLBCount - 1 Step 1
        LBfun.RemoveItem 0
    Next I
End If
LBfun.AddItem "Square(f)" , 0
LBfun.AddItem "Cube(f)" , 1
LBfun.ListIndex = 0
End Sub

Sub OperPB_Click (Index As Integer)
```

```
ngLastErrValue = 0
On Error GoTo OperErr

' get T-Register contents...
    szgTRegTxt = LTrim$(t.Caption)
    szgSaveTRegTxt = szgTRegTxt
    dgTValue = Val(szgTRegTxt)

' get F-Register contents...
    szgFRegTxt = LTrim$(f.Caption)
    szgSaveFRegTxt = szgFRegTxt
    dgFValue = Val(szgFRegTxt)

' check for calculation in progress...if there is one then complete it...
Select Case ngLastOperatorIdx
    Case 0    ' last operator was EQUALS...
    ' note: COPY F to T and display in result in F and T...
        dgSubTotal = dgFValue
    Case 1    ' last operator was ADD...
    ' note: ADD F to T and display result in F and T...
        dgSubTotal = dgTValue + dgFValue
        If (ngLastErrValue > 0) Then
            ResetOperator
            Exit Sub
        End If

    Case 2    ' last operator was SUBTRACT...
```

```
        ' note: SUBTRACT F from T and display result in F and T...
        dgSubTotal = dgTValue - dgFValue
        If (ngLastErrValue > 0) Then
            ResetOperator
            Exit Sub
        End If

    Case 3    ' last operator was MULTIPLY...
        ' note: MULTIPLY F to T and display result in F and T...
        dgSubTotal = dgTValue * dgFValue
        If (ngLastErrValue > 0) Then
            ResetOperator
            Exit Sub
        End If

    Case 4    ' last operator was DIVIDE...
        ' note: DIVIDE T to F and display result in F and T...
        If dgFValue = 0 Then
            ' ERROR-> cannot divide by ZERO...
            MsgBox22
            Exit Sub
        End If
        dgSubTotal = dgTValue / dgFValue
        If (ngLastErrValue > 0) Then
            ResetOperator
            Exit Sub
        End If
```

End Select

```
' if completing a calculation in progress then put the results into
' the F-Register and T-Register...using values from calculation above...
Select Case ngLastOperatorIdx
    Case 0, 1, 2, 3, 4
        ' copy result to T-Register...
        If (dgSubTotal < 999999999.999999) Then
            szgTRegTxt = Format$(dgSubTotal, "#########0.00####")
        Else
            szgTRegTxt = Format$(dgSubTotal, "#########0.00####E+0##")
        End If

        szgRJustTxt = Space$(22)
        RSet szgRJustTxt = Left$(szgTRegTxt, 22)
        t.Caption = szgRJustTxt

        ' also...copy it to F-Register...
        f.Caption = szgRJustTxt

        ngResetDecPoint = 0
        ngLastOperatorIdx = -1
End Select

' NOTE-> there are NO CALCULATIONS in PROGRESS as this point and we can
'        therefore get the current contents of the registers...
```

```vb
    '
    ' get T-Register contents...    ' not really needed...
    szgTRegTxt = LTrim$(t.Caption)  ' not really needed...
    dgTValue = Val(szgTRegTxt)      ' not really needed...

    ' get F-Register contents...
    szgFRegTxt = LTrim$(f.Caption)
    dgFValue = Val(szgFRegTxt)

    ' set SUBTOTAL to F-Register...
    dgSubTotal = dgFValue

    ' record the operator...
    Select Case Index
        Case 1
            ngLastOperatorIdx = 1    ' ADDITION...
        Case 2
            ngLastOperatorIdx = 2    ' SUBTRACTION...
        Case 3
            ngLastOperatorIdx = 3    ' MULTIPLICATION...
        Case 4
            ngLastOperatorIdx = 4    ' DIVISION...
    End Select

    ' copy SUBTOTAL to T-Register...
    If (dgSubTotal < 999999999.999999) Then
        szgTRegTxt = Format$(dgSubTotal, "#########0.00####")
```

```
    Else
        szgTRegTxt = Format$(dgSubTotal, "########0.00####E+0##")
    End If
    szgRJustTxt = Space$(22)
    RSet szgRJustTxt = Left$(szgTRegTxt, 22)
    t.Caption = szgRJustTxt

    ngResetDecPoint = 0      ' clear DECIMAL POINT ENTERED indicator...
    ngResetFReg = 0          ' clear F-Register RESET indicator...
    Exit Sub

OperErr:
    ngLastErrValue = Err
    MsgBox2001
    Resume Next

End Sub

Sub cPB_Click ()
    szgRJustTxt = Space$(16)
    RSet szgRJustTxt = "0"
    f.Caption = Left$(szgRJustTxt, 16)
    t.Caption = Left$(szgRJustTxt, 16)
    x.Caption = Left$(szgRJustTxt, 16)
    y.Caption = Left$(szgRJustTxt, 16)
    z.Caption = Left$(szgRJustTxt, 16)
```

```
m.Caption = Left$(szgRJustTxt, 16)
ngResetDecPoint = 0
ngSign = 1
ngLastOperatorIdx = 0
szgTRegTxt = "0"
szgXRegTxt = "0"
szgYRegTxt = "0"
szgZRegTxt = "0"
szgMRegTxt = "0"
dgFValue = 0
dgTValue = 0
dgXValue = 0
dgYValue = 0
dgZValue = 0
dgMValue = 0
dgSubTotal = 0
End Sub
```

Sub EqualsPB_Click ()

```
ngLastErrValue = 0
On Error GoTo EqualsErr

    szgTRegTxt = LTrim$(t.Caption)
    szgSaveTRegTxt = szgTRegTxt
    dgTValue = Val(szgTRegTxt)
```

```
szgFRegTxt = LTrim$(f.Caption)
szgSaveFRegTxt = szgFRegTxt
dgFValue = Val(szgFRegTxt)

Select Case ngLastOperatorIdx
    Case 0
        ' note: COPY T to F and display in F and T...
        dgSubTotal = dgTValue
        ' note: COPY F to T and display in F and T...
        dgSubTotal = dgFValue
    Case 1
        ' note: ADD F to T and display result in F and T...
        dgSubTotal = dgTValue + dgFValue
        If (ngLastErrValue > 0) Then
            ResetEquals
            Exit Sub
        End If
    Case 2
        ' note: SUBTRACT F from T and display result in F and T...
        dgSubTotal = dgTValue - dgFValue
        If (ngLastErrValue > 0) Then
            ResetEquals
            Exit Sub
        End If
    Case 3
```

```
        ' note: MULTIPLY F to T and display result in F and T...
        dgSubTotal = dgTValue * dgFValue
        If (ngLastErrValue > 0) Then
            ResetEquals
            Exit Sub
        End If
    Case 4
        ' note: DIVIDE T to F and display result in F and T...
        If dgFValue = 0 Then
            ' ERROR-> cannot divide by ZERO...
            MsgBox22
            Exit Sub
        End If
        dgSubTotal = dgTValue / dgFValue
        If (ngLastErrValue > 0) Then
            ResetEquals
            Exit Sub
        End If
End Select
If (dgSubTotal < 999999999.999999) Then
    szgTRegTxt = Format$(dgSubTotal, "#########0.00####")
Else
    szgTRegTxt = Format$(dgSubTotal, "#########0.00####E+0##")
End If
szgRJustTxt = Space$(22)
```

```
    RSet szgRJustTxt = Left$(szgTRegTxt, 22)
    t.Caption = szgRJustTxt

    ' also…copy it to F-Register…
    f.Caption = szgRJustTxt

    ngResetDecPoint = 0
    ngLastOperatorIdx = -1
    Exit Sub

EqualsErr:
    ngLastErrValue = Err
    MsgBox2001
    Resume Next

End Sub

Sub LT_Click ()
    szgRJustTxt = Space$(22)
    RSet szgRJustTxt = "0"
    t.Caption = Left$(szgRJustTxt, 22)
End Sub

Sub LM_Click ()
    szgRJustTxt = Space$(22)
    RSet szgRJustTxt = "0"
```

m.Caption = Left$(szgRJustTxt, 22)
End Sub

Sub LX_Click 0
szgRJustTxt = Space$(22)
RSet szgRJustTxt = "0"
x.Caption = Left$(szgRJustTxt, 22)
End Sub

Sub LY_Click 0
szgRJustTxt = Space$(22)
RSet szgRJustTxt = "0"
y.Caption = Left$(szgRJustTxt, 22)
End Sub

Sub LZ_Click 0
szgRJustTxt = Space$(22)
RSet szgRJustTxt = "0"
z.Caption = Left$(szgRJustTxt, 22)
End Sub

Sub LF_Click 0
szgRJustTxt = Space$(22)
RSet szgRJustTxt = "0"
f.Caption = Left$(szgRJustTxt, 22)

```
ngResetDecPoint = 0
ngSign = 1
ngLastOperatorIdx = 0
ngResetFReg = 1
ngLastErrValue = 0
End Sub
```

Sub SignPB_Click ()

```
ngLastErrValue = 0
On Error GoTo SignErr

szgFRegTxt = LTrim$(f.Caption)
szgSaveFRegTxt = szgFRegTxt
    dgFValue = Val(szgFRegTxt)

If ngSign < 1 Then
    ' sign is negative...so make it POSITIVE...
    ngSign = 1
Else
    ' sign is positive...so make it NEGATIVE...
    ngSign = 0
End If

' note: MULTIPLY F by -1 and display result in F...
dgSubTotal = dgFValue * (-1)
If (ngLastErrValue > 0) Then
```

```
    ResetSign
    Exit Sub
End If

' copy SUBTOTAL to F-Register...
If (dgSubTotal < 999999999.999999) Then
    szgFRegTxt = Format$(dgSubTotal, "##########.######")
Else
    szgFRegTxt = Format$(dgSubTotal, "#########0.######E+0##")
End If
szgRJustTxt = Space$(22)
RSet szgRJustTxt = Left$(szgFRegTxt, 22)
dgSubTotal = Val(szgRJustTxt)
If (dgSubTotal = 0) Then
    szgRJustTxt = Space$(22)
    RSet szgRJustTxt = Left$("0", 22)
    f.Caption = szgRJustTxt
    ngResetDecPoint = 0     ' clear DECIMAL POINT ENTERED indicator...
Else
    nDecPtLoc% = InStr(1, szgRJustTxt, ".")
    If (nDecPtLoc% > 0) Then
        nRetVal% = Len(szgRJustTxt)
        nLen% = nRetVal% - nDecPtLoc%
        nStart% = nDecPtLoc% + 1
        szFrac$ = Mid$(szgRJustTxt, nStart%, nLen%)
        nFrac% = Val(szFrac$)
        If (nFrac% = 0) Then
```

```
        If (ngResetDecPoint < 1) Then
            nStart% = nDecPtLoc% - 1
            szInt$ = Left$(szRJustTxt, nStart%)
            szgRJustTxt = Space$(22)
            RSet szgRJustTxt = Left$(szInt$, 22)
            ngResetDecPoint = 0    ' clear DECIMAL POINT ENTERED indicator...
        Else
            ngResetDecPoint = 1    ' set DECIMAL POINT ENTERED indicator...
        End If

    Else
        ngResetDecPoint = 1    ' set DECIMAL POINT ENTERED indicator...
    End If
Else
    ngResetDecPoint = 0    ' set DECIMAL POINT ENTERED indicator...
End If
f.Caption = szgRJustTxt

End If

Exit Sub

SignErr:
ngLastErrValue = Err
MsgBox 2001
Resume Next
```

End Sub

Sub MOperPB_Click (Index As Integer)
ngLastErrValue = 0
On Error GoTo MemoryErr

Select Case ngCurrMType
    Case 1
        ' get f-Register contents...
        szgRRegTxt = LTrim$(f.Caption)
    Case 2
        ' get t-Register contents...
        szgRRegTxt = LTrim$(t.Caption)
    Case 3
        ' get x-Register contents...
        szgRRegTxt = LTrim$(x.Caption)
    Case 4
        ' get y-Register contents...
        szgRRegTxt = LTrim$(y.Caption)
    Case 5
        ' get z-Register contents...
        szgRRegTxt = LTrim$(z.Caption)
    Case 6
        ' get M-Register contents...
        szgRRegTxt = LTrim$(m.Caption)
End Select

```
        dgRValue = Val(szgRRegTxt)
        szgSaveRRegTxt = szgRRegTxt

    ' get F-Register contents...
        szgFRegTxt = LTrim$(f.Caption)
        szgSaveFRegTxt = szgFRegTxt
        dgFValue = Val(szgFRegTxt)

    ' perform the calculation...
        Select Case Index
            Case 1
                ' note: ADD F to R and display result in R...
                dgSubTotal = dgRValue + dgFValue
                If (ngLastErrValue > 0) Then
                    ResetMemory
                    Exit Sub
                End If
            Case 2
                ' note: SUBTRACT F from R and display result in R...
                dgSubTotal = dgRValue - dgFValue
                If (ngLastErrValue > 0) Then
                    ResetMemory
                    Exit Sub
                End If
            Case 3
                ' note: MULTIPLY R by F and display result in R...
                dgSubTotal = dgRValue * dgFValue
```

```
        If (ngLastErrValue > 0) Then
            ResetMemory
            Exit Sub
        End If
    Case 4
    ' note: DIVIDE R to F and display result in F...
        If dgFValue = 0 Then
            ' ERROR-> cannot divide by ZERO...
            MsgBox22
            Exit Sub
        End If
        dgSubTotal = dgRValue / dgFValue
        If (ngLastErrValue > 0) Then
            ResetMemory
            Exit Sub
        End If
End Select

If (dgSubTotal < 999999999.999999) Then
    szgRRegTxt = Format$(dgSubTotal, "#########0.00####")
Else
    szgRRegTxt = Format$(dgSubTotal, "#########0.00####E+0##")
End If

szgRJustTxt = Space$(22)
RSet szgRJustTxt = Left$(szgRRegTxt, 22)
```

```
Select Case ngCurrMType
    Case 1
        f.Caption = szgRJustTxt
    Case 2
        t.Caption = szgRJustTxt
    Case 3
        x.Caption = szgRJustTxt
    Case 4
        y.Caption = szgRJustTxt
    Case 5
        z.Caption = szgRJustTxt
    Case 6
        m.Caption = szgRJustTxt
End Select

ngResetDecPoint = 0      ' clear DECIMAL POINT ENTERED indicator...
ngResetFReg = 0          ' clear F-Register RESET indicator...
Exit Sub

MemoryErr:
ngLastErrValue = Err
MsgBox2001
Resume Next

End Sub
```

Sub xPB_Click ()
' get contents of X-Register...
szgXRegTxt = LTrim$(RTrim$(x.Caption))

' copy contents of X-Register to F-Register...
szgRJustTxt = Space$(22)
RSet szgRJustTxt = Left$(szgXRegTxt, 22)
f.Caption = szgRJustTxt

ngResetDecPoint = 1   ' set DECIMAL POINT ENTERED indicator...
ngResetFReg = 0   ' clear F-Register RESET indicator...
End Sub

Sub yPB_Click ()
' get contents of Y-Register...
szgYRegTxt = LTrim$(RTrim$(y.Caption))

' copy contents of Y-Register to F-Register...
szgRJustTxt = Space$(22)
RSet szgRJustTxt = Left$(szgYRegTxt, 22)
f.Caption = szgRJustTxt

ngResetDecPoint = 1   ' set DECIMAL POINT ENTERED indicator...
ngResetFReg = 0   ' clear F-Register RESET indicator...
End Sub

Sub zPB_Click ()
' get contents of Z-Register...
szgZRegTxt = LTrim$(RTrim$(z.Caption))

' copy contents of Z-Register to F-Register...
szgRJustTxt = Space$(22)
RSet szgRJustTxt = Left$(szgZRegTxt, 22)
f.Caption = szgRJustTxt

ngResetDecPoint = 1   ' set DECIMAL POINT ENTERED indicator...
ngResetFReg = 0   ' clear F-Register RESET indicator...
End Sub

Sub MPB_Click ()
' get contents of M-Register...
szgMRegTxt = LTrim$(RTrim$(m.Caption))

' copy contents of M-Register to F-Register...
szgRJustTxt = Space$(22)
RSet szgRJustTxt = Left$(szgMRegTxt, 22)
f.Caption = szgRJustTxt

ngResetDecPoint = 1   ' set DECIMAL POINT ENTERED indicator...
ngResetFReg = 0   ' clear F-Register RESET indicator...
End Sub

```
Sub x_Click ()
MOperPB(1).Caption = " x+"
MOperPB(2).Caption = " x-"
MOperPB(3).Caption = " x*"
MOperPB(4).Caption = " x/"
RmPB.Caption = " Rx"
f.BackColor = WHITE
t.BackColor = WHITE
x.BackColor = YELLOW
y.BackColor = WHITE
z.BackColor = WHITE
m.BackColor = BLUE
m.ForeColor = WHITE
ngCurrMType = 3
End Sub

Sub y_Click ()
MOperPB(1).Caption = " y+"
MOperPB(2).Caption = " y-"
MOperPB(3).Caption = " y*"
MOperPB(4).Caption = " y/"
RmPB.Caption = " Ry"
f.BackColor = WHITE
t.BackColor = WHITE
x.BackColor = WHITE
y.BackColor = YELLOW
```

```
    z.BackColor = WHITE
    m.BackColor = BLUE
    m.ForeColor = WHITE
    ngCurrMType = 4
End Sub

Sub z_Click ()
    MOperPB(1).Caption = " z+"
    MOperPB(2).Caption = " z-"
    MOperPB(3).Caption = " z*"
    MOperPB(4).Caption = " z/"
    RmPB.Caption = " Rz"
    f.BackColor = WHITE
    t.BackColor = WHITE
    x.BackColor = WHITE
    y.BackColor = WHITE
    z.BackColor = YELLOW
    m.BackColor = BLUE
    m.ForeColor = WHITE
    ngCurrMType = 5
End Sub

Sub M_Click ()
    MOperPB(1).Caption = " M+"
    MOperPB(2).Caption = " M-"
    MOperPB(3).Caption = " M*"
```

```
    MOperPB(4).Caption = " M/"
    RmPB.Caption = " RM"
    f.BackColor = WHITE
    t.BackColor = WHITE
    x.BackColor = WHITE
    y.BackColor = WHITE
    z.BackColor = WHITE
    m.BackColor = YELLOW
    m.ForeColor = BLUE
    ngCurrMType = 6
End Sub

Sub t_Click ()
    MOperPB(1).Caption = " t+"
    MOperPB(2).Caption = " t-"
    MOperPB(3).Caption = " t*"
    MOperPB(4).Caption = " t/"
    RmPB.Caption = " Rt"
    f.BackColor = WHITE
    t.BackColor = YELLOW
    x.BackColor = WHITE
    y.BackColor = WHITE
    z.BackColor = WHITE
    m.BackColor = BLUE
    m.ForeColor = WHITE
    ngCurrMType = 2
```

End Sub

Sub f_Click ()
```
MOperPB(1).Caption = " f+"
MOperPB(2).Caption = " f-"
MOperPB(3).Caption = " f*"
MOperPB(4).Caption = " f/"
RmPB.Caption = " Rf"
f.BackColor = YELLOW
t.BackColor = WHITE
x.BackColor = WHITE
y.BackColor = WHITE
z.BackColor = WHITE
m.BackColor = BLUE
m.ForeColor = WHITE
ngCurrMType = 1
End Sub
```

Sub RmPB_Click ()
```
Select Case ngCurrMType
  Case 1
    ' get f-Register contents…
    szgRRegTxt = LTrim$(f.Caption)
  Case 2
    ' get t-Register contents…
    szgRRegTxt = LTrim$(t.Caption)
```

```
        Case 3
            ' get x-Register contents…
            szgRRegTxt = LTrim$(x.Caption)
        Case 4
            ' get y-Register contents…
            szgRRegTxt = LTrim$(y.Caption)
        Case 5
            ' get z-Register contents…
            szgRRegTxt = LTrim$(z.Caption)
        Case 6
            ' get M-Register contents…
            szgRRegTxt = LTrim$(m.Caption)
    End Select
    dgRValue = Val(szgRRegTxt)

    ' now…copy contents to F-Register…
    If (dgRValue < 999999999.999999) Then
        szgRRegTxt = Format$(dgRValue, "#########0.00####")
    Else
        szgRRegTxt = Format$(dgRValue, "#########0.00####E+0##")
    End If

    szgRJustTxt = Space$(22)
    RSet szgRJustTxt = Left$(szgRRegTxt, 22)
    f.Caption = szgRJustTxt
    ngResetFReg = 1
```

End Sub

Sub tPB_Click ()
```
' get contents of t-Register...
szgTRegTxt = LTrim$(RTrim$(t.Caption))

' copy contents of T-Register to F-Register...
szgRJustTxt = Space$(22)
RSet szgRJustTxt = Left$(szgTRegTxt, 22)
f.Caption = szgRJustTxt

ngResetDecPoint = 1    ' set DECIMAL POINT ENTERED indicator...
ngResetFReg = 0        ' clear F-Register RESET indicator...
```
End Sub

Sub ExitPB_Click ()
End
End Sub

Sub functPB_Click ()
```
ngLastErrValue = 0
On Error GoTo ErrorHandler
' get F-Register contents...
szgFRegTxt = LTrim$(f.Caption)
```

```
szSaveFRegTxt$ = szgFRegTxt
dgFValue = Val(szgFRegTxt)

' perform the currently selected function on the F-Register...
nFunctIdx% = LBfun.ListIndex
Select Case nFunctIdx%
    Case 0    ' Square(f)...
        dgSubTotal = dgFValue * dgFValue
        If (ngLastErrValue > 0) Then
            szgFRegTxt = szSaveFRegTxt$
            szgRJustTxt = Space$(22)
            RSet szgRJustTxt = Left$(szgFRegTxt, 22)
            f.Caption = szgRJustTxt
            Exit Sub
        End If
    Case 1    ' Cube(f)...
        dgSubTotal = dgFValue * dgFValue
        If (ngLastErrValue > 0) Then
            szgFRegTxt = szSaveFRegTxt$
            szgRJustTxt = Space$(22)
            RSet szgRJustTxt = Left$(szgFRegTxt, 22)
            f.Caption = szgRJustTxt
            Exit Sub
        End If
        dgSubTotal = dgSubTotal * dgFValue
        If (ngLastErrValue > 0) Then
            szgFRegTxt = szSaveFRegTxt$
```

```
            szgRJustTxt = Space$(22)
            RSet szgRJustTxt = Left$(szgFRegTxt, 22)
            f.Caption = szgRJustTxt
            Exit Sub
        End If
End Select
' copy result to F-Register...
If (dgSubTotal < 999999999.999999) Then
    szgFRegTxt = Format$(dgSubTotal, "##########0.00####")
Else
    szgFRegTxt = Format$(dgSubTotal, "##########0.00####E+0##")
End If
szgRJustTxt = Space$(22)
RSet szgRJustTxt = Left$(szgFRegTxt, 22)
f.Caption = szgRJustTxt
dgSubTotal = Val(szgRJustTxt)
If dgSubTotal = 0 Then
    ngResetFReg = 0
End If
ngResetFReg = 0
Exit Sub

ErrorHandler:
ngLastErrValue = Err
MsgBox2001
Resume Next
```

End Sub

Sub MsgBox2001 ()
   Const MB_OK = 0
   Const MB_ICONSTOP = 16
   Title$ = "XPR Calculator"
   Msg$ = "FUNCTION caused an ERROR!"
   DgDef% = MB_OK + MB_ICONSTOP
   Response% = MsgBox(Msg$, DgDef%, Title$)
End Sub

Sub ResetOperator ()
   szgFRegTxt = szgSaveFRegTxt
   szgRJustTxt = Space$(22)
   RSet szgRJustTxt = Left$(szgFRegTxt, 22)
   XPRCALC.f.Caption = szgRJustTxt
   szgTRegTxt = szgSaveTRegTxt
   szgRJustTxt = Space$(22)
   RSet szgRJustTxt = Left$(szgTRegTxt, 22)
   XPRCALC.t.Caption = szgRJustTxt
End Sub

Sub ResetEquals ()

```
szgFRegTxt = szgSaveFRegTxt
szgRJustTxt = Space$(22)
RSet szgRJustTxt = Left$(szgFRegTxt, 22)
XPRCALC.f.Caption = szgRJustTxt
szgTRegTxt = szgSaveTRegTxt
szgRJustTxt = Space$(22)
RSet szgRJustTxt = Left$(szgTRegTxt, 22)
XPRCALC.t.Caption = szgRJustTxt
```

End Sub

Sub ResetSign ()
```
szgFRegTxt = szgSaveFRegTxt
szgRJustTxt = Space$(22)
RSet szgRJustTxt = Left$(szgFRegTxt, 22)
XPRCALC.f.Caption = szgRJustTxt
End Sub
```

Sub ResetMemory ()
```
szgFRegTxt = szgSaveFRegTxt
szgRJustTxt = Space$(22)
RSet szgRJustTxt = Left$(szgFRegTxt, 22)
XPRCALC.f.Caption = szgRJustTxt

szgRRegTxt = szgSaveRRegTxt
szgRJustTxt = Space$(22)
```

```
    szgFRegTxt = szgSaveFRegTxt
    szgRJustTxt = Space$(22)
    RSet szgRJustTxt = Left$(szgFRegTxt, 22)
    XPRCALC.f.Caption = szgRJustTxt
    szgTRegTxt = szgSaveTRegTxt
    szgRJustTxt = Space$(22)
    RSet szgRJustTxt = Left$(szgTRegTxt, 22)
    XPRCALC.t.Caption = szgRJustTxt
End Sub

Sub ResetSign ()
    szgFRegTxt = szgSaveFRegTxt
    szgRJustTxt = Space$(22)
    RSet szgRJustTxt = Left$(szgFRegTxt, 22)
    XPRCALC.f.Caption = szgRJustTxt
End Sub

Sub ResetMemory ()
    szgFRegTxt = szgSaveFRegTxt
    szgRJustTxt = Space$(22)
    RSet szgRJustTxt = Left$(szgFRegTxt, 22)
    XPRCALC.f.Caption = szgRJustTxt

    szgRRegTxt = szgSaveRRegTxt
    szgRJustTxt = Space$(22)
```

```
RSet szgRJustTxt = Left$(szgRRegTxt, 22)
Select Case ngCurrMType
    Case 1
        ' restore f-Register contents…
        XPRCALC.f.Caption = szgRJustTxt
    Case 2
        ' get t-Register contents…
        XPRCALC.t.Caption = szgRJustTxt
    Case 3
        ' get x-Register contents…
        XPRCALC.x.Caption = szgRJustTxt
    Case 4
        ' get y-Register contents…
        XPRCALC.y.Caption = szgRJustTxt
    Case 5
        ' get z-Register contents…
        XPRCALC.z.Caption = szgRJustTxt
    Case 6
        ' get M-Register contents…
        XPRCALC.m.Caption = szgRJustTxt
End Select
```

End Sub

Sub MsgBox2002 ()

```
Const MB_OK = 0
Const MB_ICONSTOP = 16
Title$ = "XPR Calculator"
Msg$ = "NUMBER is TOO LARGE!"
DgDef% = MB_OK + MB_ICONSTOP
Response% = MsgBox(Msg$, DgDef%, Title$)
End Sub
```

Sub MsgBox22 ()

```
Const MB_OK = 0
Const MB_ICONSTOP = 16
Title$ = "XPR Calculator"
Msg$ = "Division by ZERO is UNDEFINED!"
DgDef% = MB_OK + MB_ICONSTOP
Response% = MsgBox(Msg$, DgDef%, Title$)
End Sub
```

The Text Viewer

Type TxtFileStruct
  szTxt As String
  lSeekPos As Long
End Type

```
' NOTE-> nNumOfDisplayRows is set in Form_Load...
' WARNING-> if the number of display rows is changed it
'           MUST match the TxtFileRec array AND the actual
'           number of rows on the form...
Dim nNumOfDisplayRows As Integer
Dim TxtFileRec(1 To 15)  As TxtFileStruct
' NOTE-> nFileBufferBytes is set in Form_Load...
' WARNING-> szGetString length MUST equal value used
'           for nFileBufferBytes...
Dim nFileBufferBytes As Integer
Dim szGetString As String * 1024
Dim TitleRec(1 To 2)  As TxtFileStruct
Dim nTitleON As Integer      '0 = OFF, 1 = ON...
Dim nLineLen As Integer
Dim nMaxLineLen As Integer
Dim nInitialLoad As Integer
Dim nFoundOne As Integer
Dim nTxtFileNum As Integer
Dim nChkForPartial As Integer
Dim nCurrBufferStart As Integer
Dim nPrevBufferStart As Integer
Dim nPartialLine As Integer
Dim nEOF As Integer
Dim nIdx As Integer
Dim nTxtFileTotalRecs As Integer
Dim nNoMoreLines As Integer
Dim nSaveVSRValue As Integer
```

```
Dim nSaveHSRValue As Integer
Dim nCurrHSRMax As Integer
Dim nCurrVSRMax As Integer
Dim nResetHSR As Integer
Dim nResetVSR As Integer
Dim nCurrLineLength As Integer
Dim nBytesRead As Integer
Dim nSaveBufferStart As Integer
Dim nSaveBytesRead As Integer
Dim nSaveEOF As Integer
Dim nMatchFound As Integer

Dim lCurrLowSeekPos As Long
Dim lCurrSeekPos As Long
Dim lNextSeekPos As Long
Dim lFileLength As Long
Dim lUnReadLength As Long
Dim lSaveSeekPos As Long
Dim lSaveUnReadLength As Long

Dim szSubTxt As String
Dim szNewLine As String

Const TRUE = -1
Const FALSE = 0
```

```
Sub OpenFilePB_Click 0
    If nTxtFileNum = 0 Then
        nTxtFileNum = FreeFile
    End If
    szFile$ = "C:\VBMC2\DATA\VIEW.TXT"
    Match$ = Dir$(szFile$)    ' Find first match.
    If (Len(Match$) < 1) Then
        MsgBox2001
        Exit Sub
    End If
    Open "C:\VBMC2\DATA\VIEW.TXT" For Binary Access Read As nTxtFileNum
    lCurrSeekPos = 1
    nCurrBufferStart = 1
    lFileLength = LOF(nTxtFileNum)
    lUnReadLength = lFileLength
    nBytesRead = 0
    nEOF = 0
    nSaveVSRValue = 0
    nSaveHSRValue = 0
    nChkForPartial = 0
    nInitialLoad = 0
    OpenFilePB.Enabled = FALSE
    CloseFilePB.Enabled = TRUE
    For I = 1 To nNumOfDisplayRows Step 1
        TxtFileRec(I).szTxt = ""
        TxtFileRec(I).lSeekPos = 0
```

```
    Next I
    For I = 1 To 2 Step 1
        TitleRec(I).szTxt = ""
        TitleRec(I).lSeekPos = 0
    Next I
    GetTotalNumOfRecs
    HSR.Max = nMaxLineLen        'NOTE-> see alternative way to do this
    nCurrHSRMax = nMaxLineLen '          below…can RESET HSR.Max each time…
    nInitialLoad = 1
    For I = 1 To nNumOfDisplayRows Step 1
        nIdx = I
        GetNextLine
        If nMoreLines Then
            Exit For
        End If
    Next I
    nInitialLoad = 0
    For I = 1 To 2 Step 1
        TitleRec(I).szTxt = TxtFileRec(I).szTxt
        nLength = Len(TitleRec(I).szTxt)
        If nLength < HSR.Value Then
            LTT(I).Caption = ""
        Else
            szSubTxt = Mid$(TitleRec(I).szTxt, HSR.Value, 60)
            LTT(I).Caption = Left$(szSubTxt, 60)
        End If
    Next I
```

```
' can we scroll...
VSR.Enabled = TRUE
nResetVSR = 0  ' used to make VSR.Change IGNORE the following change...
nCurrVSRMax = nTxtFileTotalRecs  ' from GetTotalNumOfRecs...
VSR.Max = nCurrVSRMax
'VSR.Value = nNumOfDisplayRows  ' value is nNumOfDisplayRows because we have nNumOfDisplayRows rows...
'nSaveVSRValue = nNumOfDisplayRows
VSR.Value = 1
nSaveVSRValue = 1
nResetVSR = 1  ' set VSR.Change behavior to normal...
'.................
' get length of LONGEST record on DISPLAY...
' For I = 1 To nNumOfDisplayRows Step 1
'     nLength = Len(TxtFileRec(I).szTxt)
'     If nLength > nCurrHSRMax Then
'         nCurrHSRMax = nLength
'     End If
' Next I
' HSR.Max = nCurrHSRMax
'.................
HSR.Enabled = TRUE
nResetHSR = 0  ' used to make HSR.Change IGNORE the following change...
HSR.Value = 1
nResetHSR = 1  ' set HSR.Change behavior to normal...
End Sub
```

Sub Form_Load ()
```
szNewLine = Chr$(13) + Chr$(10)
nTxtFileNum = 0
nBytesRead = 0
lUnReadLength = 0
lCurrSeekPos = 1
nEOF = 0
nSaveVSRValue = 0
nSaveHSRValue = 0
HSR.Max = 0
nChkForPartial = 0
nInitialLoad = 0
nFileBufferBytes = 1024
nNumOfDisplayRows = 15
nTitleON = 0
FBT.Visible = FALSE
End Sub
```

Sub CloseFilePB_Click ()
```
Close nTxtFileNum
lCurrSeekPos = 1
nCurrBufferStart = 1
lFileLength = 0
lUnReadLength = 0
nBytesRead = 0
nEOF = 0
```

```
For I = 1 To 2 Step 1
    LTT(I).Caption = ""
Next I
For I = 1 To nNumOfDisplayRows Step 1
    LT(I).Caption = ""
Next I
VSR.Enabled = FALSE
HSR.Enabled = FALSE
OpenFilePB.Enabled = TRUE
CloseFilePB.Enabled = FALSE
nTitleON = 0
FBT.Visible = FALSE
End Sub
```

Sub GetNextBuffer ()

```
lUnReadLength = (lFileLength - lNextSeekPos) + 1
If lUnReadLength > 0 Then
    Get nTxtFileNum, , szGetString
    lCurrSeekPos = lNextSeekPos
    If lUnReadLength > = nFileBufferBytes Then
        lNextSeekPos = lCurrSeekPos + nFileBufferBytes
        nBytesRead = nFileBufferBytes
    Else
        lNextSeekPos = lCurrSeekPos + lUnReadLength
        nBytesRead = lUnReadLength
        ' we are at EOF...so remember where we are...
```

```
        nEOF = 1
    End If
    nCurrBufferStart = 1
Else
    ' we are at EOF...so remember where we are...
    nEOF = 1
End If
End Sub
```

Sub GetNextLine ()

```
If nEOF > 0 Then ' we are at EOF...
If nPartialLine > 0 Then 'we are working on a LINE...so COMPLETE it...
    nPartialLine = 0
    LT(nIdx).Caption = Left$(TxtFileRec(nIdx).szTxt, 60)   'write the partial line...
    nNoMoreLines = 1   ' there are no more lines...we are at EOF...
End If
' WARNING-> although it would appear to be logical to
-             exit this subroutine at this time be cause
-             the nEOF indicator tells us that we are at
-             the logical EOF...we MUST continue with the
-             process BECAUSE IT IS RECURSIVE and where
-             we APPEAR to be is not necessarily where
-             we ACTUALLY are...
-                 this is---of course--abstruse but then so
-                 is this algorithm...
End If
```

```
        If nBytesRead < nCurrBufferStart Then
            If ((nBytesRead < 1) And (nEOF > 0)) Then     ' NEW…for EOF
                Exit Sub           ' NEW…for EOF
            End If                 ' NEW…for EOF
            GetNextBuffer
        End If

        If nPartialLine < 1 Then
        ' we are NOT working on a partial line…
        ' NOTE-> because we MAY have scrolled UP…the CURRENT POINTERS may
        '        be out of synch…so we need to get them from the LAST line
        '        in the TxtFileRec structure array…and thereby KNOW that we
        '        are getting CORRECT CURRENCY INFORMATION…else we will be
        '        GREATLY CONFUSED…also note that we should check for no more
        '        data which will be indicated by TxtFileRec(nNumOfDisplayRows).lSeekPos being
        '        equal to ZERO---which is NOT A VALID SEEK VALUE for VB binary
        '        reads…
        '………NEW……………………………………………
            If nInitialLoad = 0 Then
                If (TxtFileRec((nNumOfDisplayRows - 1)).lSeekPos < 1) Then
                    ' we CANNOT scroll down…
                    Exit Sub
                End If
                lCurrSeekPos = TxtFileRec((nNumOfDisplayRows - 1)).lSeekPos
                lNextSeekPos = lCurrSeekPos
                Seek nTxtFileNum, lCurrSeekPos
```

```
GetNextBuffer
' now SKIP the FIRST LINE in the NEW buffer...because it is ITEM nNumOfDisplayRows...
nRetVal = InStr(nCurrBufferStart, szGetString, szNewLine)
If nRetVal > 0 Then
    nCurrBufferStart = nRetVal + 2
    nPartialLine = 0
Else
    ' ERROR-> or PROBABLY an error...
End If
End If
'............NEW...................................................................

nRetVal = InStr(nCurrBufferStart, szGetString, szNewLine)
If nRetVal > 0 Then
    ' we have a COMPLETE LINE...
    nCurrLineLength = nRetVal - nCurrBufferStart
    TxtFileRec(nIdx).szTxt = Mid$(szGetString, nCurrBufferStart, nCurrLineLength)
    TxtFileRec(nIdx).lSeekPos = lCurrSeekPos + (nCurrBufferStart - 1)
    nLength = Len(TxtFileRec(nIdx).szTxt)
    If nLength < HSR.Value Then
        LT(nIdx).Caption = ""
    Else
        szSubTxt = Mid$(TxtFileRec(nIdx).szTxt, HSR.Value, 60)
        LT(nIdx).Caption = Left$(szSubTxt, 60)
    End If
    nCurrBufferStart = nRetVal + 2
    nPartialLine = 0
```

```
        Else
                ' we have a PARTIAL LINE...
                nCurrLength = (nBytesRead - nCurrBufferStart) + 1
                TxtFileRec(nIdx).szTxt = Mid$(szGetString, nCurrBufferStart, nCurrLineLength)
                TxtFileRec(nIdx).lSeekPos = lCurrSeekPos + (nCurrBufferStart - 1)
                nPartialLine = 1
                nBytesRead = 0   ' to force next buffer read...
                ' so click the NextLinePB...
                GetNextLine    'WARNING-> this is RECURSIVE...
                '               and REQUIRES lines in the file
                '               to be <CR><LF> terminated...
                '                  ('0D0A' in HEX)...
        End If
    Else
        ' WORKING on a PARTIAL LINE...i.e...the SECOND PART...
        nRetVal = InStr(nCurrBufferStart, szGetString, szNewLine)
        If nRetVal > 0 Then
            ' we have the SECOND PART of the partial line...
            nCurrLineLength = nRetVal - nCurrBufferStart
            szSubTxt = Mid$(szGetString, nCurrBufferStart, nCurrLineLength)
            TxtFileRec(nIdx).szTxt = TxtFileRec(nIdx).szTxt + szSubTxt
            ' do NOT need to change the TxtFileRec.lSeekPos value...
            nLength = Len(TxtFileRec(nIdx).szTxt)
            If nLength < HSR.Value Then
                LT(nIdx).Caption = ""
            Else
                szSubTxt = Mid$(TxtFileRec(nIdx).szTxt, HSR.Value, 60)
```

```
            LT(nIdx).Caption = Left$(szSubTxt, 60)
        End If
        nCurrBufferStart = nRetVal + 2
        nPartialLine = 0
    Else
        ' we have a PARTIAL LINE…AND A LONG ONE…may be an ERROR(???)
        nCurrLength = (nBytesRead - nCurrBufferStart) + 1
        szSubTxt = Mid$(szGetString, nCurrBufferStart, nCurrLineLength)
        TxtFileRec(nIdx).szTxt = TxtFileRec(nIdx).szTxt + szSubTxt
        ' do NOT need to change the TxtFileRec.lSeekPos value…
        nPartialLine = 1
        nBytesRead = 0   ' to force next buffer read…
        GetNextLine 'WARNING-> this is RECURSIVE…
        '                     and REQUIRES lines in the file
        '                     to be <CR> <LF> terminated…
        '                     ('0D0A' in HEX)…

    End If
  End If
End Sub

Sub HSR_Change ()
    If nResetHSR < 1 Then
        nResetHSR = 1
        Exit Sub
    End If
    ' now horizontally scroll the title lines…
```

255

```
    For I = 1 To 2 Step 1
        nLength = Len(TitleRec(I).szTxt)
        If nLength < HSR.Value Then
            LTT(I).Caption = ""
        Else
            szSubTxt = Mid$(TitleRec(I).szTxt, HSR.Value, 60)
            LTT(I).Caption = Left$(szSubTxt, 60)
        End If
    Next I
    ' now horizontally scroll the data...
    For I = 1 To nNumOfDisplayRows Step 1
        nLength = Len(TxtFileRec(I).szTxt)
        If nLength < HSR.Value Then
            LT(I).Caption = ""
        Else
            szSubTxt = Mid$(TxtFileRec(I).szTxt, HSR.Value, 60)
            LT(I).Caption = Left$(szSubTxt, 60)
        End If
    Next I
End Sub

Sub VSR_Change ()
    If nResetVSR < 1 Then
        nResetVSR = 1
        Exit Sub
    End If
```

```
If VSR.Value >= nSaveVSRValue Then
    ' we are scrolling UP...
    nDiff = VSR.Value - nSaveVSRValue
    If nDiff = 1 Then   ' we are incrementing by ONE...
        For I = 2 To nNumOfDisplayRows Step 1
            TxtFileRec(I - 1).szTxt = TxtFileRec(I).szTxt
            TxtFileRec(I - 1).lSeekPos = TxtFileRec(I).lSeekPos
        Next I
        For I = 1 To (nNumOfDisplayRows - 1) Step 1
            nLength = Len(TxtFileRec(I).szTxt)
            If nLength < HSR.Value Then
                LT(I).Caption = ""
            Else
                szSubTxt = Mid$(TxtFileRec(I).szTxt, HSR.Value, 60)
                LT(I).Caption = Left$(szSubTxt, 60)
            End If
        Next I
        TxtFileRec(nNumOfDisplayRows).szTxt = ""
        TxtFileRec(nNumOfDisplayRows).lSeekPos = 0
        LT(nNumOfDisplayRows).Caption = ""
        nIdx = nNumOfDisplayRows
        GetNextLine
        nSaveVSRValue = VSR.Value
    Else
        ' we have JUMPED by MORE THAN ONE...so we have to START FROM THE TOP
        ' and SKIP over (VSR.Value -1) CR/LF's or something like that...
        ' WARNING-> add this function...
```

```
            ReloadDisplayLines
            nSaveVSRValue = VSR.Value
        End If
    Else
        nDiff = nSaveVSRValue - VSR.Value
        If nDiff = 1 Then    ' we are decrementing by ONE...
            If VSR.Value <= (nNumOfDisplayRows - 1) Then
                ' special case-> treat this as a JUMP...
                ReloadDisplayLines
                nSaveVSRValue = VSR.Value
                Exit Sub
            End If
            For I = (nNumOfDisplayRows - 1) To 1 Step -1
                TxtFileRec(I + 1).szTxt = TxtFileRec(I).szTxt
                TxtFileRec(I + 1).lSeekPos = TxtFileRec(I).lSeekPos
            Next I
            For I = 2 To nNumOfDisplayRows Step 1
                nLength = Len(TxtFileRec(I).szTxt)
                If nLength < HSR.Value Then
                    LT(I).Caption = ""
                Else
                    szSubTxt = Mid$(TxtFileRec(I).szTxt, HSR.Value, 60)
                    LT(I).Caption = Left$(szSubTxt, 60)
                End If
            Next I
            TxtFileRec(1).szTxt = ""
            TxtFileRec(1).lSeekPos = 0
```

```
        LT(1).Caption = ""
        GetPreviousLine
        nSaveVSRValue = VSR.Value
    Else
        ' we have JUMPED by MORE THAN ONE...so we have to START FROM THE TOP
        ' and SKIP over (VSR.Value -1) CR/LF's or something like that...
        ' WARNING-> add this function...
        ' we have JUMPED by MORE THAN ONE...so we have to START FROM THE TOP
        ' and SKIP over (VSR.Value -1) CR/LF's or something like that...
        ' WARNING-> add this function...
        ReloadDisplayLines
        nSaveVSRValue = VSR.Value
    End If
End If
End Sub

Sub GetPreviousLine ()
If nChkForPartial > 0 Then
    ' FORCE to get ANOTHER BUFFER...
    GetPrevLineFromPrevBuffer
Else
    ' looking for a FIRST MATCH...
    lCurrLowSeekPos = TxtFileRec(2).lSeekPos
    If lCurrLowSeekPos > lCurrSeekPos Then
        ' MUST get SOME or ALL of previous line...
        If nChkForPartial < 1 Then
```

```
            ' should NOT be used if nChkForPartial is set...
            GetPrevLineFromCurrBuffer
        End If
    Else
        ' MAY be used if nChkForPartial is set...
        GetPrevLineFromPrevBuffer
    End If
    If nChkForPartial > 0 Then
        GetPreviousLine  'WARNING-> this is RECURSIVE...so watch out...
    End If
End If
End Sub

Sub GetTotalNumOfRecs ()
lSaveSeekPos = lCurrSeekPos
nSaveBufferStart = nCurrBufferStart
lSaveUnReadLength = lUnReadLength
nSaveBytesRead = nBytesRead
nSaveEOF = nEOF
lCurrSeekPos = 1
nCurrBufferStart = 1
lUnReadLength = lFileLength
nBytesRead = 0
nEOF = 0
nDone = 0
nMaxLineLen = 0
```

```
nLineLen = 0
nTxtFileTotalRecs = 0
Do While nDone = 0
    If lUnReadLength > 0 Then
        Get nTxtFileNum, , szGetString
        If lUnReadLength >= nFileBufferBytes Then
            lCurrSeekPos = lCurrSeekPos + nFileBufferBytes
            nBytesRead = nFileBufferBytes
            lUnReadLength = lUnReadLength - nBytesRead
        Else
            lCurrSeekPos = lCurrSeekPos + lUnReadLength
            nBytesRead = lUnReadLength
            ' we are at EOF...so remember where we are...
            lUnReadLength = 0              '???
            nEOF = 1
            nDone = 1
        End If
        nCurrBufferStart = 1
        nScanDone = 0
        Do While nScanDone = 0
            nRetVal = InStr(nCurrBufferStart, szGetString, szNewLine)
            If nRetVal > 0 Then
                ' we FOUND a CR/LF (i.e., '0D0A')...
                nLineLen = nLineLen + (nRetVal - nCurrBufferStart)
                If nLineLen > nMaxLineLen Then
                    nMaxLineLen = nLineLen
                End If
```

```
              nTxtFileTotalRecs = nTxtFileTotalRecs + 1
              nCurrBufferStart = nRetVal + 2
              nLineLen = 0
          Else
              nLineLen = nLineLen + ((nBytesRead - nCurrBufferStart) + 1)
              nScanDone = 1
          End If
      Loop
      If nLineLen > nMaxLineLen Then
          nMaxLineLen = nLineLen
      End If
  Else
      ' we need this to exit the loop if file is EMPTY…
      ' we are at EOF…so remember where we are…
      nEOF = 1
      nDone = 1
  End If
Loop
' MsgBox19  ' display the total number of records…for testing…
' restore previous state…and provide for using this after OpenFilePB…
lCurrSeekPos = 1
Seek nTxtFileNum, lCurrSeekPos
lUnReadLength = lFileLength
nBytesRead = 0
nEOF = 0
If lUnReadLength > 0 Then
    Get nTxtFileNum, , szGetString
```

```
        If lUnReadLength > = nFileBufferBytes Then
            lCurrSeekPos = lCurrSeekPos + nFileBufferBytes
            nBytesRead = nFileBufferBytes
            lUnReadLength = lUnReadLength - nBytesRead
        Else
            lCurrSeekPos = lCurrSeekPos + lUnReadLength
            nBytesRead = lUnReadLength
            ' we are at EOF…so remember where we are…
            lUnReadLength = 0      '???
            nEOF = 1
        End If
        nCurrBufferStart = 1
    End If
End Sub
```

Sub MsgBox19 ()

```
    Const MB_OK = 0, MB_OKCANCEL = 1      'Define buttons
    Const MB_YESNOCANCEL = 3, MB_YESNO = 4
    Const MB_ICONSTOP = 16, MB_ICONQUESTION = 32     ' Define Icons.
    Const MB_ICONEXCLAMATION = 48, MB_ICONINFORMATION = 64
    Const MB_DEFBUTTON2 = 256, IDYES = 6, IDNO = 7  ' Define other.
    Title$ = "GetTotalNumOfRecs"
    Msg$ = "nTxtFileTotalRecs = "
    Msg$ = Msg$ + Str$(nTxtFileTotalRecs)
    DgDef% = MB_YESNO + MB_ICONSTOP + MB_DEFBUTTON2 ' Describe dialog.
```

```
Response% = MsgBox(Msg$, DgDef%, Title$)    ' Get user response.
If Response% = IDYES Then    ' Evaluate response
    ' YES action goes here...
Else
    ' NO action goes here...
End If
End Sub
```

Sub GetPrevLineFromCurrBuffer ()

```
' SOME or ALL of the previous line is in the CURRENT
' szGetString buffer...so start at the BEGINNING of
' the current buffer and skip CR/LF's until we get to
' lCurrLowSeekPos and then use the previous line info
' to get that line...noting that we have to save the
' previous line info as we skip from the start...
' also note that this will affect the code for
' GetNextLine...
nCurrBufferStart = 1
nScanDone = 0
Do While nScanDone = 0
    nRetVal = InStr(nCurrBufferStart, szGetString, szNewLine)
    If nRetVal > 0 Then
        ' we FOUND a CR/LF (i.e., '0D0A')...
        lPrevLowSeekPos = lCurrSeekPos + (nCurrBufferStart - 1)
        nPrevBufferStart = nCurrBufferStart
        nCurrBufferStart = nRetVal + 2
```

```
lNextLowSeekPos = lCurrSeekPos + (nCurrBufferStart - 1)
If lNextLowSeekPos = lCurrLowSeekPos Then   'we found a MATCH...
    ' we found a MATCH with a PREVIOUS LINE in the current buffer...
    ' therefore...all we need to do is get it and adjust the
    ' pointers...and any affected code in GetNextLine...
    ' GET THE PREVIOUS LINE NOW...
    nCurrBufferStart = nPrevBufferStart
    nRetVal = InStr(nCurrBufferStart, szGetString, szNewLine)
    If nRetVal > 0 Then
        If lPrevLowSeekPos = lCurrSeekPos Then
            If lPrevLowSeekPos > 1 Then
                ' this may be a PARTIAL LINE...have to CHECK IT...
                nChkForPartial = 1
            Else
                ' lPrevLowSeekPos AND lCurrSeekPos are
                ' most probably equal to 1...and we are
                ' therefore trying to get the FIRST LINE
                ' and are starting from the BEGINNING
                ' of the file and DO NOT HAVE TO DO
                ' ANYTHING regarding PARTIAL LINES...
                ' or so we think...
            End If
        Else
            ' we have a COMPLETE LINE...
            nChkForPartial = 0
        End If
        nCurrLineLength = nRetVal - nCurrBufferStart
```

```
            TxtFileRec(1).szTxt = Mid$(szGetString, nCurrBufferStart, nCurrLineLength)
            TxtFileRec(1).lSeekPos = lPrevLowSeekPos
            nLength = Len(TxtFileRec(1).szTxt)
            If nChkForPartial < 1 Then
                ' this is a COMPLETE LINE...
                If nLength < HSR.Value Then
                    LT(1).Caption = ""
                Else
                    szSubTxt = Mid$(TxtFileRec(1).szTxt, HSR.Value, 60)
                    LT(1).Caption = Left$(szSubTxt, 60)
                End If
                nCurrBufferStart = nRetVal + 2
                nPartialLine = 0
            Else
                nScanDone = 1
                nMatchFound = 1
                Exit Do
            End If
        End If
        nScanDone = 1
        nMatchFound = 1
    Else
        If lNextLowSeekPos >= (lCurrSeekPos + nFileBufferBytes) Then
            ' ERROR-> we should have found one in this buffer...
            nScanDone = 1
            nMatchFound = 0
        End If
```

```
        End If
    Else
        nScanDone = 1
        nMatchFound = 0
    End If
Loop
If nMatchFound < 1 Then
    ' ERROR-> did NOT find a previous line when we should have...
End If
End Sub
```

Sub GetPrevLineFromPrevBuffer ()
' BACK UP from the lCurrLowSeekPos...but first determine HOW FAR...

```
If (lCurrLowSeekPos - nFileBufferBytes) >= 1 Then
    ' we can back up by nFileBufferBytes..
    lCurrSeekPos = (lCurrLowSeekPos - nFileBufferBytes)
    Seek nTxtFileNum, lCurrSeekPos
    lUnReadLength = (lFileLength - lCurrSeekPos) + 1
    nBytesRead = nFileBufferBytes
Else
    ' we can only back up by LESS THAN nFileBufferBytes...so go to the START...
    lCurrSeekPos = 1
    Seek nTxtFileNum, lCurrSeekPos
    If lFileLength >= nFileBufferBytes Then
        lUnReadLength = (lFileLength - lCurrSeekPos) + 1
```

```
        nBytesRead = nFileBufferBytes
    Else
        lUnReadLength = lFileLength
        nBytesRead = lUnReadLength
    End If
End If

If lUnReadLength > 0 Then
    Get nTxtFileNum, , szGetString
    lNextSeekPos = lCurrLowSeekPos
    ' now scan this buffer for a match with lCurrLowSeekPos
    ' and if we find one then the previous line is the one we
    ' want...if not then must be a long line...
    nCurrBufferStart = 1
    lPrevLowSeekPos = lCurrSeekPos
    nScanDone = 0
    nFoundOne = 0
    Do While nScanDone = 0
        nRetVal = InStr(nCurrBufferStart, szGetString, szNewLine)
        If nRetVal > 0 Then
            nFoundOne = 1
            ' we FOUND a CR/LF (i.e., '0D0A')...
            lPrevLowSeekPos = lCurrSeekPos + (nCurrBufferStart - 1)
            nPrevBufferStart = nCurrBufferStart
            nCurrBufferStart = nRetVal + 2
            lNextLowSeekPos = lCurrSeekPos + (nCurrBufferStart - 1)
            'NOTE-> added the second part of this COMPLEX test to handle FIRST LINE...
```

```
    'If ((lNextLowSeekPos = lCurrLowSeekPos) Or ((nChkForPartial > 0) And (TxtFileRec(1).lSeekPos < 22))) Then
'we found a MATCH…
        If (lNextLowSeekPos = lCurrLowSeekPos) Then
        ' we found a MATCH with a PREVIOUS LINE in the current buffer…
        ' therefore…all we need to do is get it and adjust the
        ' pointers…and any affected code in GetNextLine…
        ' GET THE PREVIOUS LINE NOW…
            nCurrBufferStart = nPrevBufferStart
            nRetVal = InStr(nCurrBufferStart, szGetString, szNewLine)
            If nRetVal > 0 Then
            ' we have a COMPLETE LINE…
                nCurrLineLength = nRetVal - nCurrBufferStart
                TxtFileRec(1).szTxt = Mid$(szGetString, nCurrBufferStart, nCurrLineLength)
                TxtFileRec(1).lSeekPos = lPrevLowSeekPos
                nLength = Len(TxtFileRec(1).szTxt)
                If nLength < HSR.Value Then
                    LT(1).Caption = ""
                Else
                    szSubTxt = Mid$(TxtFileRec(1).szTxt, HSR.Value, 60)
                    LT(1).Caption = Left$(szSubTxt, 60)
                End If
                nCurrBufferStart = nRetVal + 2
                nPartialLine = 0
                nChkForPartial = 0    ' added this as QUICK FIX…???
            End If
            nScanDone = 1
            nMatchFound = 1
```

```
        Else
            If lNextLowSeekPos >= (lCurrSeekPos + nFileBufferBytes) Then
                ' ERROR-> we should have found one in this buffer...
                nScanDone = 1
                nMatchFound = 0
            End If
        End If
    Else
        If ((nFoundOne > 0) And (nChkForPartial > 0)) Then
            ' we need to start from the LAST CR/LF we found and read to
            ' the END of the current buffer to get the FIRST part of
            ' the PARTIAL LINE we now have in TxtFileRec.szTxt(1)...
            lPrevLowSeekPos = lCurrSeekPos + (nCurrBufferStart - 1)
            nPrevBufferStart = nCurrBufferStart
            ' everything now points to the start of the LAST BLOCK we
            ' checked for CR/LF and did NOT find one...so this block is
            ' the FIRST part of the PARTIAL LINE we are building...
            ' so get it...and INSERT it to the string we already have...
            nCurrLineLength = nBytesRead - nCurrBufferStart
            szSubTxt = Mid$(szGetString, nCurrBufferStart, nCurrLineLength)
            ' NOTE-> we are INSERTING szSubTxt...NOT APPENDING it...
            TxtFileRec(1).szTxt = szSubTxt + TxtFileRec(1).szTxt
            ' NOTE-> we want to use the START of the COMPLETE LINE...NOT the partial...
            TxtFileRec(1).lSeekPos = lPrevLowSeekPos
            nLength = Len(TxtFileRec(1).szTxt)
            If nLength < HSR.Value Then
                LT(1).Caption = ""
```

270

```
            Else
                szSubTxt = Mid$(TxtFileRec(1).szTxt, HSR.Value, 60)
                LT(1).Caption = Left$(szSubTxt, 60)
            End If
            nCurrBufferStart = nRetVal + 2
            nPartialLine = 0
            nMatchFound = 1
            nChkForPartial = 0
        Else
            nMatchFound = 0
        End If
        nScanDone = 1
    End If
Loop
If nMatchFound < 1 Then
    ' ERROR-> did NOT find a previous line when we should have…
End If
Else
    ' we are lost….
End If
End Sub

Sub ReloadDisplayLines ()
For I = 1 To nNumOfDisplayRows Step 1
    TxtFileRec(I).szTxt = ""
    TxtFileRec(I).lSeekPos = 0
```

```
        LT(I).Caption = " "
    Next I
    nPartialLine = 0
    nMoreLines = 0
    JumpToVSRLine
    nInitialLoad = 1
    For I = 1 To nNumOfDisplayRows Step 1
        nIdx = I
        GetNextLine
        If nMoreLines Then
            Exit For
        End If
    Next I
    nInitialLoad = 0
End Sub

Sub JumpToVSRLine ()
    lCurrSeekPos = 1
    lNextSeekPos = 1
    nCurrBufferStart = 1
    nBytesRead = 0
    nEOF = 0
    nDone = 0
    Seek nTxtFileNum, lCurrSeekPos    'jump to START...
    lUnReadLength = lFileLength
    nSkippedRecCount = 0
```

```
If VSR.Value <= 1 Then
' If VSR.Value <= nNumOfDisplayRows Then
    If lUnReadLength > 0 Then
        Get nTxtFileNum, , szGetString
        lCurrSeekPos = lNextSeekPos
        If lUnReadLength >= nFileBufferBytes Then
            lNextSeekPos = lNextSeekPos + nFileBufferBytes
            nBytesRead = nFileBufferBytes
            lUnReadLength = lUnReadLength - nBytesRead
        Else
            lNextSeekPos = lNextSeekPos + lUnReadLength
            nBytesRead = lUnReadLength
            ' we are at EOF…so remember where we are…
            lUnReadLength = 0
            nEOF = 1
        End If
        nCurrBufferStart = 1
    End If
    Exit Sub
End If

Do While nDone = 0
    If lUnReadLength > 0 Then
        Get nTxtFileNum, , szGetString
        lCurrSeekPos = lNextSeekPos
        If lUnReadLength >= nFileBufferBytes Then
            lNextSeekPos = lNextSeekPos + nFileBufferBytes
```

```
                nBytesRead = nFileBufferBytes
                lUnReadLength = lUnReadLength - nBytesRead
            Else
                lNextSeekPos = lNextSeekPos + lUnReadLength
                nBytesRead = lUnReadLength
                ' we are at EOF…so remember where we are…
                lUnReadLength = 0
                nEOF = 1
                nDone = 1
            End If
            nCurrBufferStart = 1
            nScanDone = 0
            Do While nScanDone = 0
                nRetVal = InStr(nCurrBufferStart, szGetString, szNewLine)
                If nRetVal > 0 Then
                    ' we FOUND a CR/LF (i.e., '0D0A')…
                    nSkippedRecCount = nSkippedRecCount + 1
                    nCurrBufferStart = nRetVal + 2
                    If (nSkippedRecCount = (VSR.Value - 1)) Then
                        ' we are now pointing to the first line to display…
                        ' because we just jumped over the CR/LF of the previous line…
                        nScanDone = 1
                        nDone = 1
                    End If
                Else
                    nScanDone = 1
                End If
```

```
       Loop
    Else
       ' we need this to exit the loop if file is EMPTY...
       ' we are at EOF...so remember where we are...
       nEOF = 1
       nDone = 1
    End If
  Loop
End Sub

Sub TPB_Click ()
If nTitleON = 0 Then
   nTitleON = 1        ' ON...
   FBT.Visible = TRUE
Else
   nTitleON = 0
   FBT.Visible = FALSE
End If                  ' OFF...
End Sub

Sub ExitPB_Click ()
Close nTxtFileNum
End
End Sub
```

```
Sub MsgBox2001 ()
    Const MB_OK = 0          'Define buttons
    Const MB_ICONSTOP = 16   ' Define Icons.
    Title$ = "Text File Viewer"
    Msg$ = "ERROR-> C:\VBMC2\DATA\VIEW.TXT was not found!"
    DgDef% = MB_OK + MB_ICONSTOP ' Describe dialog.
    Response% = MsgBox(Msg$, DgDef%, Title$)    ' Get user response.
End Sub
```

The SQL Select Generator

Sub Form_Load 0
SqlFrm.WindowState = 2
Screen.MousePointer = 11

HelpCtl.Visible = FALSE ' SQL statement DISPLAY listbox....
FBCB.Visible = FALSE   ' CONDITION box....
FBSB.Visible = TRUE   ' SELECTION box....

nNoSelClrMsgs = 1
InitNewSQLSelList
InitNewSQLCndList

nSqlFrmReallyVisible = 1
ResetSqlFrm

GenerateSqlPB.Visible = TRUE
GenerateSqlPB.Enabled = TRUE

' WARNING-> DO NOT ALLOW CONDITIONS UNTIL USER SELECTS A
'   TBL/VIEW....
'ConditionsPB.SymBackColor = LIGHTGRAY
'ConditionsPB.FontColor = WHITE
ConditionsPB.Enabled = FALSE

nNoSelClrMsgs = 0
Screen.MousePointer = 0

```
fhOldQryFile = 0    ' clear the OLD .QRY file handle
fhQryFile = 0       ' clear the NEW .QRY file handle

End Sub

Sub GenerateSqlPB_Click ()

GenerateSimpleSQL

'--FOR TESTING-----------------------------
HelpCtl.Text = szSqlCmdStr
HelpCtl.Visible = TRUE
HelpCtl.SetFocus
'--FOR TESTING-----------------------------

End Sub

Sub ExecuteSqlPB_Click ()
    ' Generate the SQL commands...
    GenerateSimpleSQL
    ' NOTE-> to actually use this with SQL Server...
    '        run the SQL Server command from here...

End Sub

Sub ViewSqlPB_Click ()
```

```
' NOTE-> a form to view the SQL results can be attached here...
End Sub

Sub TvRcVSR_Change ()
If nResetTvRcVSR = 0 Then
   Exit Sub
Else
   For I = 1 To 5 Step 1
      TvRcData(I).szTblColName = ""
      TvRcData(I).szTblName = ""
      TvRcData(I).nData = 0
      TVRC(I).Caption = ""
      TVRC(I).BackColor = WHITE
   Next I
   For I = 1 To 5 Step 1
      If TvRcVSR.Value < 1 Then
         nIdx = TvRcVSR.Value + I
      Else
         nIdx = TvRcVSR.Value + (I - 1)
      End If
      If (nIdx <= TvRcVSR.Max) Then
         TVRC(I).Caption = TblCols(nIdx).szTblColName
         If TblCols(nIdx).nData > 0 Then
            TVRC(I).BackColor = LIGHTGRAY
         End If
         TvRcData(I).szTblColName = TblCols(nIdx).szTblColName
```

```
            TvRcData(I).szTblName = TblCols(nIdx).szTblName
            TvRcData(I).nData = nIdx
        Else
            Exit For
        End If
    Next I
End Sub

Sub TblViewCB_Click ()
If (FBSB.Visible = TRUE) Then
    If ngLoadingViaSqlAdHoc = 1 Then
        ' already checked for OK to continue...so skip it...
    Else
        nRetVal = MsgBox2002()
        If (nRetVal = FALSE) Then
            Exit Sub
        End If
    End If
End If

Screen.MousePointer = 11
'-----------------------------------------
For I = 1 To 100 Step 1
    TblCols(I).szTblName = ""
    TblCols(I).szTblColName = ""
```

```
        TblCols(I).nData = 0
    Next I
'───────────────
    For I = 1 To 5 Step 1
        TVRC(I).Caption = " "
        TvRcData(I).szTblColName = ""
        TvRcData(I).szTblName = ""
        TvRcData(I).nData = 0
    Next I
    TvRcVSR.Min = 0
    TvRcVSR.Max = 0
    nResetTvRcVSR = 0
    TvRcVSR.Value = 0
    nTblIdx = SqlFrm.TblViewCB.ListIndex
    szCurrTblName = LTrim$(RTrim$(SqlFrm.TblViewCB.LIST(nTblIdx)))
    GetTblViewColumns
    If nCurrColCount > 0 Then
        For I = 1 To 5 Step 1
            If I <= nCurrColCount Then
                TvRcData(I).szTblColName = TblCols(I).szTblColName
                TvRcData(I).szTblName = szCurrTblName
                TvRcData(I).nData = I
                TVRC(I).Caption = TvRcData(I).szTblColName
                TVRC(I).Enabled = TRUE
            Else
                Exit For
            End If
```

```
    Next I
    TvRcVSR.Min = 1
    TvRcVSR.Max = nCurrColCount
    TvRcVSR.Enabled = TRUE
    nResetTvRcVSR = 1
    TvRcVSR.Value = 1
    nResetTvRcVSR = 1
End If
'CountPB.SymBackColor = LIGHTGRAY
'CountDistinctPB.SymBackColor = LIGHTGRAY
'ColTitleIsPB.SymBackColor = LIGHTGRAY
'RemoveRedRowPB.SymBackColor = LIGHTGRAY
'CountPB.FontColor = WHITE
'CountDistinctPB.FontColor = WHITE
'ColTitleIsPB.FontColor = WHITE
'RemoveRedRowPB.FontColor = WHITE
CountPB.Enabled = FALSE
CountDistinctPB.Enabled = FALSE
RemoveRedRowPB.Enabled = FALSE
ColTitleIsPB.Enabled = FALSE
ColTitleIsTxt.Enabled = FALSE
ColTitleIsTxt.Text = ""
ColTitleIsTxt.BackColor = WHITE
ColTitleIsTxt.ForeColor = DARKGRAY
'CountPB.SymBackColor = LIGHTGRAY
'CountDistinctPB.SymBackColor = LIGHTGRAY
'ColTitleIsPB.SymBackColor = LIGHTGRAY
```

```
'RemoveRedRowPB.SymBackColor = LIGHTGRAY
'CountPB.FontColor = WHITE
'CountDistinctPB.FontColor = WHITE
'ColTitleIsPB.FontColor = WHITE
'RemoveRedRowPB.FontColor = WHITE
For I = 1 To 5 Step 1
    SLRC(I).BackColor = WHITE
    SLRC(I).ForeColor = BLUE
    SLRC(I).Caption = ""
    SIRcData(I).szTblColName = ""
    SIRcData(I).szTblName = ""
    SIRcData(I).szColTitle = ""
    SIRcData(I).nData = 0
    SIRcData(I).nCount = 0
    SIRcData(I).nCountDistinct = 0
    SIRcData(I).nFlag = 0
Next I
SLRC(1).Caption = ""
nResetSIRcVSR = 0
SIRcVSR.Min = 0
SIRcVSR.Max = 0
SIRcVSR.Value = 0
nResetSIRcVSR = 1   ' WARNING-> MUST do this to enable scrolling…
'CountPB.SymBackColor = LIGHTGRAY
'CountDistinctPB.SymBackColor = LIGHTGRAY
'ColTitleIsPB.SymBackColor = LIGHTGRAY
'RemoveRedRowPB.SymBackColor = LIGHTGRAY
```

```
'CountPB.FontColor = WHITE
'CountDistinctPB.FontColor = WHITE
'ColTitleIsPB.FontColor = WHITE
'RemoveRedRowPB.FontColor = WHITE
For I = 1 To 100 Step 1
    SelList(I).szTblColName = ""
    SelList(I).szTblName = ""
    SelList(I).szColTitle = ""
    SelList(I).nData = 0
    SelList(I).nCount = 0
    SelList(I).nCountDistinct = 0
    SelList(I).nFlag = 0
Next I

InitNewSQLCndList

FindSelTxt.Text = ""
If nSqlFrmReallyVisible > 0 Then
    If FBSB.Visible = TRUE Then
        If FindSelTxt.Enabled = TRUE Then
            FindSelTxt.Enabled = TRUE
        Else
        End If
        FindSelTxt.SetFocus
        ConditionsPB.Enabled = TRUE
        'ConditionsPB.SymBackColor = DARKPURPLE
        'ConditionsPB.FontColor = WHITE
```

```
        End If
    End If
    Screen.MousePointer = 0
End Sub

Sub TVRC_Click (Index As Integer)
    nIdx = TvRcData(Index).nData
    If nIdx < 1 Then
        ' there is NO DATA for this row...so exit...
        Exit Sub
    End If
    If (TblCols(nIdx).nData < 1) Then
        TblCols(nIdx).nData = 1
        TVRC(Index).BackColor = LIGHTGRAY
        ' NOTE-> ADD to the SLRC...(append at FIRST ZERO loc)...
        For I = 1 To 100 Step 1
            ' change the SelList items to WHITE if they are BLUE...
            If SelList(I).nFlag = 1 Then
                ' it is BLUE...so make it WHITE...
                SelList(I).nFlag = 0
            End If
            If (SelList(I).nData = 0) Then
                SelList(I).szTblColName = TblCols(nIdx).szTblColName
                SelList(I).szTblName = TblCols(nIdx).szTblName
                SelList(I).szColTitle = ""
                SelList(I).nData = TvRcData(Index).nData
```

```
SelList(I).nCount = 0
SelList(I).nCountDistinct = 0
SelList(I).nFlag = 1     ' set to BLUE as DEFAULT...
```

' use this to set scroll position to NEW item...

```
'nResetSIRcVSR = 1
'SIRcVSR.Min = 1
'SIRcVSR.Max = I
'SIRcVSR.Value = I
```

' use the following to set scroll position to TOP...

```
nAtLeastOne = 0
'CountPB.SymBackColor = LIGHTGRAY
'CountDistinctPB.SymBackColor = LIGHTGRAY
'ColTitleIsPB.SymBackColor = LIGHTGRAY
'RemoveRedRowPB.SymBackColor = LIGHTGRAY
'CountPB.FontColor = WHITE
'CountDistinctPB.FontColor = WHITE
'ColTitleIsPB.FontColor = WHITE
'RemoveRedRowPB.FontColor = WHITE
CountPB.Enabled = FALSE
CountDistinctPB.Enabled = FALSE
RemoveRedRowPB.Enabled = FALSE
ColTitleIsPB.Enabled = FALSE
ColTitleIsTxt.Enabled = FALSE
```

```
ColTitleIsTxt.Text = ""
ColTitleIsTxt.BackColor = WHITE
ColTitleIsTxt.ForeColor = DARKGRAY
'CountPB.FontColor = WHITE
'CountDistinctPB.FontColor = WHITE
'ColTitleIsPB.FontColor = WHITE
'RemoveRedRowPB.FontColor = WHITE
For J = 1 To 5 Step 1
    If (SelList(J).nData > 0) Then
        nAtLeastOne = 1
        SIRcData(J).szTblColName = SelList(J).szTblColName
        SIRcData(J).szTblName = SelList(J).szTblName
        SIRcData(J).nData = J
        SIRcData(J).szColTitle = SelList(J).szColTitle
        Col$ = LTrim$(RTrim$(SIRcData(J).szColTitle))
        nLength = Len(Col$)
        If nLength > 0 Then
            Title$ = Col$ + " = "
        Else
            Title$ = ""
        End If
        SIRcData(J).nCount = SelList(J).nCount
        SIRcData(J).nCountDistinct = SelList(J).nCountDistinct
        SIRcData(J).nFlag = SelList(J).nFlag
        Select Case SIRcData(J).nFlag
            Case 0
                SLRC(J).BackColor = WHITE
```

```
            SLRC(J).ForeColor = BLUE
        Case 1
            SLRC(J).BackColor = BLUE
            SLRC(J).ForeColor = WHITE
            CountPB.Enabled = TRUE
            CountDistinctPB.Enabled = TRUE
            ColTitleIsPB.Enabled = TRUE
            ColTitleIsTxt.Enabled = TRUE
            ColTitleIsTxt.BackColor = BLUE
            ColTitleIsTxt.ForeColor = WHITE
            ColTitleIsTxt.Text = SlRcData(J).szColTitle
            ColTitleIsTxt.SetFocus
            ColTitleIsTxt.SelStart = 0
            'CountPB.SymBackColor = BLUE
            'CountDistinctPB.SymBackColor = BLUE
            'ColTitleIsPB.SymBackColor = BLUE
        Case 2
            SLRC(J).BackColor = RED
            SLRC(J).ForeColor = WHITE
            RemoveRedRowPB.Enabled = TRUE
            'RemoveRedRowPB.SymBackColor = RED
    End Select
    Col$ = LTrim$(RTrim$(SlRcData(J).szTblColName))
    If Col$ <> "*" Then
        tmp$ = LTrim$(RTrim$(SlRcData(J).szTblName))
        tmp$ = tmp$ + "."
        tmp$ = tmp$ + Col$
```

```
            Else
                tmp$ = Col$
            End If
            ' check for COUNT or COUNT DISTINCT...if ON...then add to DISPLAY...
            If SIRcData(J).nCount > 0 Then
                tmp$ = "Count(" + tmp$ + ")"
            Else
                If SIRcData(J).nCountDistinct > 0 Then
                    tmp$ = "Count(Distinct(" + tmp$ + "))"
                End If
            End If
            tmp$ = Title$ + tmp$
            SLRC(J).Caption = LTrim$(RTrim$(tmp$))
            SLRC(J).Enabled = TRUE
        Else
            SIRcData(J).szTblColName = ""
            SIRcData(J).szTblName = ""
            SIRcData(J).nData = 0
            SIRcData(J).szColTitle = ""
            SIRcData(J).nCount = 0
            SIRcData(J).nCountDistinct = 0
            SIRcData(J).nFlag = 0
            SLRC(J).Caption = ""
            SLRC(J).BackColor = WHITE
            SLRC(J).ForeColor = BLUE
            SLRC(J).Enabled = FALSE
        End If
```

```
        Next J
        nResetSIRcVSR = 0
        If nAtLeastOne > 0 Then
            SIRcVSR.Enabled = TRUE
            SIRcVSR.Min = 1
            SIRcVSR.Max = I
            SIRcVSR.Value = 1
        Else
            ' ERROR-> should NOT occur...is same as: SIRcVSR.Value = 0
            '           which at this point would cause an error...
        End If
        nResetSIRcVSR = 1
        Exit For
      End If
   Next I
   Else
   ' WARNING-> cannot REMOVE or UNSELECT from TVRC...
   '             MUST DO THIS FROM SLRC...
   ' NOTE-> if REMOVE LAST ITEM then set SIRcVSR.Min to
   '          ZERO...set SIRcVSR.Max to new MAX regardless...
   End If
   'CountPB.FontColor = WHITE
   'CountDistinctPB.FontColor = WHITE
   'ColTitleIsPB.FontColor = WHITE
   'RemoveRedRowPB.FontColor = WHITE
End Sub
```

Sub SIRcVSR_Change ()
```
If nResetSIRcVSR = 0 Then
    Exit Sub
Else
    For I = 1 To 5 Step 1
        SIRcData(I).szTblColName = ""
        SIRcData(I).szTblName = ""
        SIRcData(I).nData = 0
        SIRcData(I).szColTitle = ""
        SIRcData(I).nCount = 0
        SIRcData(I).nCountDistinct = 0
        SIRcData(I).nFlag = 0
        SLRC(I).BackColor = WHITE
        SLRC(I).ForeColor = BLUE
        SLRC(I).Caption = ""
    Next I
    'CountPB.SymBackColor = LIGHTGRAY
    'CountDistinctPB.SymBackColor = LIGHTGRAY
    'ColTitleIsPB.SymBackColor = LIGHTGRAY
    'RemoveRedRowPB.SymBackColor = LIGHTGRAY
    'CountPB.FontColor = WHITE
    'CountDistinctPB.FontColor = WHITE
    'ColTitleIsPB.FontColor = WHITE
    'RemoveRedRowPB.FontColor = WHITE
    CountPB.Enabled = FALSE
```

```
CountDistinctPB.Enabled = FALSE
RemoveRedRowPB.Enabled = FALSE
ColTitleIsPB.Enabled = FALSE
ColTitleIsTxt.Enabled = FALSE
ColTitleIsTxt.BackColor = WHITE
ColTitleIsTxt.ForeColor = DARKGRAY
ColTitleIsTxt.Text = ""
For I = 1 To 5 Step 1
    If (SlRcVSR.Value = 0) Then
        nIdx = SlRcVSR.Value + I
    Else
        nIdx = SlRcVSR.Value + (I - 1)
    End If
    If (nIdx <= SlRcVSR.Max) Then
        SlRcData(I).szTblColName = SelList(nIdx).szTblColName
        SlRcData(I).szTblName = SelList(nIdx).szTblName
        SlRcData(I).nData = nIdx
        SlRcData(I).szColTitle = SelList(nIdx).szColTitle
        Col$ = LTrim$(RTrim$(SlRcData(I).szColTitle))
        nLength = Len(Col$)
        If nLength > 0 Then
            Title$ = Col$ + " = "
        Else
            Title$ = ""
        End If
        SlRcData(I).nCount = SelList(nIdx).nCount
        SlRcData(I).nCountDistinct = SelList(nIdx).nCountDistinct
```

```
SlRcData(I).nFlag = SelList(nIdx).nFlag
Select Case SlRcData(I).nFlag
    Case 0
        SLRC(I).BackColor = WHITE
        SLRC(I).ForeColor = BLUE
    Case 1
        CountPB.Enabled = TRUE
        CountDistinctPB.Enabled = TRUE
        ColTitleIsPB.Enabled = TRUE
        ColTitleIsTxt.Enabled = TRUE
        ColTitleIsTxt.BackColor = BLUE
        ColTitleIsTxt.ForeColor = WHITE
        ColTitleIsTxt.Text = SlRcData(I).szColTitle
        ColTitleIsTxt.SetFocus
        ColTitleIsTxt.SelStart = 0
        SLRC(I).BackColor = BLUE
        SLRC(I).ForeColor = WHITE
        'CountPB.SymBackColor = BLUE
        'CountDistinctPB.SymBackColor = BLUE
        'ColTitleIsPB.SymBackColor = BLUE
    Case 2
        RemoveRedRowPB.Enabled = TRUE
        'RemoveRedRowPB.SymBackColor = RED
        SLRC(I).BackColor = RED
        SLRC(I).ForeColor = WHITE
End Select
' check for COUNT or COUNT DISTINCT…if ON…then add to DISPLAY…
```

```
            Col$ = LTrim$(RTrim$(SelList(SIRcData(I).nData).szTblColName))
            If Col$ <> "*" Then
                tmp$ = LTrim$(RTrim$(SelList(SIRcData(I).nData).szTblName))
                tmp$ = tmp$ + "."
                tmp$ = tmp$ + Col$
            Else
                tmp$ = Col$
            End If
            If SIRcData(I).nCount > 0 Then
                tmp$ = "Count(" + tmp$ + ")"
            Else
                If SIRcData(I).nCountDistinct > 0 Then
                    tmp$ = "Count(Distinct(" + tmp$ + "))"
                End If
            End If
            tmp$ = Title$ + tmp$
            SLRC(I).Caption = LTrim$(RTrim$(tmp$))
        Else
            Exit For
        End If
    Next I
End If
'CountPB.FontColor = WHITE
'CountDistinctPB.FontColor = WHITE
'ColTitleIsPB.FontColor = WHITE
'RemoveRedRowPB.FontColor = WHITE
```

End Sub

Sub SLRC_Click (Index As Integer)

```
nSLRCIdx = SIRcData(Index).nData
If nSLRCIdx < 1 Then
    ' there is NO DATA for this display row...so exit...
    Exit Sub
End If
If (SelList(nSLRCIdx).nData < 1) Then
    ' this row is EMPTY...so do nothing...
    Exit Sub
Else
    Select Case SelList(nSLRCIdx).nFlag
        Case 0
            ' this row is currently WHITE...so change it to RED...
            SelList(nSLRCIdx).nFlag = 2
            SIRcData(Index).nFlag = 2
            SLRC(Index).BackColor = RED
            SLRC(Index).ForeColor = WHITE
            ' NOTE-> there can ONLY be ONE RED ROW and ONLY ONE RED SelList
            '        item at a time...so change the other RED item WHITE...
            For I = 1 To 5 Step 1
                ' change to other DISPLAY rows to WHITE if they are RED...
                If I <> Index Then
                    If SIRcData(I).nFlag = 2 Then
                        SIRcData(I).nFlag = 0
```

295

```
            SLRC(I).BackColor = WHITE
            SLRC(I).ForeColor = BLUE
         End If
      End If
   Next I
   For I = 1 To 100 Step 1
      ' change the SelList items to WHITE if they are RED...
      If SelList(I).nData = 0 Then
         ' there are no more...so exit the loop...
         Exit For
      Else
         If nSLRCIdx <> I Then
            ' this item is NOT the one we just changed to RED...
            If SelList(I).nFlag = 2 Then
               ' it is RED...so make it WHITE...
               SelList(I).nFlag = 0
            End If
         End If
      End If
   Next I
   ' NOTE-> we now have a RED ROW...and since we can REMOVE A RED ROW...
   '        we need to enable the REMOVE RED ROW button...
   RemoveRedRowPB.Enabled = TRUE
   'RemoveRedRowPB.SymBackColor = RED

Case 1
```

```
' this row is currently BLUE...so change it to WHITE...
SelList(nSLRCIdx).nFlag = 0
SIRcData(Index).nFlag = 0
SLRC(Index).BackColor = WHITE
SLRC(Index).ForeColor = BLUE
' NOTE-> and since there can ONLY be ONE RED row and there are
'        NO RED ROWS NOW...and since we can ONLY REMOVE A RED ROW...
'        we need to disable the REMOVE RED ROW button...
CountPB.Enabled = FALSE
CountDistinctPB.Enabled = FALSE
ColTitleIsPB.Enabled = FALSE
ColTitleIsTxt.Enabled = FALSE
ColTitleIsTxt.BackColor = WHITE
ColTitleIsTxt.ForeColor = DARKGRAY
ColTitleIsTxt.Text = ""
SIRcVSR.SetFocus
'CountPB.SymBackColor = LIGHTGRAY
'CountDistinctPB.SymBackColor = LIGHTGRAY
'ColTitleIsPB.SymBackColor = LIGHTGRAY

Case 2
' this row is currently RED...so change it to BLUE...
SelList(nSLRCIdx).nFlag = 1
SIRcData(Index).nFlag = 1
SLRC(Index).BackColor = BLUE
SLRC(Index).ForeColor = WHITE
CountPB.Enabled = TRUE
```

```
CountDistinctPB.Enabled = TRUE
ColTitleIsPB.Enabled = TRUE
ColTitleIsTxt.Enabled = TRUE
ColTitleIsTxt.BackColor = BLUE
ColTitleIsTxt.ForeColor = WHITE
ColTitleIsTxt.Text = SIRcData(Index).szColTitle
ColTitleIsTxt.SetFocus
ColTitleIsTxt.SelStart = 0
'CountPB.SymBackColor = BLUE
'CountDistinctPB.SymBackColor = BLUE
'ColTitleIsPB.SymBackColor = BLUE
' NOTE-> there can ONLY be ONE BLUE ROW and ONLY ONE BLUE SelList
'       item at a time...so change the other BLUE item WHITE...
For I = 1 To 5 Step 1
    ' change to other DISPLAY rows to WHITE if they are BLUE...
    If I <> Index Then
        If SIRcData(I).nFlag = 1 Then
            SIRcData(I).nFlag = 0
            SLRC(I).BackColor = WHITE
            SLRC(I).ForeColor = BLUE
        End If
    End If
Next I
For I = 1 To 100 Step 1
    ' change the SelList items to WHITE if they are BLUE...
    If SelList(I).nData = 0 Then
        ' there are no more...so exit the loop...
```

```
            Exit For
         Else
            If nSLRCIdx < > I Then
               ' this item is NOT the one we just changed to BLUE...
               If SelList(I).nFlag = 1 Then
                  ' it is BLUE...so make it WHITE...
                  SelList(I).nFlag = 0
               End If
            End If
         End If
      Next I
      RemoveRedRowPB.Enabled = FALSE
      'RemoveRedRowPB.SymBackColor = LIGHTGRAY
      SlRcVSR.SetFocus
   End Select
End If
'CountPB.FontColor = WHITE
'CountDistinctPB.FontColor = WHITE
'ColTitlelsPB.FontColor = WHITE
'RemoveRedRowPB.FontColor = WHITE
End Sub

Sub ExitSqlFrmPB_Click ()
End
End Sub
```

Sub RemoveRedRowPB_Click ()
RemoveRedSlRcItem
RemoveRedRowPB.Enabled = FALSE
End Sub

Sub CountPB_Click ()
For I = 1 To 5 Step 1
  If (SlRcData(I).nFlag = 1) Then
    ' this is the BLUE row…and the one to change…
    ' but first…reset the COLUMN TITLE to the STORED VALUE…
    ColTitleIsTxt.Text = SlRcData(I).szColTitle
    Col$ = LTrim$(RTrim$(SlRcData(I).szColTitle))
    nLength = Len(Col$)
    If nLength > 0 Then
      Title$ = Col$ + " = "
    Else
      Title$ = ""
    End If
    Col$ = LTrim$(RTrim$(SlRcData(I).szTblColName))
    If Col$ <> "*" Then
      tmp$ = LTrim$(RTrim$(SlRcData(I).szTblName))
      tmp$ = tmp$ + "."
      tmp$ = tmp$ + Col$
    Else
      tmp$ = Col$
    End If

```
            If SlRcData(I).nCount < 1 Then
                ' make it COUNT()...
                SlRcData(I).nCount = 1
                SlRcData(I).nCountDistinct = 0
                SelList(SlRcData(I).nData).nCount = 1
                SelList(SlRcData(I).nData).nCountDistinct = 0
                tmp$ = "Count(" + tmp$ + ")"
            Else
                ' clear the COUNT()...
                SlRcData(I).nCount = 0
                SlRcData(I).nCountDistinct = 0
                SelList(SlRcData(I).nData).nCount = 0
                SelList(SlRcData(I).nData).nCountDistinct = 0
            End If
            ' NOTE-> leave the color as BLUE…make the user change it…
            tmp$ = Title$ + tmp$
            SLRC(I).Caption = LTrim$(RTrim$(tmp$))
            Exit For
        End If
    Next I
    ColTitleIsTxt.SetFocus
    ColTitleIsTxt.SelStart = 0
End Sub

Sub CountDistinctPB_Click ()
    For I = 1 To 5 Step 1
```

```
If (SIRcData(I).nFlag = 1) Then
   ' this is the BLUE row…and the one to change…
   ' but first…reset the COLUMN TITLE to the STORED VALUE…
   ColTitleIsTxt.Text = SIRcData(I).szColTitle
   Col$ = LTrim$(RTrim$(SIRcData(I).szColTitle))
   nLength = Len(Col$)
   If nLength > 0 Then
      Title$ = Col$ + " = "
   Else
      Title$ = ""
   End If
   Col$ = LTrim$(RTrim$(SIRcData(I).szTblColName))

   Col$ = LTrim$(RTrim$(SelList(SIRcData(I).nData).szTblColName))
   If Col$ <> "*" Then
      tmp$ = LTrim$(RTrim$(SelList(SIRcData(I).nData).szTblColName))
      tmp$ = tmp$ + ","
      tmp$ = tmp$ + Col$
   Else
      tmp$ = Col$
   End If
   If SIRcData(I).nCountDistinct < 1 Then
      ' make it COUNT(DISTINCT()…
      SIRcData(I).nCount = 0
      SIRcData(I).nCountDistinct = 1
      SelList(SIRcData(I).nData).nCount = 0
      SelList(SIRcData(I).nData).nCountDistinct = 1
```

```
        tmp$ = "Count(Distinct(" + tmp$ + "))"
    Else
        ' clear the COUNT(DISTINCT()...
        SIRcData(I).nCount = 0
        SIRcData(I).nCountDistinct = 0
        SelList(SIRcData(I).nData).nCount = 0
        SelList(SIRcData(I).nData).nCountDistinct = 0
    End If
    ' NOTE-> leave the color as BLUE...make the user change it...
    tmp$ = Title$ + tmp$
    SLRC(I).Caption = LTrim$(RTrim$(tmp$))
    Exit For
  End If
Next I
ColTitleIsTxt.SetFocus
ColTitleIsTxt.SelStart = 0
End Sub

Sub SLRC_Change (Index As Integer)
HelpCtl.Text = ""
End Sub

Sub ColTitleIsPB_click ()
nFoundABlueRow = 0
For I = 1 To 5 Step 1
    If SIRcData(I).nFlag = 1 Then
```

```
            nFoundABlueRow = 1
            nSLRCIdx = SIRcData(I).nData
            Exit For
        End If
    Next I
    If nFoundABlueRow < 1 Then
    ' the BLUE ROW is NOT currently visible…and CANNOT BE TITLED…
        Exit Sub
    End If
    SIRcData(nSLRCIdx).szColTitle = ColTitleIsTxt.Text
    SelList(SIRcData(nSLRCIdx).nData).szColTitle = ColTitleIsTxt.Text
    Col$ = LTrim$(RTrim$(SIRcData(nSLRCIdx).szColTitle))
    nLength = Len(Col$)
    If nLength > 0 Then
        Title$ = Col$ + " = "
    Else
        Title$ = ""
    End If
    ' check for COUNT or COUNT DISTINCT…if ON…then add to DISPLAY…
    Col$ = LTrim$(RTrim$(SIRcData(nSLRCIdx).szTblColName))
    If Col$ <> "*" Then
        tmp$ = LTrim$(RTrim$(SIRcData(nSLRCIdx).szTblName))
        tmp$ = tmp$ + "."
        tmp$ = tmp$ + Col$
    Else
        tmp$ = tmp$ + Col$
    End If
```

```
        If SlRcData(nSLRCIdx).nCount > 0 Then
            tmp$ = "Count(" + tmp$ + ")"
        Else
            If SlRcData(nSLRCIdx).nCountDistinct > 0 Then
                tmp$ = "Count(Distinct(" + tmp$ + "))"
            End If
        End If
        tmp$ = Title$ + tmp$
        SLRC(I).Caption = LTrim$(RTrim$(tmp$))
        ColTitleIsTxt.SetFocus
        ColTitleIsTxt.SelStart = 0
End Sub

Sub CndTVRC_Click (Index As Integer)
    nIdx = CndTvRcData(Index).nData
    If nIdx < 1 Then
        ' there is NO DATA for this row…so exit…
        Exit Sub
    End If
    ' NOTE-> ADD to the CndSLRC…(append at FIRST ZERO loc)…
    For I = 1 To 100 Step 1
        ' change the CndSelList items to WHITE if they are YELLOW…
        If CndSelList(I).nFlag = 3 Then
            ' it is YELLOW…so make it WHITE…
            CndSelList(I).nFlag = 0
        End If
```

```
If (CndSelList(I).nData = 0) Then
    CndSelList(I).szTblColName = CndTblCols(nIdx).szTblColName
    CndSelList(I).szTblName = CndTblCols(nIdx).szTblName
    CndSelList(I).szColTitle = ""
    CndSelList(I).szCndValue = ""
    CndSelList(I).nData = CndTvRcData(Index).nData
    CndSelList(I).nConnector = 1    ' WARNING-> default is 'AND'
    CndSelList(I).nRelation = 1     ' WARNING=> default is 'IS ANY VALUE'
    CndSelList(I).nLeftFunction = 0
    CndSelList(I).nRightFunction = 0
    CndSelList(I).nCount = 0
    CndSelList(I).nCountDistinct = 0
    CndSelList(I).nFlag = 3         ' WARNING-> default is 'YELLOW"
    nAtLeastOne = 0
    RemoveCndRedRowPB.Enabled = FALSE
    'RemoveCndRedRowPB.SymBackColor = LIGHTGRAY
    'RemoveCndRedRowPB.FontColor = WHITE
    FBXL.Visible = FALSE
    'RelTxtPB.SymBackColor = LIGHTGRAY
    'RelTxtPB.FontColor = WHITE
    RelTxtPB.Enabled = FALSE
    RelTxt.BackColor = LIGHTGRAY
    RelTxt.ForeColor = WHITE
    RelTxt.Text = ""
    RelTxt.Enabled = FALSE
    FBXR.Visible = FALSE
    For J = 1 To 5 Step 1
```

```
If (CndSelList(J).nData > 0) Then
    nAtLeastOne = 1
    CndSlRcData(J).szTblColName = CndSelList(J).szTblColName
    CndSlRcData(J).szTblName = CndSelList(J).szTblName
    CndSlRcData(J).szColTitle = CndSelList(J).szColTitle
    CndSlRcData(J).szCndValue = CndSelList(J).szCndValue
    CndSlRcData(J).nData = J
    CndSlRcData(J).nConnector = CndSelList(J).nConnector
    CndSlRcData(J).nRelation = CndSelList(J).nRelation
    CndSlRcData(J).nLeftFunction = CndSelList(J).nLeftFunction
    CndSlRcData(J).nRightFunction = CndSelList(J).nRightFunction
    CndSlRcData(J).nCount = CndSelList(J).nCount
    CndSlRcData(J).nCountDistinct = CndSelList(J).nCountDistinct
    CndSlRcData(J).nFlag = CndSelList(J).nFlag
    nCndIdx = J
    BuildCndString
    Select Case CndSlRcData(J).nFlag
        Case 0
            CndSLRC(J).BackColor = WHITE
            CndSLRC(J).ForeColor = BLUE
        Case 1
            CndSLRC(J).BackColor = BLUE
            CndSLRC(J).ForeColor = WHITE
            FBXR.Visible = TRUE
            RelCB.ListIndex = CndSlRcData(J).nRelation - 1
            If (CndSlRcData(J).szCndValue < > "") Then
                RelTxt.Text = CndSlRcData(J).szCndValue
```

```
        Else
            RelTxt.Text = " "
        End If
        If ((CndSIRcData(J).nRelation > 1) And (CndSIRcData(J).nRelation < 12)) Then
            RelTxtPB.Enabled = TRUE
            'RelTxtPB.SymBackColor = BLUE
            'RelTxtPB.FontColor = WHITE
            RelTxt.Enabled = TRUE
            RelTxt.BackColor = BLUE
            RelTxt.ForeColor = WHITE
            RelTxt.SetFocus
            RelTxt.SelStart = 0
        End If
    Case 2
        CndSLRC(J).BackColor = RED
        CndSLRC(J).ForeColor = WHITE
        RemoveCndRedRowPB.Enabled = TRUE
        'RemoveCndRedRowPB.SymBackColor = RED
        'RemoveCndRedRowPB.FontColor = WHITE
    Case 3
        CndSLRC(J).BackColor = YELLOW
        CndSLRC(J).ForeColor = BLUE
        FBXL.Visible = TRUE
        If CndSIRcData(J).nConnector = 1 Then
            LogCB.ListIndex = 0
        Else
            LogCB.ListIndex = 1
```

```
            End If
        End Select
        CndSLRC(J).Caption = LTrim$(RTrim$(szTempCndStr))
    Else
        CndSlRcData(J).szTblColName = ""
        CndSlRcData(J).szTblName = ""
        CndSlRcData(J).szColTitle = ""
        CndSlRcData(J).szCndValue = ""
        CndSlRcData(J).nData = 0
        CndSlRcData(J).nConnector = 0
        CndSlRcData(J).nRelation = 0
        CndSlRcData(J).nLeftFunction = 0
        CndSlRcData(J).nRightFunction = 0
        CndSlRcData(J).nCount = 0
        CndSlRcData(J).nCountDistinct = 0
        CndSlRcData(J).nFlag = 0
        CndSLRC(J).Caption = ""
        CndSLRC(J).BackColor = WHITE
        CndSLRC(J).ForeColor = BLUE
    End If
Next J
nResetCndSlRcVSR = 0
If nAtLeastOne > 0 Then
    CndSlRcVSR.Min = 1
    CndSlRcVSR.Max = I
    CndSlRcVSR.Value = 1
Else
```

```
        ' ERROR-> should NOT occur...is same as:  CndSlRcVSR.Value = 0
        '         which at this point would cause an error...
        End If
        nResetCndSlRcVSR = 1
        Exit For
    End If
    Next I
End Sub

## Sub CndSLRC_Click (Index As Integer)
nCndSLRCIdx = CndSlRcData(Index).nData
If nCndSLRCIdx < 1 Then
    ' there is NO DATA for this display row...so exit...
    Exit Sub
End If
If (CndSelList(nCndSLRCIdx).nData < 1) Then
    ' this row is EMPTY...so do nothing...
    Exit Sub
Else
    Select Case CndSelList(nCndSLRCIdx).nFlag
    Case 0
        ' this row is currently WHITE...so change it to RED...
        CndSelList(nCndSLRCIdx).nFlag = 2
        CndSlRcData(Index).nFlag = 2
        CndSLRC(Index).BackColor = RED
        CndSLRC(Index).ForeColor = WHITE
```

```
' NOTE-> there can ONLY be ONE RED ROW and ONLY ONE RED CndSelList
'         item at a time…so change the other RED item WHITE…
For I = 1 To 5 Step 1
    ' change to other DISPLAY rows to WHITE if they are RED…
    If I <> Index Then
        If CndSIRcData(I).nFlag = 2 Then
            CndSIRcData(I).nFlag = 0
            CndSLRC(I).BackColor = WHITE
            CndSLRC(I).ForeColor = BLUE
        End If
    End If
Next I
For I = 1 To 100 Step 1
    ' change the CndSelList items to WHITE if they are RED…
    If CndSelList(I).nData = 0 Then
        ' there are no more…so exit the loop…
        Exit For
    Else
        If nCndSLRCIdx <> I Then
            ' this item is NOT the one we just changed to RED…
            If CndSelList(I).nFlag = 2 Then
                ' it is RED…so make it WHITE…
                CndSelList(I).nFlag = 0
            End If
        End If
    End If
Next I
```

311

```
' NOTE-> we now have a RED ROW...and since we can REMOVE A RED ROW...
'              we need to enable the REMOVE RED ROW button...
        RemoveCndRedRowPB.Enabled = TRUE
       'RemoveCndRedRowPB.SymBackColor = RED
       'RemoveCndRedRowPB.FontColor = WHITE
        RemoveCndRedRowPB.SetFocus

Case 1
    ' this row is currently BLUE...so change it to WHITE...
        CndSelList(nCndSLRCIdx).nFlag = 0
        CndSlRcData(Index).nFlag = 0
        CndSLRC(Index).BackColor = WHITE
        CndSLRC(Index).ForeColor = BLUE
       'RelTxtPB.SymBackColor = LIGHTGRAY
       'RelTxtPB.FontColor = WHITE
        RelTxtPB.Enabled = FALSE
        RelTxt.BackColor = LIGHTGRAY
        RelTxt.ForeColor = WHITE
        RelTxt.Enabled = FALSE
        RelTxt.Text = ""
        FBXR.Visible = FALSE

Case 2
    ' this row is currently RED...so change it to YELLOW...
        CndSelList(nCndSLRCIdx).nFlag = 3
        CndSlRcData(Index).nFlag = 3
        CndSLRC(Index).BackColor = YELLOW
```

```
            CndSLRC(Index).ForeColor = BLUE
            FBXL.Visible = TRUE
            If CndSlRcData(Index).nConnector = 1 Then
               LogCB.ListIndex = 0
            Else
               LogCB.ListIndex = 1
            End If
   ' NOTE-> there can ONLY be ONE YELLOW ROW and ONLY ONE YELLOW CndSelList
   '        item at a time...so change the other YELLOW item WHITE...
            For I = 1 To 5 Step 1
             ' change to other DISPLAY rows to WHITE if they are YELLOW...
               If I <> Index Then
                  If CndSlRcData(I).nFlag = 3 Then
                     CndSlRcData(I).nFlag = 0
                     CndSLRC(I).BackColor = WHITE
                     CndSLRC(I).ForeColor = BLUE
                  End If
               End If
            Next I
            For I = 1 To 100 Step 1
             ' change the CndSelList items to WHITE if they are YELLOW...
               If CndSelList(I).nData = 0 Then
                ' there are no more...so exit the loop...
                  Exit For
               Else
                  If nCndSLRCIdx <> I Then
                   ' this item is NOT the one we just changed to YELLOW...
```

```
            If CndSelList(I).nFlag = 3 Then
                ' it is YELLOW...so make it WHITE...
                CndSelList(I).nFlag = 0
            End If
        End If
    End If
Next I
' NOTE-> since the ONLY way this row got to be YELLOW was by FIRST
'        being RED and since there is ONLY ONE RED ROW at a time
'        there is NOT A RED ROW NOW...so disable the RED buttons...
RemoveCndRedRowPB.Enabled = FALSE
'RemoveCndRedRowPB.SymBackColor = LIGHTGRAY
'RemoveCndRedRowPB.FontColor = WHITE

Case 3
    ' this row is currently YELLOW...so change it to BLUE...
    CndSelList(nCndSLRCIdx).nFlag = 1
    CndSlRcData(Index).nFlag = 1
    CndSLRC(Index).BackColor = BLUE
    CndSLRC(Index).ForeColor = WHITE
    FBXR.Visible = TRUE
    RelTxtPB.Enabled = TRUE
    'RelTxtPB.SymBackColor = BLUE
    'RelTxtPB.FontColor = WHITE
    RelTxt.Enabled = TRUE
    RelTxt.BackColor = BLUE
    RelTxt.ForeColor = WHITE
```

```
If CndSlRcData(Index).szCndValue < > "" Then
    RelTxt.Text = CndSlRcData(Index).szCndValue
Else
    RelTxt.Text = ""
End If
If ((CndSlRcData(Index).nRelation > 1) And (CndSlRcData(Index).nRelation < 12)) Then
    RelTxt.SetFocus
    RelTxt.SelStart = 0
Else
    'RelTxtPB.SymBackColor = LIGHTGRAY
    'RelTxtPB.FontColor = WHITE
    RelTxt.BackColor = LIGHTGRAY
    RelTxt.ForeColor = WHITE
    RelTxt.Enabled = FALSE
    RelTxtPB.Enabled = FALSE
    RelCB.SetFocus
End If
' NOTE-> there can ONLY be ONE BLUE ROW and ONLY ONE BLUE CndSelList
'        item at a time…so change the other BLUE item WHITE…
For I = 1 To 5 Step 1
    ' change to other DISPLAY rows to WHITE if they are BLUE…
    If I < > Index Then
        If CndSlRcData(I).nFlag = 1 Then
            CndSlRcData(I).nFlag = 0
            CndSLRC(I).BackColor = WHITE
            CndSLRC(I).ForeColor = BLUE
        End If
```

```
            End If
         Next I
         For I = 1 To 100 Step 1
            ' change the CndSelList items to WHITE if they are BLUE…
            If CndSelList(I).nData = 0 Then
               ' there are no more…so exit the loop…
               Exit For
            Else
               If nCndSLRCIdx < > I Then
                  ' this item is NOT the one we just changed to BLUE…
                  If CndSelList(I).nFlag = 1 Then
                     ' it is BLUE…so make it WHITE…
                     CndSelList(I).nFlag = 0
                  End If
               End If
            End If
         Next I
         RelCB.ListIndex = CndSlRcData(Index).nRelation - 1
         ' NOTE-> there can ONLY be ONE YELLOW ROW and ONLY ONE YELLOW CndSelList
         '        item at a time…so there is NOT A YELLOW ROW anymore…
         '        so disable the YELLOW buttons…
         FBXL.Visible = FALSE
   End Select
   End If
End Sub
```

Sub RemoveCndRedRowPB_Click ()

```
RemoveRedCndSlRcItem
RemoveCndRedRowPB.Enabled = FALSE
End Sub
```

Sub CndTvRcVSR_Change ()

```
If nResetCndTvRcVSR = 0 Then
    Exit Sub
Else
    For I = 1 To 5 Step 1
        CndTvRcData(I).szTblColName = ""
        CndTvRcData(I).szTblName = ""
        CndTvRcData(I).nData = 0
        CndTVRC(I).Caption = ""
        CndTVRC(I).BackColor = WHITE
    Next I
    For I = 1 To 5 Step 1
        If CndTvRcVSR.Value < 1 Then
            nIdx = CndTvRcVSR.Value + I
        Else
            nIdx = CndTvRcVSR.Value + (I - 1)
        End If
        If (nIdx <= CndTvRcVSR.Max) Then
            CndTVRC(I).Caption = CndTblCols(nIdx).szTblColName
            If CndTblCols(nIdx).nData > 0 Then
                ' set to DIFFERENT color HERE...for NOW...leave it WHITE...
```

```
            CndTVRC(I).BackColor = WHITE
        End If
        CndTvRcData(I).szTblColName = CndTblCols(nIdx).szTblColName
        CndTvRcData(I).szTblName = CndTblCols(nIdx).szTblName
        CndTvRcData(I).nData = nIdx
    Else
        Exit For
    End If
Next I
End If
End Sub

Sub CndSlRcVSR_Change ()
If nResetCndSlRcVSR = 0 Then
    Exit Sub
Else
    For I = 1 To 5 Step 1
        CndSlRcData(I).szTblColName = ""
        CndSlRcData(I).szTblName = ""
        CndSlRcData(I).szColTitle = ""
        CndSlRcData(I).szCndValue = ""
        CndSlRcData(I).nData = 0
        CndSlRcData(I).nConnector = 0
        CndSlRcData(I).nRelation = 0
        CndSlRcData(I).nLeftFunction = 0
        CndSlRcData(I).nRightFunction = 0
```

```
CndSlRcData(I).nCount = 0
CndSlRcData(I).nCountDistinct = 0
CndSlRcData(I).nFlag = 0
CndSLRC(I).BackColor = WHITE
CndSLRC(I).ForeColor = BLUE
CndSLRC(I).Caption = ""
Next I
nFoundABlue = 0
nFoundARed = 0
nFoundAYellow = 0
For I = 1 To 5 Step 1
    If (CndSlRcVSR.Value = 0) Then
        nIdx = CndSlRcVSR.Value + I
    Else
        nIdx = CndSlRcVSR.Value + (I - 1)
    End If
    If (nIdx <= CndSlRcVSR.Max) Then
        CndSlRcData(I).szTblColName = CndSelList(nIdx).szTblColName
        CndSlRcData(I).szTblName = CndSelList(nIdx).szTblName
        CndSlRcData(I).szColTitle = CndSelList(nIdx).szColTitle
        CndSlRcData(I).szCndValue = CndSelList(nIdx).szCndValue
        CndSlRcData(I).nData = nIdx
        CndSlRcData(I).nConnector = CndSelList(nIdx).nConnector
        CndSlRcData(I).nRelation = CndSelList(nIdx).nRelation
        CndSlRcData(I).nLeftFunction = CndSelList(nIdx).nLeftFunction
        CndSlRcData(I).nRightFunction = CndSelList(nIdx).nRightFunction
        CndSlRcData(I).nCount = CndSelList(nIdx).nCount
```

```
CndSlRcData(I).nCountDistinct = CndSelList(nIdx).nCountDistinct
CndSlRcData(I).nFlag = CndSelList(nIdx).nFlag
nCndIdx = I
BuildCndString
Select Case CndSlRcData(I).nFlag
    Case 0
        CndSLRC(I).BackColor = WHITE
        CndSLRC(I).ForeColor = BLUE
    Case 1
        CndSLRC(I).BackColor = BLUE
        CndSLRC(I).ForeColor = WHITE
        FBXR.Visible = TRUE
        If ((CndSlRcData(I).nRelation > 1) And (CndSlRcData(I).nRelation < 12)) Then
            RelTxtPB.Enabled = TRUE
            'RelTxtPB.SymBackColor = BLUE
            'RelTxtPB.FontColor = WHITE
            RelTxt.Enabled = TRUE
            RelTxt.BackColor = BLUE
            RelTxt.ForeColor = WHITE
            If (CndSlRcData(I).szCndValue <> "") Then
                RelTxt.Text = CndSlRcData(I).szCndValue
            Else
                RelTxt.Text = " "
            End If
            RelTxt.SetFocus
            RelTxt.SelStart = 0
        Else
```

```
        'RelTxtPB.SymBackColor = LIGHTGRAY
        'RelTxtPB.FontColor = WHITE
        RelTxtPB.Enabled = FALSE
        RelTxt.BackColor = LIGHTGRAY
        RelTxt.ForeColor = WHITE
        If (CndSlRcData(I).szCndValue < > "") Then
            RelTxt.Text = CndSlRcData(I).szCndValue
        Else
            RelTxt.Text = " "
        End If
        RelTxt.Enabled = FALSE
    End If
    nFoundABlue = I     'WARNING-> set to I so we KNOW which
                        '          RelCB.ListIndex to use...LATER...
Case 2
    RemoveCndRedRowPB.Enabled = TRUE
    'RemoveCndRedRowPB.SymBackColor = RED
    'RemoveCndRedRowPB.FontColor = WHITE
    CndSLRC(I).BackColor = RED
    CndSLRC(I).ForeColor = WHITE
    nFoundARed = 1
Case 3
    CndSLRC(I).BackColor = YELLOW
    CndSLRC(I).ForeColor = BLUE
    FBXL.Visible = TRUE
    If CndSlRcData(I).nConnector = 1 Then
        LogCB.ListIndex = 0
```

```
                Else
                    LogCB.ListIndex = 1
                End If
                nFoundAYellow = 1
            End Select
            CndSLRC(I).Caption = szTempCndStr
        Else
            Exit For
        End If
    Next I
    If nFoundABlue < 1 Then
        'RelTxtPB.SymBackColor = LIGHTGRAY
        'RelTxtPB.FontColor = WHITE
        RelTxtPB.Enabled = FALSE
        RelTxt.BackColor = LIGHTGRAY
        RelTxt.ForeColor = WHITE
        RelTxt.Text = ""
        RelTxt.Enabled = FALSE
        FBXR.Visible = FALSE
    Else
        RelCB.ListIndex = CndSlRcData(nFoundABlue).nRelation - 1
    End If
    If nFoundARed < 1 Then
        RemoveCndRedRowPB.Enabled = FALSE
        'RemoveCndRedRowPB.SymBackColor = LIGHTGRAY
        'RemoveCndRedRowPB.FontColor = WHITE
    End If
```

```
        If nFoundAYellow < 1 Then
            FBXL.Visible = FALSE
        End If
    End If
End Sub

Sub CndTblViewCB_Click 0
    If (FBCB.Visible = TRUE) Then
        nRetVal = MsgBox2001()
        If (nRetVal = FALSE) Then
            Exit Sub
        End If
    End If
    For I = 1 To 5 Step 1
        CndTVRC(I).Caption = " "
        CndTvRcData(I).szTblColName = ""
        CndTvRcData(I).szTblName = ""
        CndTvRcData(I).nData = 0
    Next I
    CndTvRcVSR.Min = 0
    CndTvRcVSR.Max = 0
    nResetCndTvRcVSR = 0
    CndTvRcVSR.Value = 0

    For I = 1 To 100 Step 1
        CndTblCols(I).szTblName = ""
```

```
            CndTblCols(I).szTblColName = ""
            CndTblCols(I).nData = 0
        Next I
        '_____
        nCndTblIdx = SqlFrm.CndTblViewCB.ListIndex
        szCurrCndTblName = LTrim$(RTrim$(SqlFrm.CndTblViewCB.LIST(nCndTblIdx)))
        GetCndTblViewColumns
        If nCurrCndColCount > 0 Then
            For I = 1 To 5 Step 1
                If I <= nCurrCndColCount Then
                    CndTvRcData(I).szTblColName = CndTblCols(I).szTblColName
                    CndTvRcData(I).szTblName = szCurrCndTblName
                    CndTvRcData(I).nData = I
                    CndTVRC(I).Caption = CndTvRcData(I).szTblColName
                Else
                    Exit For
                End If
            Next I
            CndTvRcVSR.Min = 1
            CndTvRcVSR.Max = nCurrCndColCount
            nResetTvRcVSR = 1
            CndTvRcVSR.Value = 1
            nResetCndTvRcVSR = 1
        End If
        For I = 1 To 5 Step 1
            CndSLRC(I).BackColor = WHITE
            CndSLRC(I).ForeColor = BLUE
```

```
CndSLRC(I).Caption = ""
CndSlRcData(I).szTblColName = ""
CndSlRcData(I).szTblName = ""
CndSlRcData(I).szColTitle = ""
CndSlRcData(I).szCndValue = ""
CndSlRcData(I).nData = 0
CndSlRcData(I).nConnector = 0
CndSlRcData(I).nRelation = 0
CndSlRcData(I).nLeftFunction = 0
CndSlRcData(I).nRightFunction = 0
CndSlRcData(I).nCount = 0
CndSlRcData(I).nCountDistinct = 0
CndSlRcData(I).nFlag = 0
Next I
CndSLRC(1).Caption = ""
For I = 1 To 100 Step 1
    CndSelList(I).szTblColName = ""
    CndSelList(I).szTblName = ""
    CndSelList(I).szColTitle = ""
    CndSelList(I).szCndValue = ""
    CndSelList(I).nData = 0
    CndSelList(I).nConnector = 0
    CndSelList(I).nRelation = 0
    CndSelList(I).nLeftFunction = 0
    CndSelList(I).nRightFunction = 0
    CndSelList(I).nCount = 0
    CndSelList(I).nCountDistinct = 0
```

```
        CndSelList(I).nFlag = 0
    Next I
    nResetCndSlRcVSR = 0
    CndSlRcVSR.Min = 0
    CndSlRcVSR.Max = 0
    CndSlRcVSR.Value = 0
    nResetCndSlRcVSR = 1    ' WARNING-> MUST do this to enable scrolling…
    FBXL.Visible = FALSE
    FBXR.Visible = FALSE
    RelTxt.Text = ""
    RemoveCndRedRowPB.Enabled = FALSE
    'RemoveCndRedRowPB.SymBackColor = LIGHTGRAY
    'RemoveCndRedRowPB.FontColor = WHITE
    FindCndTxt.Text = ""
    If nSqlFrmReallyVisible > 0 Then
        If FBCB.Visible = TRUE Then
            FindCndTxt.SetFocus
        End If
    End If
End Sub

Sub ConditionsPB_Click ()
'ConditionsPB.SymBackColor = LIGHTGRAY
'ConditionsPB.FontColor = WHITE
'-------------------------------------
'CountPB.SymBackColor = LIGHTGRAY
```

```
'CountDistinctPB.SymBackColor = LIGHTGRAY
'ColTitleIsPB.SymBackColor = LIGHTGRAY
'RemoveRedRowPB.SymBackColor = LIGHTGRAY
'CountPB.FontColor = WHITE
'CountDistinctPB.FontColor = WHITE
'ColTitleIsPB.FontColor = WHITE
'RemoveRedRowPB.FontColor = WHITE
'
CountPB.Enabled = FALSE
CountDistinctPB.Enabled = FALSE
ColTitleIsPB.Enabled = FALSE
RemoveRedRowPB.Enabled = FALSE
'
'CountPB.SymBackColor = LIGHTGRAY
'CountDistinctPB.SymBackColor = LIGHTGRAY
'ColTitleIsPB.SymBackColor = LIGHTGRAY
'RemoveRedRowPB.SymBackColor = LIGHTGRAY
'CountPB.FontColor = WHITE
'CountDistinctPB.FontColor = WHITE
'ColTitleIsPB.FontColor = WHITE
'RemoveRedRowPB.FontColor = WHITE
'
FBSB.Enabled = FALSE
FBCB.Visible = TRUE
FBCB.Enabled = TRUE
'ConditionsPB.SymBackColor = LIGHTGRAY
'ConditionsPB.FontColor = WHITE
```

```
'CountPB.SymBackColor = LIGHTGRAY
'CountDistinctPB.SymBackColor = LIGHTGRAY
'ColTitleIsPB.SymBackColor = LIGHTGRAY
'RemoveRedRowPB.SymBackColor = LIGHTGRAY
'CountPB.FontColor = WHITE
'CountDistinctPB.FontColor = WHITE
'ColTitleIsPB.FontColor = WHITE
'RemoveRedRowPB.FontColor = WHITE
For I = 1 To 5 Step 1
    Select Case SLRC(I).BackColor
        Case WHITE
            SaveSlRcPaint(I).nColor = 0
        Case BLUE
            SaveSlRcPaint(I).nColor = 1
        Case RED
            SaveSlRcPaint(I).nColor = 2
        Case Else
            SaveSlRcPaint(I).nColor = 0
    End Select
    SLRC(I).BackColor = WHITE
    SLRC(I).ForeColor = DARKGRAY
Next I
For I = 1 To 5 Step 1
    Select Case TVRC(I).BackColor
        Case WHITE
            SaveTvRcPaint(I).nColor = 0
        Case LIGHTGRAY
```

```
            SaveTvRcPaint(I).nColor = 1
        Case Else
            SaveTvRcPaint(I).nColor = 0
        End Select
        TVRC(I).BackColor = WHITE
        TVRC(I).ForeColor = DARKGRAY
    Next I
    'ConditionsPB.SymBackColor = LIGHTGRAY
    'ConditionsPB.FontColor = WHITE
    'CountPB.SymBackColor = LIGHTGRAY
    'CountDistinctPB.SymBackColor = LIGHTGRAY
    'ColTitleIsPB.SymBackColor = LIGHTGRAY
    'RemoveRedRowPB.SymBackColor = LIGHTGRAY
    'CountPB.FontColor = WHITE
    'CountDistinctPB.FontColor = WHITE
    'ColTitleIsPB.FontColor = WHITE
    'RemoveRedRowPB.FontColor = WHITE
    ColTitleIsTxt.BackColor = WHITE
    ColTitleIsTxt.ForeColor = DARKGRAY
    LX.BackColor = WHITE
    LX.ForeColor = DARKGRAY
    RcTitle.BackColor = WHITE
    RcTitle.ForeColor = DARKGRAY
    TblViewCB.BackColor = WHITE
    TblViewCB.ForeColor = DARKGRAY
    TblViewCB.Enabled = FALSE
    TvRcVSR.Enabled = FALSE
```

```
SIRcVSR.Enabled = FALSE
ConditionsPB.Enabled = FALSE
FindCndTxt.SetFocus
End Sub

Sub SelectionsPB_Click 0
FBSB.Enabled = TRUE
FBCB.Visible = FALSE
ConditionsPB.Enabled = TRUE
'ConditionsPB.SymBackColor = DARKPURPLE
'ConditionsPB.FontColor = WHITE
For I = 1 To 5 Step 1
Select Case SaveSIRcPaint(I).nColor
    Case 0
        SLRC(I).BackColor = WHITE
        SLRC(I).ForeColor = BLUE
    Case 1
        SLRC(I).BackColor = BLUE
        SLRC(I).ForeColor = WHITE
'--------------------------------
        CountPB.Enabled = TRUE
        CountDistinctPB.Enabled = TRUE
        ColTitleIsPB.Enabled = TRUE
'--------------------------------
        'CountPB.SymBackColor = BLUE
        'CountDistinctPB.SymBackColor = BLUE
```

```
        'ColTitleIsPB.SymBackColor = BLUE
        'CountPB.FontColor = WHITE
        'CountDistinctPB.FontColor = WHITE
        'ColTitleIsPB.FontColor = WHITE
        ColTitleIsTxt.SetFocus
        ColTitleIsTxt.SelStart = 0
        ColTitleIsTxt.BackColor = BLUE
        ColTitleIsTxt.ForeColor = WHITE
    Case 2
        SLRC(I).BackColor = RED
        SLRC(I).ForeColor = WHITE
    '_____
        RemoveRedRowPB.Enabled = TRUE
    '_____
        'RemoveRedRowPB.SymBackColor = RED
        'RemoveRedRowPB.FontColor = WHITE
    Case Else
        SLRC(I).BackColor = WHITE
        SLRC(I).ForeColor = BLUE
    End Select
Next I
For I = 1 To 5 Step 1
    Select Case SaveTvRcPaint(I).nColor
        Case 0
            TVRC(I).BackColor = WHITE
            TVRC(I).ForeColor = BLUE
        Case 1
```

```
            TVRC(I).BackColor = LIGHTGRAY
            TVRC(I).ForeColor = BLUE
        Case Else
            TVRC(I).BackColor = WHITE
            TVRC(I).ForeColor = BLUE
        End Select
    Next I
    LX.BackColor = CYAN
    LX.ForeColor = BLUE
    RcTitle.BackColor = CYAN
    RcTitle.ForeColor = BLUE
    TblViewCB.BackColor = WHITE
    TblViewCB.ForeColor = BLUE
    TblViewCB.Enabled = TRUE
    TvRcVSR.Enabled = TRUE
    SIRcVSR.Enabled = TRUE
    If FindSelTxt.Enabled = TRUE Then
        FindSelTxt.SetFocus
    Else
        TblViewCB.SetFocus
    End If
    ConditionsPB.Enabled = TRUE
End Sub

Sub LogCB_Click ()
For I = 1 To 5 Step 1
```

```
    If (CndSlRcData(I).nFlag = 3) Then
      ' this is the YELLOW row…and the one to change…
      If LogCB.ListIndex = 0 Then
        CndSlRcData(I).nConnector = 1
        CndSelList(CndSlRcData(I).nData).nConnector = 1
      Else
        CndSlRcData(I).nConnector = 2
        CndSelList(CndSlRcData(I).nData).nConnector = 2
      End If
      nCndIdx = I
      BuildCndString
      ' NOTE-> leave the color as YELLOW…make the user change it…
      SqlFrm.CndSLRC(I).Caption = szTempCndStr
      Exit For
    End If
  Next I
End Sub

Sub RelTxtPB_click ()
  For I = 1 To 5 Step 1
    If (CndSlRcData(I).nFlag = 1) Then
      ' this is the BLUE row…and the one to change…
      tmp$ = RelTxt.Text
      nLength = Len(tmp$)
      If nLength > 0 Then
        CndSlRcData(I).szCndValue = tmp$
```

```
            CndSelList(CndSIRcData(I).nData).szCndValue = tmp$
      Else
            CndSIRcData(I).szCndValue = ""
            CndSelList(CndSIRcData(I).nData).szCndValue = ""
      End If
      nCndIdx = I
      BuildCndString
      ' NOTE-> leave the color as BLUE...make the user change it...
      SqlFrm.CndSLRC(I).Caption = szTempCndStr
      RelTxt.Enabled = TRUE
      RelTxt.SetFocus
      RelTxt.SelStart = 0
      Exit For
   End If
Next I
End Sub

Sub RelCB_Click ()
For I = 1 To 5 Step 1
   If (CndSIRcData(I).nFlag = 1) Then
      ' this is the BLUE row...and the one to change...
      Select Case RelCB.ListIndex
         Case 0
            CndSIRcData(I).nRelation = 1
            CndSelList(CndSIRcData(I).nData).nRelation = 1
            RelTxt.Text = ""
```

```
            CndSelList(CndSlRcData(I).nData).szCndValue = ""
            CndSlRcData(I).szCndValue = ""
            'RelTxtPB.SymBackColor = LIGHTGRAY
            'RelTxtPB.FontColor = WHITE
            RelTxt.BackColor = LIGHTGRAY
            RelTxt.ForeColor = WHITE
            RelTxt.Enabled = FALSE
            RelTxtPB.Enabled = FALSE
        Case 1
            CndSlRcData(I).nRelation = 2
            CndSelList(CndSlRcData(I).nData).nRelation = 2
            RelTxt.Enabled = TRUE
            RelTxtPB.Enabled = TRUE
            RelTxt.Text = CndSlRcData(I).szCndValue
            'RelTxtPB.SymBackColor = BLUE
            'RelTxtPB.FontColor = WHITE
            RelTxt.BackColor = BLUE
            RelTxt.ForeColor = WHITE
            RelTxt.SetFocus
            RelTxt.SelStart = 0
        Case 2
            CndSlRcData(I).nRelation = 3
            CndSelList(CndSlRcData(I).nData).nRelation = 3
            RelTxt.Enabled = TRUE
            RelTxtPB.Enabled = TRUE
            RelTxt.Text = CndSlRcData(I).szCndValue
            'RelTxtPB.SymBackColor = BLUE
```

```
'RelTxtPB.FontColor = WHITE
RelTxt.BackColor = BLUE
RelTxt.ForeColor = WHITE
RelTxt.SetFocus
RelTxt.SelStart = 0
Case 3
    CndSlRcData(I).nRelation = 4
    CndSelList(CndSlRcData(I).nData).nRelation = 4
    RelTxt.Enabled = TRUE
    RelTxtPB.Enabled = TRUE
    RelTxt.Text = CndSlRcData(I).szCndValue
    'RelTxtPB.SymBackColor = BLUE
    'RelTxtPB.FontColor = WHITE
    RelTxt.BackColor = BLUE
    RelTxt.ForeColor = WHITE
    RelTxt.SetFocus
    RelTxt.SelStart = 0
Case 4
    CndSlRcData(I).nRelation = 5
    CndSelList(CndSlRcData(I).nData).nRelation = 5
    RelTxt.Enabled = TRUE
    RelTxtPB.Enabled = TRUE
    RelTxt.Text = CndSlRcData(I).szCndValue
    'RelTxtPB.SymBackColor = BLUE
    'RelTxtPB.FontColor = WHITE
    RelTxt.BackColor = BLUE
    RelTxt.ForeColor = WHITE
```

```
        RelTxt.SetFocus
        RelTxt.SelStart = 0
    Case 5
        CndSlRcData(I).nRelation = 6
        CndSelList(CndSlRcData(I).nData).nRelation = 6
        RelTxt.Enabled = TRUE
        RelTxtPB.Enabled = TRUE
        RelTxt.Text = CndSlRcData(I).szCndValue
        'RelTxtPB.SymBackColor = BLUE
        'RelTxtPB.FontColor = WHITE
        RelTxt.BackColor = BLUE
        RelTxt.ForeColor = WHITE
        RelTxt.SetFocus
        RelTxt.SelStart = 0
    Case 6
        CndSlRcData(I).nRelation = 7
        CndSelList(CndSlRcData(I).nData).nRelation = 7
        RelTxt.Enabled = TRUE
        RelTxtPB.Enabled = TRUE
        RelTxt.Text = CndSlRcData(I).szCndValue
        'RelTxtPB.SymBackColor = BLUE
        'RelTxtPB.FontColor = WHITE
        RelTxt.BackColor = BLUE
        RelTxt.ForeColor = WHITE
        RelTxt.SetFocus
        RelTxt.SelStart = 0
    Case 7
```

```
        CndSIRcData(I).nRelation = 8
        CndSelList(CndSIRcData(I).nData).nRelation = 8
        RelTxt.Enabled = TRUE
        RelTxtPB.Enabled = TRUE
        RelTxt.Text = CndSIRcData(I).szCndValue
        'RelTxtPB.SymBackColor = BLUE
        'RelTxtPB.FontColor = WHITE
        RelTxt.BackColor = BLUE
        RelTxt.ForeColor = WHITE
        RelTxt.SetFocus
        RelTxt.SelStart = 0
    Case 8
        CndSIRcData(I).nRelation = 9
        CndSelList(CndSIRcData(I).nData).nRelation = 9
        RelTxt.Enabled = TRUE
        RelTxtPB.Enabled = TRUE
        RelTxt.Text = CndSIRcData(I).szCndValue
        'RelTxtPB.SymBackColor = BLUE
        'RelTxtPB.FontColor = WHITE
        RelTxt.BackColor = BLUE
        RelTxt.ForeColor = WHITE
        RelTxt.SetFocus
        RelTxt.SelStart = 0
    Case 9
        CndSIRcData(I).nRelation = 10
        CndSelList(CndSIRcData(I).nData).nRelation = 10
        RelTxt.Enabled = TRUE
```

```
            RelTxtPB.Enabled = TRUE
            RelTxt.Text = CndSlRcData(I).szCndValue
            'RelTxtPB.SymBackColor = BLUE
            'RelTxtPB.FontColor = WHITE
            RelTxt.BackColor = BLUE
            RelTxt.ForeColor = WHITE
            RelTxt.SetFocus
            RelTxt.SelStart = 0
        Case 10
            CndSlRcData(I).nRelation = 11
            CndSelList(CndSlRcData(I).nData).nRelation = 11
            RelTxt.Enabled = TRUE
            RelTxtPB.Enabled = TRUE
            RelTxt.Text = CndSlRcData(I).szCndValue
            'RelTxtPB.SymBackColor = BLUE
            'RelTxtPB.FontColor = WHITE
            RelTxt.BackColor = BLUE
            RelTxt.ForeColor = WHITE
            RelTxt.SetFocus
            RelTxt.SelStart = 0
        Case 11
            CndSlRcData(I).nRelation = 12
            CndSelList(CndSlRcData(I).nData).nRelation = 12
            RelTxt.Text = ""
            CndSelList(CndSlRcData(I).nData).szCndValue = ""
            CndSlRcData(I).szCndValue = ""
            'RelTxtPB.SymBackColor = LIGHTGRAY
```

```
            'RelTxtPB.FontColor = WHITE
            RelTxt.BackColor = LIGHTGRAY
            RelTxt.ForeColor = WHITE
            RelTxt.Enabled = FALSE
            RelTxtPB.Enabled = FALSE
        Case 12
            CndSlRcData(I).nRelation = 13
            CndSelList(CndSlRcData(I).nData).nRelation = 13
            RelTxt.Text = ""
            CndSelList(CndSlRcData(I).nData).szCndValue = ""
            CndSlRcData(I).szCndValue = ""
            'RelTxtPB.SymBackColor = LIGHTGRAY
            'RelTxtPB.FontColor = WHITE
            RelTxt.BackColor = LIGHTGRAY
            RelTxt.ForeColor = WHITE
            RelTxt.Enabled = FALSE
            RelTxtPB.Enabled = FALSE
        End Select
        nCndIdx = I
        BuildCndString
        ' NOTE-> leave the color as BLUE…make the user change it…
        SqlFrm.CndSLRC(I).Caption = szTempCndStr
        Exit For
    End If
Next I
End Sub
```

Sub RelTxt_KeyDown (KeyCode As Integer, Shift As Integer)
```
If KeyCode = KEY_RETURN Then
    Call RelTxtPB_click
    KeyCode = 0
End If
End Sub
```

Sub ColTitleIsTxt_KeyDown (KeyCode As Integer, Shift As Integer)
```
If KeyCode = KEY_RETURN Then
    Call ColTitleIsPB_click
    KeyCode = 0
End If
End Sub
```

Sub FindSelTxt_Change ()
```
szTxt = LTrim$(RTrim$(FindSelTxt.Text))
FindSelString
If nRowMatchIdx < 1 Then
Else
    ' Found index, reshuffle rowdata.  Index is in nRowMatchIdx
    SqlFrm.TvRcVSR.Value = nRowMatchIdx
End If
End Sub
```

```
Sub FindCndTxt_Change ()
    szTxt = LTrim$(RTrim$(FindCndTxt.Text))
    FindCndString.
    If nRowMatchIdx < 0 Then
    Else
        ' Found index, reshuffle rowdata. Index is in nRowMatchIdx
        SqlFrm.CndTvRcVSR.Value = nRowMatchIdx
    End If
End Sub

Sub FindSelTxt_KeyPress (KeyAscii As Integer)
    If ((KeyAscii > 96) And (KeyAscii < 123)) Then
        KeyAscii = KeyAscii - 32
    End If
End Sub

Sub FindCndTxt_KeyPress (KeyAscii As Integer)
    If ((KeyAscii > 96) And (KeyAscii < 123)) Then
        KeyAscii = KeyAscii - 32
    End If
End Sub

Sub NewSqlPB_Click ()
    nRetVal = MsgBox2003()
    If (nRetVal = FALSE) Then
```

```
    Exit Sub
  End If
  nNoSelClrMsgs = 1
  Screen.MousePointer = 11
  Form_Load
  Screen.MousePointer = 0
  nNoSelClrMsgs = 0
End Sub
```

Sub SaveSqlAsPB_Click ()

```
'----------------------------------------
' NOTE: The FIRST thing we need to do is GENERATE the SQL
'       SELECT statement...
' WARNING-> the GENERATE function MUST also generate the
'           TOKENIZED version of the SELECT statement...
'----------------------------------------

  GenerateSimpleSQL

'---FOR TESTING--------------------------
  HelpCtl.Text = szTokenSqlCmdStr
  HelpCtl.Visible = TRUE
  HelpCtl.SetFocus
'---FOR TESTING--------------------------
'----------------------------------------
```

```
'NOTE: NEXT...we need to do is SAVE the TOKENIZED version
'       of the SELECT statement in a FILE...and since this
'       is the SAVE AS push button we need to provide a
'       dialog box to let the user specify a FILE NAME...
'-------
    SaveAs.Show 1
End Sub

Sub OpenSqlPB_Click 0
' FIRST...give user the option of NOT DOING THIS...
    nRetVal = MsgBox2003()
    If (nRetVal = FALSE) Then
        Exit Sub
    End If
' THEN...since we are continuing...clear the screen...
    fhSaveOldQryFile% = fhOldQryFile ' because Form_Load clears it...
    nNoSelClrMsgs = 1
    Screen.MousePointer = 11
    Form_Load
    Screen.MousePointer = 0
    nNoSelClrMsgs = 0

    ngSqlAdHocOpenSuccessful = 0
    FileForm.Show 1
    If ngSqlAdHocOpenSuccessful > 0 Then
        fhOldQryFile = fhSaveOldQryFile% 'restore fhOldQryFile...
```

```
If (fhOldQryFile > 0) Then
    ' we no longer need the OLD .QRY file handle...
    fhOldQryFile = 0
End If
'---FOR TESTING---------------------------
HelpCtl.Text = szTokenSqlCmdStr
HelpCtl.Visible = TRUE
HelpCtl.SetFocus
'---FOR TESTING---------------------------
'---PARSE THE SQL statement---------------
' Note-> the SQL statement is in szTokenSqlCmdStr...
ParseAndLoadSqlAdHocStmt
'-----------------------------------------
' NOTE-> because TvRcVSR.Value was PRESET to 1, we cannot
'        force this HYBRID object to refresh itself by
'        setting its VALUE to its CURRENT value...we have
'        to set its value to any OTHER value and then set
'        it back to the desired value...this will cause
'        the VALUE to CHANGE and that will trigger the
'        REFRESH...since this is a HYBRID object, it does
'        not have a REFRESH property...so we have to
'        emulate the appropriate behavior...it is easy, but
'        it means that it actually does TWO scroll steps...
'        ONE FORWARD and ONE BACKWARD...but it WORKS...
'-----------------------------------------
TvRcVSR.Value = 2    ' set to DIFFERENT value...
TvRcVSR.Value = 1    ' then..set to CORRECT value...
```

```vb
    '
    SIRcVSR.Value = 1
    '----PARSE THE SQL Select statement----------
End If

End Sub

Sub Command1_Click ()
' NOTE-> this is the little, square button located at
'        the lower right-hand corner of the Condition
'        Selection List...it currently does not do
'        anything...but it could do something...it is
'        primarily here to make the scroll bars look
'        good...
End Sub
```

Sub GetTblViewNames ()

```
'--NON-SQL TESTING-----------------------------
GetLocTblViewNames
'--NON-SQL TESTING-----------------------------
```

End Sub

Sub GetTblViewColumns ()

```
'--NON-SQL TESTING-----------------------------
GetLocTblViewColumns
'--NON-SQL TESTING-----------------------------
```

End Sub

Sub GetLocTblViewColumns ()

```
nIdx = SqlFrm.TblViewCB.ListIndex
If nIdx < 0 Then
    Exit Sub
End If
szSubTxt = LTrim$(RTrim$(SqlFrm.TblViewCB.LIST(nIdx)))
szCurrTblName = LTrim$(RTrim$(szSubTxt))
'-----------------------------------------------

For I = 1 To 100 Step 1
    TblCols(I).szTblName = ""
```

```
        TblCols(I).szTblColName = ""
        TblCols(I).nData = 0
    Next I
    '_____
    I = 1
    TblCols(I).szTblColName = "*"
    TblCols(I).szTblName = szCurrTblName
    nCurrColCount = 1
    For I = 2 To 21 Step 1
        TblCols(I).szTblColName = "Col" + LTrim$(RTrim$(Str$(I)))
        TblCols(I).szTblName = szCurrTblName
        TblCols(I).nData = 0
        nCurrColCount = nCurrColCount + 1
    Next I
End Sub

Sub GetLocTblViewNames ()
nLBCount = SqlFrm.TblViewCB.ListCount
If nLBCount > 0 Then
    For I = 1 To nLBCount Step 1
        SqlFrm.TblViewCB.RemoveItem 0
    Next I
End If
'..........................................................
SqlFrm.TblViewCB.AddItem "VIEW_001" ' for NON-SQL TESTING...
'..........................................................
```

End Sub

Sub GetLocCndTblViewColumns ()
```
nIdx = SqlFrm.CndTblViewCB.ListIndex
If nIdx < 0 Then
    Exit Sub
End If
szSubTxt = LTrim$(RTrim$(SqlFrm.CndTblViewCB.LIST(nIdx)))
szCurrCndTblName = LTrim$(RTrim$(szSubTxt))
'--------------------------------------
For I = 1 To 100 Step 1
    CndTblCols(I).szTblName = ""
    CndTblCols(I).szTblColName = ""
    CndTblCols(I).nData = 0
Next I
'--------------------------------------
I = 1
CndTblCols(I).szTblColName = "*"
CndTblCols(I).szTblName = szCurrCndTblName
nCurrCndColCount = 1
For I = 2 To 21 Step 1
    CndTblCols(I).szTblColName = "Col" + LTrim$(RTrim$(Str$(I)))
    CndTblCols(I).szTblName = szCurrCndTblName
    CndTblCols(I).nData = 0
    nCurrCndColCount = nCurrCndColCount + 1
Next I
```

End Sub

Sub GetLocCndTblViewNames ()
```
nLBCount = SqlFrm.CndTblViewCB.ListCount
If nLBCount > 0 Then
    For I = 1 To nLBCount Step 1
        SqlFrm.CndTblViewCB.RemoveItem 0
    Next I
End If
'..............................................
SqlFrm.CndTblViewCB.AddItem "VIEW_001" ' for NON-SQL TESTING...
'..............................................
```
End Sub

Sub GetCndTblViewColumns ()
```
'---NON-SQL TESTING-------------------------------------
GetLocCndTblViewColumns
'---NON-SQL TESTING-------------------------------------
```
End Sub

Sub GetCndTblViewNames ()
```
'---NON-SQL TESTING-------------------------------------
```

GetLocCndTblViewNames
'---NON-SQL TESTING------

End Sub

Sub GenerateSimpleSQL 0

'---USE WHEN ADD SQL COMPUTE CLAUSE------
' LoadSqlCalcStmt
'---USE WHEN ADD SQL COMPUTE CLAUSE------
' WARNING-> the code will currently allow the user to select "*" and
'   none or more of the columns…in the event that a column
'   is selected it may be STUPID to include the "*" and if so
'   the easy way to remove it is via InStr() and Mid$() with
'   intermediate substrings on the FINAL szSqlCmdStr…in other
'   words…build it STUPIDLY and then CORRECT IT…rather than
'   add the INTELLIGENCE to earlier code…TOO BIZARRE…might
'   want to display a MSG NOTE that we are doing this…
szTokenSqlCmdStr = ""
szSqlCmdStr = ""
szSqlCmdStr = LTrim$("SELECT ")
szTokenSqlCmdStr = LTrim$("SELECT> sc<")
' now…generate the SELECTION LIST CLAUSE…
If (SelList(1).nData = 0) Then
    ' there is NO SELECTION LIST…and the DEFAULT is ALL(i.e., "*")…

```
                szSqlCmdStr = szSqlCmdStr + "*"
                szTokenSqlCmdStr = szTokenSqlCmdStr + "*"
                szTokenSqlCmdStr = szTokenSqlCmdStr + "##"
                szTokenSqlCmdStr = szTokenSqlCmdStr + " >endsc <"
        Else
                ' there is a SELECTION LIST…so get it…
                nFirstOne = 0
                For I = 1 To 100 Step 1
                    If SelList(I).nData > 0 Then
                        ' found one…
                        If nFirstOne > 0 Then
                            szSqlCmdStr = szSqlCmdStr + ", "
                        Else
                            nFirstOne = 1
                        End If
                        Col$ = LTrim$(RTrim$(SelList(I).szColTitle))
                        nLength = Len(Col$)
                        If nLength > 0 Then
                            Title$ = Col$ + " = "
                        Else
                            Title$ = ""
                        End If
                        Col$ = LTrim$(RTrim$(SelList(I).szTblColName))
                        If Col$ <> "*" Then
                            tmp$ = LTrim$(RTrim$(SelList(I).szTblName))
                            tmp$ = tmp$ + "."
                            tmp$ = tmp$ + Col$
```

```
        Else
            tmp$ = Col$
        End If
        ' check for COUNT or COUNT DISTINCT…if ON…then add to DISPLAY…
        If SelList(I).nCount > 0 Then
            tmp$ = "Count(" + tmp$ + ")"
        Else
            If SelList(I).nCountDistinct > 0 Then
                tmp$ = "Count(Distinct(" + tmp$ + "))"
            End If
        End If
        tmp$ = Title$ + tmp$
        szSqlCmdStr = szSqlCmdStr + LTrim$(RTrim$(tmp$))
        szTokenSqlCmdStr = szTokenSqlCmdStr + tmp$
        szTokenSqlCmdStr = szTokenSqlCmdStr + "##"
    Else
        ' no more…
        szSqlCmdStr = szSqlCmdStr + " "
        szTokenSqlCmdStr = szTokenSqlCmdStr + " >endsc< "
        Exit For
    End If
Next I
End If
' now…generate the FROM clause…
szSqlCmdStr = szSqlCmdStr + "FROM "
szTokenSqlCmdStr = szTokenSqlCmdStr + "FROM"
szTokenSqlCmdStr = szTokenSqlCmdStr + " >fc< "
```

```
szSqlCmdStr = szSqlCmdStr + LTrim$(RTrim$(szCurrTblName))
szTokenSqlCmdStr = szTokenSqlCmdStr + LTrim$(RTrim$(szCurrTblName))
szTokenSqlCmdStr = szTokenSqlCmdStr + "##"
szTokenSqlCmdStr = szTokenSqlCmdStr + ">endfc<"
' now...generate the WHERE clause...if there NEEDS to be ONE...
If (CndSelList(1).nData > 0) Then
    ' there is a WHERE clause...so build it...
    szSqlCmdStr = szSqlCmdStr + " "
    szSqlCmdStr = szSqlCmdStr + "WHERE "
    szTokenSqlCmdStr = szTokenSqlCmdStr + "WHERE"
    szTokenSqlCmdStr = szTokenSqlCmdStr + ">wc<"
    nFirstOne = 0
    nDone = 0
    For I = 1 To 100 Step 1
        If (CndSelList(I).nData > 0) Then
            nCndIdx = I
            BuildSqlCndString
            If nFirstOne = 0 Then
                ' this is the FIRST ONE...
                nLength = Len(szTempCndStr)
                nLength = nLength - 3
                tmp$ = Mid$(szTempCndStr, 4, nLength)
                szSqlCmdStr = szSqlCmdStr + tmp$
                szSqlCmdStr = szSqlCmdStr + " "   ' append a BLANK...no harm...
                nFirstOne = 1
                ' WARNING-> we want the LOGICAL OPERATOR for the FIRST ITEM
```

354

- in the TOKENIZED string...actually the FIRST ITEM
- should NOT have a logical operator because it simply
- is...i.e., it is not really determined until a
- SECOND ITEM is added...or more correctly it is
- REQUIRED if alone...but dependent if used as part of
- a group...the correct way to deal with this is to
- NOT ALLOW A LOGICAL OPERATOR on the FIRST ITEM...

```
                szTokenSqlCmdStr = szTokenSqlCmdStr + szTempCndStr
                szTokenSqlCmdStr = szTokenSqlCmdStr + "##"
            Else
                szSqlCmdStr = szSqlCmdStr + szTempCndStr
                szSqlCmdStr = szSqlCmdStr + " "    ' append a BLANK...no harm...
                szTokenSqlCmdStr = szTokenSqlCmdStr + szTempCndStr
                szTokenSqlCmdStr = szTokenSqlCmdStr + "##"
            End If
        Else
            ' we are done...
            nDone = 1
            szTokenSqlCmdStr = szTokenSqlCmdStr + " >endwc< "
            Exit For
        End If
    Next I
End If
' NOTE-> all done for the present...
' WARNING-> see WARNING at TOP about doing STUPID things...
End Sub
```

Sub InitSqlCalc ()
' NOTE-> this is one way to list EVERYTHING in SQL Server...
'Functs.AddItem "ABS(", 0
'Functs.AddItem "ACOS(", 1
'Functs.AddItem "ASCII(", 2
'Functs.AddItem "ASIN(", 3
'Functs.AddItem "ATAN(", 4
'Functs.AddItem "ATN2(", 5
'Functs.AddItem "AVG(", 6
'Functs.AddItem "AVG(DISTINCT   ", 7
'Functs.AddItem "CEILING(", 8
'Functs.AddItem "CHAR(", 9
'Functs.AddItem "CHARINDEX(", 10
'Functs.AddItem "CONVERT(", 11
'Functs.AddItem "COS(", 12
'Functs.AddItem "COT(", 13
'Functs.AddItem "COUNT(", 14
'Functs.AddItem "COUNT(DISTINCT ", 15
'Functs.AddItem "COUNT(*)   ", 16
'Functs.AddItem "DATALENGTH(", 17
'Functs.AddItem "DATENAME(", 18
'Functs.AddItem "DATEPART(", 19
'Functs.AddItem "DATEDIFF(", 20
'Functs.AddItem "DATEADD(", 21
'Functs.AddItem "DEGREES(", 22

```
'Functs.AddItem "DIFFERENCE(  ", 23
'Functs.AddItem "FLOOR(  ", 24
'Functs.AddItem "GETDATE(  ", 25
'Functs.AddItem "LOG(  ", 26
'Functs.AddItem "LOG10(  ", 27
'Functs.AddItem "LOWER(  ", 28
'Functs.AddItem "LTRIM(  ", 29
'Functs.AddItem "MIN(  ", 30
'Functs.AddItem "MAX(  ", 31
'Functs.AddItem "PI(  ", 32
'Functs.AddItem "POWER(  ", 33
'Functs.AddItem "RAND(  ", 34
'Functs.AddItem "RADIANS(  ", 35
'Functs.AddItem "REPLICATE(  ", 36
'Functs.AddItem "ROUND(  ", 37
'Functs.AddItem "RTRIM(  ", 38
'Functs.AddItem "SIGN(  ", 39
'Functs.AddItem "SIN(  ", 40
'Functs.AddItem "SOUNDEX(  ", 41
'Functs.AddItem "SPACE(  ", 42
'Functs.AddItem "SQRT(  ", 43
'Functs.AddItem "STR(  ", 44
'Functs.AddItem "STUFF(  ", 45
'Functs.AddItem "SUBSTRING(  ", 46
'Functs.AddItem "SUM(  ", 47
'Functs.AddItem "SUM(DISTINCT  ", 48
'Functs.AddItem "TAN(  ", 49
```

```
'Functs.AddItem "UPPER(        ", 50
'Functs.AddItem "ISNULL(       ", 51
'Functs.ListIndex = 0
'Operator.AddItem " =  [EQUALS]            ", 0
'Operator.AddItem " >  [GREATER THAN]      ", 1
'Operator.AddItem " <  [LESS THAN]         ", 2
'Operator.AddItem " >= [GT OR EQUAL]       ", 3
'Operator.AddItem " <= [LT OR EQUAL]       ", 4
'Operator.AddItem "!=  [NOT EQUAL]         ", 5
'Operator.AddItem "!>  [NOT GREATER]       ", 6
'Operator.AddItem "!<  [NOT LESS THAN]     ", 7
'Operator.AddItem " DISTINCT               ", 8
'Operator.AddItem " ANY                    ", 9
'Operator.AddItem " * [ALL]                ", 10
'Operator.AddItem " + [CONCATENATE]        ", 11
'Operator.AddItem " AND                    ", 12
'Operator.AddItem " OR                     ", 13
'Operator.AddItem " NOT                    ", 14
'Operator.AddItem " NOT BETWEEN            ", 15
'Operator.AddItem " NOT EXISTS             ", 16
'Operator.AddItem " NOT IN                 ", 17
'Operator.AddItem " NOT LIKE...            ", 18
'Operator.AddItem " BETWEEN                ", 19
'Operator.AddItem " EXISTS                 ", 20
'Operator.AddItem " IN                     ", 21
'Operator.AddItem " [LIKE...]              ", 22
'Operator.AddItem " IS NULL                ", 23
```

```
'Operator.AddItem "   IS NOT NULL  ", 24
'Operator.AddItem "*= [L. OUTER JOIN] ", 25
'Operator.AddItem "=* [R. OUTER JOIN] ", 26
'Operator.AddItem "&  [BITWISE AND]   ", 27
'Operator.AddItem "|  [BITWISE OR]    ", 28
'Operator.AddItem "^  [BITWISE XOR]   ", 29
'Operator.AddItem "~  [BITWISE NOT]   ", 30
'Operator.AddItem "+  [ADD]           ", 31
'Operator.AddItem "-  [SUBTRACT]      ", 32
'Operator.AddItem "*  [MULTIPLY]      ", 33
'Operator.AddItem "/  [DIVIDE]        ", 34
'Operator.AddItem "%  [MODULO]        ", 35
'Operator.AddItem "(  [L. PARENTHESIS]", 36
'Operator.AddItem ")  [R. PARENTHESIS]", 37
'Operator.AddItem "ASC  [ASCENDING]   ", 38
'Operator.AddItem "DESC [DESCENDING]  ", 39
'Operator.ListIndex = 0
End Sub

Sub InitNewSQLCndList ()
Screen.MousePointer = 11
GetCndTblViewNames
nLBCount = SqlFrm.CndTblViewCB.ListCount
If nLBCount > 0 Then
    SqlFrm.CndTblViewCB.ListIndex = 0
    szCurrCndTblName = LTrim$(RTrim$(SqlFrm.CndTblViewCB.LIST(0)))
```

```
End If
For I = 1 To 5 Step 1
    SqlFrm.CndTVRC(I).Caption = ""
Next I
SqlFrm.CndTvRcVSR.Min = 1
SqlFrm.CndTvRcVSR.Max = 1
nResetCndTvRcVSR = 0
SqlFrm.CndTvRcVSR.Value = 1
For I = 1 To 5 Step 1
    SqlFrm.CndSLRC(I).Caption = ""
Next I
SqlFrm.CndSIRcVSR.Min = 1
SqlFrm.CndSIRcVSR.Max = 1
nResetCndSIRcVSR = 0
SqlFrm.CndSIRcVSR.Value = 1
nLBCount = SqlFrm.LogCB.ListCount
If nLBCount > 0 Then
    For I = 1 To nLBCount Step 1
        SqlFrm.LogCB.RemoveItem 0
    Next I
End If
SqlFrm.LogCB.AddItem "And", 0
SqlFrm.LogCB.AddItem "Or", 1
SqlFrm.LogCB.ListIndex = 0
nLBCount = SqlFrm.RelCB.ListCount
If nLBCount > 0 Then
    For I = 1 To nLBCount Step 1
```

```
        SqlFrm.RelCB.RemoveItem 0
    Next I
End If
SqlFrm.RelCB.AddItem "Is Any Value", 0
SqlFrm.RelCB.AddItem "Less Than", 1
SqlFrm.RelCB.AddItem "Less Or Equals", 2
SqlFrm.RelCB.AddItem "Equals", 3
SqlFrm.RelCB.AddItem "Greater Or Equals", 4
SqlFrm.RelCB.AddItem "Greater Than", 5
SqlFrm.RelCB.AddItem "NOT(Less Than)", 6
SqlFrm.RelCB.AddItem "NOT(Less Or Equals)", 7
SqlFrm.RelCB.AddItem "NOT(Equals)", 8
SqlFrm.RelCB.AddItem "NOT(Greater Or Equals)", 9
SqlFrm.RelCB.AddItem "NOT(Greater Than)", 10
SqlFrm.RelCB.AddItem "Is Empty", 11
SqlFrm.RelCB.AddItem "Is NOT Empty", 12

SqlFrm.RelCB.ListIndex = 0
SqlFrm.CndSLRC(1).Caption = " "

For I = 1 To 5 Step 1
    SqlFrm.CndTVRC(I).Caption = " "
    CndTvRcData(I).szTblColName = ""
    CndTvRcData(I).szTblName = ""
    CndTvRcData(I).nData = 0
Next I
SqlFrm.CndTvRcVSR.Min = 0
```

```
SqlFrm.CndTvRcVSR.Max = 0
nResetCndTvRcVSR = 0
SqlFrm.CndTvRcVSR.Value = 0
'─────────────
For I = 1 To 100 Step 1
    CndTblCols(I).szTblName = ""
    CndTblCols(I).szTblColName = ""
    CndTblCols(I).nData = 0
Next I
'─────────────
nCndTblIdx = SqlFrm.CndTblViewCB.ListIndex
szCurrCndTblName = LTrim$(RTrim$(SqlFrm.CndTblViewCB.LIST(nCndTblIdx)))
GetCndTblViewColumns
If nCurrCndColCount > 0 Then
    For I = 1 To 5 Step 1
        If I <= nCurrCndColCount Then
            CndTvRcData(I).szTblColName = CndTblCols(I).szTblColName
            CndTvRcData(I).szTblName = szCurrCndTblName
            CndTvRcData(I).nData = I
            SqlFrm.CndTVRC(I).Caption = CndTvRcData(I).szTblColName
        Else
            Exit For
        End If
    Next I
    SqlFrm.CndTvRcVSR.Min = 1
    SqlFrm.CndTvRcVSR.Max = nCurrCndColCount
    nResetTvRcVSR = 1
```

```
SqlFrm.CndTvRcVSR.Value = 1
    nResetCndTvRcVSR = 1
End If
For I = 1 To 5 Step 1
    SqlFrm.CndSLRC(I).BackColor = WHITE
    SqlFrm.CndSLRC(I).ForeColor = BLUE
    SqlFrm.CndSLRC(I).Caption = ""
    CndSlRcData(I).szTblColName = ""
    CndSlRcData(I).szTblName = ""
    CndSlRcData(I).szColTitle = ""
    CndSlRcData(I).szCndValue = ""
    CndSlRcData(I).nData = 0
    CndSlRcData(I).nConnector = 0
    CndSlRcData(I).nRelation = 0
    CndSlRcData(I).nLeftFunction = 0
    CndSlRcData(I).nRightFunction = 0
    CndSlRcData(I).nCount = 0
    CndSlRcData(I).nCountDistinct = 0
    CndSlRcData(I).nFlag = 0
Next I
SqlFrm.CndSLRC(1).Caption = ""
For I = 1 To 100 Step 1
    CndSelList(I).szTblColName = ""
    CndSelList(I).szTblName = ""
    CndSelList(I).szColTitle = ""
    CndSelList(I).szCndValue = ""
    CndSelList(I).nData = 0
```

```
            CndSelList(I).nConnector = 0
            CndSelList(I).nRelation = 0
            CndSelList(I).nLeftFunction = 0
            CndSelList(I).nRightFunction = 0
            CndSelList(I).nCount = 0
            CndSelList(I).nCountDistinct = 0
            CndSelList(I).nFlag = 0
        Next I
        nResetCndSlRcVSR = 0
        SqlFrm.CndSlRcVSR.Min = 0
        SqlFrm.CndSlRcVSR.Max = 0
        SqlFrm.CndSlRcVSR.Value = 0
        nResetCndSlRcVSR = 1   ' WARNING-> MUST do this to enable scrolling...
        SqlFrm.FBXL.Visible = FALSE
        SqlFrm.FBXR.Visible = FALSE
        SqlFrm.RelTxt.Text = ""
        SqlFrm.RemoveCndRedRowPB.Enabled = FALSE
        'SqlFrm.RemoveCndRedRowPB.SymBackColor = LIGHTGRAY
        'SqlFrm.RemoveCndRedRowPB.FontColor = WHITE
        Screen.MousePointer = 0
    End Sub
```

Sub InitNewSQLSelList ()

```
    Screen.MousePointer = 11
    For I = 1 To 100 Step 1
```

```
        TblCols(I).szTblName = ""
        TblCols(I).szTblColName = ""
        TblCols(I).nData = 0
    Next I
    For I = 1 To 100 Step 1
        SelList(I).szTblColName = ""
        SelList(I).szTblName = ""
        SelList(I).szColTitle = ""
        SelList(I).nData = 0
        SelList(I).nCount = 0
        SelList(I).nCountDistinct = 0
        SelList(I).nFlag = 0
    Next I
'----------------------------------

GetTblViewNames
    nLBCount = SqlFrm.TblViewCB.ListCount
    If nLBCount > 0 Then
        nSqlFrmReallyVisible = 0
        SqlFrm.TblViewCB.ListIndex = 0
        szCurrTblName = LTrim$(RTrim$(SqlFrm.TblViewCB.LIST(0)))
        nSqlFrmReallyVisible = 1
    End If
    For I = 1 To 5 Step 1
        SqlFrm.TVRC(I).Caption = ""
    Next I
    SqlFrm.TvRcVSR.Min = 1
```

```
SqlFrm.TvRcVSR.Max = 1
nResetTvRcVSR = 0
SqlFrm.TvRcVSR.Value = 1
For I = 1 To 5 Step 1
    SqlFrm.SLRC(I).Caption = ""
Next I
SqlFrm.SlRcVSR.Min = 1
SqlFrm.SlRcVSR.Max = 1
nResetSIRcVSR = 0
SqlFrm.SlRcVSR.Value = 1
'SqlFrm.CountPB.SymBackColor = LIGHTGRAY
'SqlFrm.CountDistinctPB.SymBackColor = LIGHTGRAY
'SqlFrm.ColTitleIsPB.SymBackColor = LIGHTGRAY
'SqlFrm.RemoveRedRowPB.SymBackColor = LIGHTGRAY
'SqlFrm.CountPB.FontColor = WHITE
'SqlFrm.CountDistinctPB.FontColor = WHITE
'SqlFrm.ColTitleIsPB.FontColor = WHITE
'SqlFrm.RemoveRedRowPB.FontColor = WHITE
SqlFrm.ColTitleIsTxt.BackColor = WHITE
SqlFrm.ColTitleIsTxt.ForeColor = DARKGRAY
SqlFrm.SLRC(1).Caption = " "
Screen.MousePointer = 0
End Sub
```

Sub RemoveRedCndSIRcItem ()

```
nFoundARedCndRow = 0
```

```
For I = 1 To 5 Step 1
    If CndSlRcData(I).nFlag = 2 Then
        nFoundARedCndRow = 1
        nCndSLRCIdx = CndSlRcData(I).nData
        Exit For
    End If
Next I
If nFoundARedCndRow < 1 Then
    ' the RED ROW is NOT currently visible...and CANNOT BE REMOVED...
    Exit Sub
End If
' the RED item needs to be REMOVED from the SELECT LIST...
' so determine whether it is in the CURRENT CndTVRC...
' and if it is then deselect it (i.e., change background
' color to white)...and remove it from the CndSelList and
' from CndSLRC...note that when the item is removed from
' CndSelList the CndSelList needs to be compacted...
szCndSelListTblName = LTrim$(RTrim$(CndSelList(nCndSLRCIdx).szTblName))
If (szCndSelListTblName = szCurrCndTblName) Then
    ' item is from CURRENT table...
    nResetCndTvRcVSR = 1
    SqlFrm.CndTvRcVSR.Value = CndSelList(nCndSLRCIdx).nData
End If
' now clear the CndSelList item...
CndSelList(nCndSLRCIdx).nData = 0
CndSelList(nCndSLRCIdx).szTblColName = ""
CndSelList(nCndSLRCIdx).szTblName = ""
```

```
CndSelList(nCndSLRCIdx).szColTitle = ""
CndSelList(nCndSLRCIdx).szCndValue = ""
CndSelList(nCndSLRCIdx).nData = 0
CndSelList(nCndSLRCIdx).nConnector = 0
CndSelList(nCndSLRCIdx).nRelation = 0
CndSelList(nCndSLRCIdx).nLeftFunction = 0
CndSelList(nCndSLRCIdx).nRightFunction = 0
CndSelList(nCndSLRCIdx).nCount = 0
CndSelList(nCndSLRCIdx).nCountDistinct = 0
CndSelList(nCndSLRCIdx).nFlag = 0
' now initialize CndTmpList...
For I = 1 To 100 Step 1
    CndTmpList(I).szTblColName = ""
    CndTmpList(I).szTblName = ""
    CndTmpList(I).szColTitle = ""
    CndTmpList(I).szCndValue = ""
    CndTmpList(I).nData = 0
    CndTmpList(I).nConnector = 0
    CndTmpList(I).nRelation = 0
    CndTmpList(I).nLeftFunction = 0
    CndTmpList(I).nRightFunction = 0
    CndTmpList(I).nCount = 0
    CndTmpList(I).nCountDistinct = 0
    CndTmpList(I).nFlag = 0
Next I
' now compact CndSelList into CndTmpList...
nBaseIdx = 1
```

```
For I = 1 To 100 Step 1
    If (CndSelList(I).nData = 0) Then
        ' SKIP this one…
    Else
        ' copy to temp list…
        CndTmpList(nBaseIdx).szTblColName = CndSelList(I).szTblColName
        CndTmpList(nBaseIdx).szTblName = CndSelList(I).szTblName
        CndTmpList(nBaseIdx).szColTitle = CndSelList(I).szColTitle
        CndTmpList(nBaseIdx).szCndValue = CndSelList(I).szCndValue
        CndTmpList(nBaseIdx).nData = CndSelList(I).nData
        CndTmpList(nBaseIdx).nConnector = CndSelList(I).nConnector
        CndTmpList(nBaseIdx).nRelation = CndSelList(I).nRelation
        CndTmpList(nBaseIdx).nLeftFunction = CndSelList(I).nLeftFunction
        CndTmpList(nBaseIdx).nRightFunction = CndSelList(I).nRightFunction
        CndTmpList(nBaseIdx).nCount = CndSelList(I).nCount
        CndTmpList(nBaseIdx).nCountDistinct = CndSelList(I).nCountDistinct
        CndTmpList(nBaseIdx).nFlag = CndSelList(I).nFlag
        nBaseIdx = nBaseIdx + 1
    End If
Next I
' now copy CndTmpList to CndSelList…
nCndSelListCount = 0
For I = 1 To 100 Step 1
    CndSelList(I).szTblColName = CndTmpList(I).szTblColName
    CndSelList(I).szTblName = CndTmpList(I).szTblName
    CndSelList(I).szColTitle = CndTmpList(I).szColTitle
    CndSelList(I).szCndValue = CndTmpList(I).szCndValue
```

```
            CndSelList(I).nData = CndTmpList(I).nData
            If (CndSelList(I).nData > 0) Then
                nCndSelListCount = nCndSelListCount + 1
            End If
            CndSelList(I).nConnector = CndTmpList(I).nConnector
            CndSelList(I).nRelation = CndTmpList(I).nRelation
            CndSelList(I).nLeftFunction = CndTmpList(I).nLeftFunction
            CndSelList(I).nRightFunction = CndTmpList(I).nRightFunction
            CndSelList(I).nCount = CndTmpList(I).nCount
            CndSelList(I).nCountDistinct = CndTmpList(I).nCountDistinct
            CndSelList(I).nFlag = CndTmpList(I).nFlag
        Next I
        nResetCndSlRcVSR = 0
        If nCndSelListCount > 0 Then
            SqlFrm.CndSlRcVSR.Min = 1
            SqlFrm.CndSlRcVSR.Max = nCndSelListCount
        Else
            SqlFrm.CndSlRcVSR.Min = 0
            SqlFrm.CndSlRcVSR.Max = 0
        End If
        ' now...clear the DISPLAY and CndSlRcData...
        For I = 1 To 5 Step 1
            CndSlRcData(I).szTblColName = ""
            CndSlRcData(I).szTblName = ""
            CndSlRcData(I).szColTitle = ""
            CndSlRcData(I).szCndValue = ""
            CndSlRcData(I).nData = 0
```

```
            CndSlRcData(I).nConnector = 0
            CndSlRcData(I).nRelation = 0
            CndSlRcData(I).nLeftFunction = 0
            CndSlRcData(I).nRightFunction = 0
            CndSlRcData(I).nCount = 0
            CndSlRcData(I).nCountDistinct = 0
            CndSlRcData(I).nFlag = 0
            SqlFrm.CndSLRC(I).Caption = ""
            SqlFrm.CndSLRC(I).BackColor = WHITE
            SqlFrm.CndSLRC(I).ForeColor = BLUE
        Next I
        ' now...LOAD the DISPLAY and CndSlRcData with the NEW CndSelList data...
        SqlFrm.RemoveCndRedRowPB.Enabled = FALSE
        'SqlFrm.RemoveCndRedRowPB.SymBackColor = LIGHTGRAY
        'SqlFrm.RemoveCndRedRowPB.FontColor = WHITE
        SqlFrm.FBXL.Visible = FALSE
        SqlFrm.FBXR.Visible = FALSE
        'SqlFrm.RelTxtPB.SymBackColor = LIGHTGRAY
        'SqlFrm.RelTxtPB.FontColor = WHITE
        SqlFrm.RelTxtPB.Enabled = FALSE
        SqlFrm.RelTxt.BackColor = LIGHTGRAY
        SqlFrm.RelTxt.ForeColor = WHITE
        SqlFrm.RelTxt.Text = ""
        SqlFrm.RelTxt.Enabled = FALSE
        For I = 1 To 5 Step 1
            If (CndSelList(I).nData > 0) Then
                CndSlRcData(I).szTblColName = CndSelList(I).szTblColName
```

371

```
CndSlRcData(I).szTblName = CndSelList(I).szTblName
CndSlRcData(I).szColTitle = CndSelList(I).szColTitle
CndSlRcData(I).szCndValue = CndSelList(I).szCndValue
CndSlRcData(I).nData = I
CndSlRcData(I).nConnector = CndSelList(I).nConnector
CndSlRcData(I).nRelation = CndSelList(I).nRelation
CndSlRcData(I).nLeftFunction = CndSelList(I).nLeftFunction
CndSlRcData(I).nRightFunction = CndSelList(I).nRightFunction
CndSlRcData(I).nCount = CndSelList(I).nCount
CndSlRcData(I).nCountDistinct = CndSelList(I).nCountDistinct
CndSlRcData(I).nFlag = CndSelList(I).nFlag
nCndIdx = I
BuildCndString
Select Case CndSlRcData(I).nFlag
    Case 0
        SqlFrm.CndSLRC(I).BackColor = WHITE
        SqlFrm.CndSLRC(I).ForeColor = BLUE
    Case 1
        SqlFrm.CndSLRC(I).BackColor = BLUE
        SqlFrm.CndSLRC(I).ForeColor = WHITE
        SqlFrm.FBXR.Visible = TRUE
        SqlFrm.RelCB.ListIndex = CndSlRcData(I).nRelation - 1
        If (CndSlRcData(I).szCndValue < > "") Then
            SqlFrm.RelTxt.Text = CndSlRcData(I).szCndValue
        Else
            SqlFrm.RelTxt.Text = " "
        End If
```

```
        If ((CndSlRcData(I).nRelation > 1) And (CndSlRcData(I).nRelation < 12)) Then
            SqlFrm.RelTxtPB.Enabled = TRUE
            'SqlFrm.RelTxtPB.SymBackColor = BLUE
            'SqlFrm.RelTxtPB.FontColor = WHITE
            SqlFrm.RelTxt.Enabled = TRUE
            SqlFrm.RelTxt.BackColor = BLUE
            SqlFrm.RelTxt.ForeColor = WHITE
            SqlFrm.RelTxt.SetFocus
            SqlFrm.RelTxt.SelStart = 0
        End If
    Case 2
' WARNING-> we can do NOTHING here ONLY because we INITIALIZED
'           CndSlRcData and the DISPLAY row prior to this...otherwise
'           the COLOR of the DISPLAY row for the item just
'           removed would still be RED...and that would be a
'           problem...
    Case 3
        SqlFrm.CndSLRC(I).BackColor = YELLOW
        SqlFrm.CndSLRC(I).ForeColor = BLUE
        SqlFrm.FBXL.Visible = TRUE
        If CndSlRcData(I).nConnector = 1 Then
            SqlFrm.LogCB.ListIndex = 0
        Else
            SqlFrm.LogCB.ListIndex = 1
        End If
End Select
Col$ = LTrim$(RTrim$(CndSlRcData(I).szTblColName))
```

```
        SqlFrm.CndSLRC(I).Caption = szTempCndStr
    Else
        CndSIRcData(I).szTblColName = ""
        CndSIRcData(I).szTblName = ""
        CndSIRcData(I).szColTitle = ""
        CndSIRcData(I).szCndValue = CndSelList(I).szCndValue
        CndSIRcData(I).nData = 0
        CndSIRcData(I).nConnector = 0
        CndSIRcData(I).nRelation = 0
        CndSIRcData(I).nLeftFunction = 0
        CndSIRcData(I).nRightFunction = 0
        CndSIRcData(I).nCount = 0
        CndSIRcData(I).nCountDistinct = 0
        CndSIRcData(I).nFlag = 0
        SqlFrm.CndSLRC(I).BackColor = WHITE
        SqlFrm.CndSLRC(I).ForeColor = BLUE
        SqlFrm.CndSLRC(I).Caption = ""
    End If
Next I
nResetCndSIRcVSR = 0
If nCndSelListCount > 0 Then
    SqlFrm.CndSIRcVSR.Value = 1
Else
    SqlFrm.CndSIRcVSR.Value = 0
End If
nResetCndSIRcVSR = 1    ' WARNING-> MUST do this to ENABLE SCROLLING...
```

End Sub

Sub RemoveRedSIRcItem ()
```
nFoundARedRow = 0
For I = 1 To 5 Step 1
    If SIRcData(I).nFlag = 2 Then
        nFoundARedRow = 1
        nSLRCIdx = SIRcData(I).nData
        Exit For
    End If
Next I
If nFoundARedRow < 1 Then
    ' the RED ROW is NOT currently visible…and CANNOT BE REMOVED…
    Exit Sub
End If
' the RED item needs to be REMOVED from the SELECT LIST…
' so determine whether it is in the CURRENT TVRC…
' and if it is then deselect it (i.e., change background
' color to white)…and remove it from the SelList and
' from SLRC…note that when the item is removed from
' SelList the SelList needs to be compacted…
szSelListTblName = LTrim$(RTrim$(SelList(nSLRCIdx).szTblName))
If (szSelListTblName = szCurrTblName) Then
    ' item is from CURRENT table…so need to deselect…
    TblCols(SelList(nSLRCIdx).nData).nData = 0
    If (TvRcData(1).nData = SelList(nSLRCIdx).nData) Then
```

```
                SqlFrm.TVRC(1).Caption = TblCols(SelList(nSLRCIdx).nData).szTblColName
                If TblCols(SelList(nSLRCIdx).nData).nData > 0 Then
                    SqlFrm.TVRC(1).BackColor = LIGHTGRAY
                Else
                    SqlFrm.TVRC(1).BackColor = WHITE
                End If
            Else
                nResetTvRcVSR = 1
                SqlFrm.TvRcVSR.Value = SelList(nSLRCIdx).nData
            End If
        End If
        ' now clear the SelList item...
        SelList(nSLRCIdx).nData = 0
        SelList(nSLRCIdx).szTblColName = ""
        SelList(nSLRCIdx).szTblName = ""
        SelList(nSLRCIdx).szColTitle = ""
        SelList(nSLRCIdx).nCount = 0
        SelList(nSLRCIdx).nCountDistinct = 0
        SelList(nSLRCIdx).nFlag = 0
        ' now initialize TmpList...
        For I = 1 To 100 Step 1
            TmpList(I).szTblColName = ""
            TmpList(I).szTblName = ""
            TmpList(I).szColTitle = ""
            TmpList(I).nData = 0
            TmpList(I).nCount = 0
            TmpList(I).nCountDistinct = 0
```

```
        TmpList(I).nFlag = 0
    Next I
    ' now compact SelList into TmpList...
    nBaseIdx = 1
    For I = 1 To 100 Step 1
        If (SelList(I).nData = 0) Then
            ' SKIP this one...
        Else
            ' copy to temp list...
            TmpList(nBaseIdx).szTblColName = SelList(I).szTblColName
            TmpList(nBaseIdx).szTblName = SelList(I).szTblName
            TmpList(nBaseIdx).szColTitle = SelList(I).szColTitle
            TmpList(nBaseIdx).nData = SelList(I).nData
            TmpList(nBaseIdx).nCount = SelList(I).nCount
            TmpList(nBaseIdx).nCountDistinct = SelList(I).nCountDistinct
            TmpList(nBaseIdx).nFlag = SelList(I).nFlag
            nBaseIdx = nBaseIdx + 1
        End If
    Next I
    ' now copy TmpList to SelList...
    nSelListCount = 0
    For I = 1 To 100 Step 1
        SelList(I).szTblColName = TmpList(I).szTblColName
        SelList(I).szTblName = TmpList(I).szTblName
        SelList(I).szColTitle = TmpList(I).szColTitle
        SelList(I).nData = TmpList(I).nData
        If (SelList(I).nData > 0) Then
```

```
            nSelListCount = nSelListCount + 1
        End If
        SelList(I).nCount = TmpList(I).nCount
        SelList(I).nCountDistinct = TmpList(I).nCountDistinct
        SelList(I).nFlag = TmpList(I).nFlag
    Next I
    nResetSIRcVSR = 0
    If nSelListCount > 0 Then
        SqlFrm.SIRcVSR.Min = 1
        SqlFrm.SIRcVSR.Max = nSelListCount
    Else
        SqlFrm.SIRcVSR.Min = 0
        SqlFrm.SIRcVSR.Max = 0
    End If
    ' now....clear the DISPLAY and SIRcData...
    For I = 1 To 5 Step 1
        SIRcData(I).szTblColName = ""
        SIRcData(I).szTblName = ""
        SIRcData(I).szColTitle = ""
        SIRcData(I).nData = 0
        SIRcData(I).nCount = 0
        SIRcData(I).nCountDistinct = 0
        SIRcData(I).nFlag = SelList(I).nFlag
        SqlFrm.SLRC(I).Caption = ""
        SqlFrm.SLRC(I).BackColor = WHITE
        SqlFrm.SLRC(I).ForeColor = BLUE
    Next I
```

```
' now...LOAD the DISPLAY and SlRcData with the NEW SelList data...
'SqlFrm.CountPB.SymBackColor = LIGHTGRAY
'SqlFrm.CountDistinctPB.SymBackColor = LIGHTGRAY
'SqlFrm.ColTitleIsPB.SymBackColor = LIGHTGRAY
'SqlFrm.RemoveRedRowPB.SymBackColor = LIGHTGRAY
SqlFrm.CountPB.Enabled = FALSE
SqlFrm.CountDistinctPB.Enabled = FALSE
SqlFrm.ColTitleIsPB.Enabled = FALSE
SqlFrm.ColTitleIsTxt.Enabled = FALSE
SqlFrm.ColTitleIsTxt.BackColor = WHITE
SqlFrm.ColTitleIsTxt.ForeColor = DARKGRAY
SqlFrm.ColTitleIsTxt.Text = ""
SqlFrm.RemoveRedRowPB.Enabled = FALSE
For I = 1 To 5 Step 1
    If (SelList(I).nData > 0) Then
        SlRcData(I).szTblColName = SelList(I).szTblColName
        SlRcData(I).szTblName = SelList(I).szTblName
        SlRcData(I).szColTitle = SelList(I).szColTitle
        Col$ = LTrim$(RTrim$(SlRcData(I).szColTitle))
        nLength = Len(Col$)
        If nLength > 0 Then
            Title$ = Col$ + " = "
        Else
            Title$ = ""
        End If
        SlRcData(I).nData = 1
        SlRcData(I).nCount = SelList(I).nCount
```

```
SlRcData(I).nCountDistinct = SelList(I).nCountDistinct
SlRcData(I).nFlag = SelList(I).nFlag
Select Case SlRcData(I).nFlag
    Case 0
        SqlFrm.SLRC(I).BackColor = WHITE
        SqlFrm.SLRC(I).ForeColor = BLUE
    Case 1
        SqlFrm.CountPB.Enabled = TRUE
        SqlFrm.CountDistinctPB.Enabled = TRUE
        SqlFrm.ColTitleIsPB.Enabled = TRUE
        SqlFrm.ColTitleIsTxt.Enabled = TRUE
        SqlFrm.ColTitleIsTxt.BackColor = BLUE
        SqlFrm.ColTitleIsTxt.ForeColor = WHITE
        SqlFrm.ColTitleIsTxt.Text = SlRcData(I).szColTitle
        SqlFrm.ColTitleIsTxt.SetFocus
        SqlFrm.ColTitleIsTxt.SelStart = 0
        SqlFrm.SLRC(I).BackColor = BLUE
        SqlFrm.SLRC(I).ForeColor = WHITE
        'SqlFrm.CountPB.SymBackColor = BLUE
        'SqlFrm.CountDistinctPB.SymBackColor = BLUE
        'SqlFrm.ColTitleIsPB.SymBackColor = BLUE
    Case 2
        ' WARNING-> we can do NOTHING here ONLY because we INITIALIZED
        '           SlRcData and the DISPLAY prior to this…otherwise
        '           the COLOR of the DISPLAY row for the item just
        '           removed would still be RED…and that would be a
        '           problem…
```

```
        End Select
        Col$ = LTrim$(RTrim$(SlRcData(I).szTblColName))
        If Col$ <> "*" Then
            tmp$ = LTrim$(RTrim$(SlRcData(I).szTblName))
            tmp$ = tmp$ + "."
            tmp$ = tmp$ + Col$
        Else
            tmp$ = Col$
        End If
        ' check for COUNT or COUNT DISTINCT...if ON...then add to DISPLAY...
        If SlRcData(I).nCount > 0 Then
            tmp$ = "Count(" + tmp$ + ")"
        Else
            If SlRcData(I).nCountDistinct > 0 Then
                tmp$ = "Count(Distinct(" + tmp$ + "))"
            End If
        End If
        tmp$ = Title$ + tmp$
        SqlFrm.SLRC(I).Caption = LTrim$(RTrim$(tmp$))
    Else
        SlRcData(I).szTblColName = ""
        SlRcData(I).szTblName = ""
        SlRcData(I).szColTitle = ""
        SlRcData(I).nData = 0
        SlRcData(I).nCount = 0
        SlRcData(I).nCountDistinct = 0
        SlRcData(I).nFlag = 0
```

```
            SqlFrm.SLRC(I).BackColor = WHITE
            SqlFrm.SLRC(I).ForeColor = BLUE
            SqlFrm.SLRC(I).Caption = ""
        End If
    Next I
    nResetSIRcVSR = 0
    If nSelListCount > 0 Then
        SqlFrm.SlRcVSR.Value = 1
    Else
        SqlFrm.SlRcVSR.Value = 0
    End If
    nResetSIRcVSR = 1    ' WARNING-> MUST do this to ENABLE SCROLLING...
    'SqlFrm.CountPB.FontColor = WHITE
    'SqlFrm.CountDistinctPB.FontColor = WHITE
    'SqlFrm.ColTitleIsPB.FontColor = WHITE
    'SqlFrm.RemoveRedRowPB.FontColor = WHITE
End Sub

Sub BuildCndString ()
' FIRST-> get the TABLE and COLUMN for the LEFT EXPRESSION...
' WARNING-> returns value via szTempCndStr...which is GLOBAL...
    Col$ = LTrim$(RTrim$(CndSelList(CndSIRcData(nCndIdx).nData).szTblColName))
    If Col$ <> "*" Then
        tmp$ = LTrim$(RTrim$(CndSelList(CndSIRcData(nCndIdx).nData).szTblName))
        tmp$ = tmp$ + "."
        tmp$ = tmp$ + Col$
```

382

```
      Else
        tmp$ = Col$
      End If
    End If
    tmp$ = tmp$ + " "
    ' SECOND-> get the RELATION OPERATOR...
    Select Case CndSlRcData(nCndIdx).nData).nRelation
      Case 0
        ' NO RELATION...Do NOTHING...
      Case 1
        ' IS ANY VALUE...NOTE-> this is STUPID...but who cares...
        tmp$ = tmp$ + "IS ANY VALUE"
      Case 2
        ' LESS THAN...
        tmp$ = tmp$ + " < "
        nLen = Len(CndSelList(CndSlRcData(nCndIdx).nData).szCndValue)
        If nLen > 0 Then
          ' there is a condition value...
          tmp$ = tmp$ + "'" + CndSelList(CndSlRcData(nCndIdx).nData).szCndValue + "'"
        Else
          ' the condition value is BLANK...
          tmp$ = tmp$ + "' '"
        End If
      Case 3
        ' LESS THAN OR EQUALS...
        tmp$ = tmp$ + " <= "
        nLen = Len(CndSelList(CndSlRcData(nCndIdx).nData).szCndValue)
        If nLen > 0 Then
```

```
            ' there is a condition value...
            tmp$ = tmp$ + "'" + CndSelList(CndSlRcData(nCndIdx).nData).szCndValue + "'"
        Else
            ' the condition value is BLANK...
            tmp$ = tmp$ + "' '"
        End If
    Case 4
        ' EQUALS...
        tmp$ = tmp$ + " = "
        nLen = Len(CndSelList(CndSlRcData(nCndIdx).nData).szCndValue)
        If nLen > 0 Then
            ' there is a condition value...
            tmp$ = tmp$ + "'" + CndSelList(CndSlRcData(nCndIdx).nData).szCndValue + "'"
        Else
            ' the condition value is BLANK...
            tmp$ = tmp$ + "' '"
        End If
    Case 5
        ' GREATER OR EQUALS...
        tmp$ = tmp$ + " >= "
        nLen = Len(CndSelList(CndSlRcData(nCndIdx).nData).szCndValue)
        If nLen > 0 Then
            ' there is a condition value...
            tmp$ = tmp$ + "'" + CndSelList(CndSlRcData(nCndIdx).nData).szCndValue + "'"
        Else
            ' the condition value is BLANK...
            tmp$ = tmp$ + "' '"
```

```
            End If
        Case 6
            ' GREATER THAN…
            tmp$ = tmp$ + " > "
            nLen = Len(CndSelList(CndSlRcData(nCndIdx).nData).szCndValue)
            If nLen > 0 Then
                ' there is a condition value…
                tmp$ = tmp$ + "'" + CndSelList(CndSlRcData(nCndIdx).nData).szCndValue + "'"
            Else
                ' the condition value is BLANK…
                tmp$ = tmp$ + "' '"
            End If
        Case 7
            ' NOT LESS THAN…
            tmp$ = tmp$ + "¦< "
            nLen = Len(CndSelList(CndSlRcData(nCndIdx).nData).szCndValue)
            If nLen > 0 Then
                ' there is a condition value…
                tmp$ = tmp$ + "'" + CndSelList(CndSlRcData(nCndIdx).nData).szCndValue + "'"
            Else
                ' the condition value is BLANK…
                tmp$ = tmp$ + "' '"
            End If
        Case 8
            ' NOT LESS THAN OR EQUALS…(i.e., GREATER THAN)…
            tmp$ = tmp$ + " > "
            nLen = Len(CndSelList(CndSlRcData(nCndIdx).nData).szCndValue)
```

```
        If nLen > 0 Then
            ' there is a condition value...
            tmp$ = tmp$ + "'" + CndSelList(CndSlRcData(nCndIdx).nData).szCndValue + "'"
        Else
            ' the condition value is BLANK...
            tmp$ = tmp$ + "''"
        End If
    Case 9
        ' NOT EQUALS...
        tmp$ = tmp$ + "!= "
        nLen = Len(CndSelList(CndSlRcData(nCndIdx).nData).szCndValue)
        If nLen > 0 Then
            ' there is a condition value...
            tmp$ = tmp$ + "'" + CndSelList(CndSlRcData(nCndIdx).nData).szCndValue + "'"
        Else
            ' the condition value is BLANK...
            tmp$ = tmp$ + "''"
        End If
    Case 10
        ' NOT (GREATER OR EQUALS)...(i.e., LESS THAN)
        tmp$ = tmp$ + "< "
        nLen = Len(CndSelList(CndSlRcData(nCndIdx).nData).szCndValue)
        If nLen > 0 Then
            ' there is a condition value...
            tmp$ = tmp$ + "'" + CndSelList(CndSlRcData(nCndIdx).nData).szCndValue + "'"
        Else
            ' the condition value is BLANK...
```

```
            tmp$ = tmp$ + "'"
          End If
        Case 11
          ' NOT GREATER THAN...(i.e., LESS THAN OR EQUALS
          tmp$ = tmp$ + " < = "
          nLen = Len(CndSelList(CndSlRcData(nCndIdx).nData).szCndValue)
          If nLen > 0 Then
            ' there is a condition value...
            tmp$ = tmp$ + "'" + CndSelList(CndSlRcData(nCndIdx).nData).szCndValue + "'"
          Else
            ' the condition value is BLANK...
            tmp$ = tmp$ + "'"
          End If
        Case 12
          ' IS EMPTY...
          tmp$ = tmp$ + "IS EMPTY"
        Case 13
          ' IS NOT EMPTY...
          tmp$ = tmp$ + "IS NOT EMPTY"
      End Select
      If CndSelList(CndSlRcData(nCndIdx).nData).nConnector = 1 Then
        tmp$ = "And (" + tmp$ + ")"
      Else
        tmp$ = "Or (" + tmp$ + ")"
      End If
      szTempCndStr = tmp$
```

End Sub

Sub BuildSqlCndString ()
```
' FIRST-> get the TABLE and COLUMN for the LEFT EXPRESSION...
' WARNING-> returns value via szTempCndStr...which is GLOBAL...
Col$ = LTrim$(RTrim$(CndSelList(nCndIdx).szTblColName))
If Col$ <> "*" Then
    tmp$ = LTrim$(RTrim$(CndSelList(nCndIdx).szTblName))
    tmp$ = tmp$ + "."
    tmp$ = tmp$ + Col$
Else
    tmp$ = Col$
End If
tmp$ = tmp$ + " "        ' NOTE-> this SPACE is VERY IMPORTANT...
' SECOND-> get the RELATION OPERATOR...
Select Case CndSelList(nCndIdx).nRelation
    Case 0
        ' NO RELATION...Do NOTHING...
    Case 1
        ' IS ANY VALUE...NOTE-> this is STUPID...but who cares...
        tmp$ = tmp$ + "IS NOT NULL OR IS NULL"
    Case 2
        ' LESS THAN...
        tmp$ = tmp$ + "< "
        nLen = Len(CndSelList(nCndIdx).szCndValue)
        If nLen > 0 Then
```

```
        ' there is a condition value...
        tmp$ = tmp$ + "'" + CndSelList(nCndIdx).szCndValue + "'"
    Else
        ' the condition value is BLANK...
        tmp$ = tmp$ + "' '"
    End If
Case 3
    ' LESS THAN OR EQUALS...
    tmp$ = tmp$ + " <= "
    nLen = Len(CndSelList(nCndIdx).szCndValue)
    If nLen > 0 Then
        ' there is a condition value...
        tmp$ = tmp$ + "'" + CndSelList(nCndIdx).szCndValue + "'"
    Else
        ' the condition value is BLANK...
        tmp$ = tmp$ + "' '"
    End If
Case 4
    ' EQUALS...
    tmp$ = tmp$ + " = "
    nLen = Len(CndSelList(nCndIdx).szCndValue)
    If nLen > 0 Then
        ' there is a condition value...
        tmp$ = tmp$ + "'" + CndSelList(nCndIdx).szCndValue + "'"
    Else
        ' the condition value is BLANK...
        tmp$ = tmp$ + "' '"
```

```
      End If
   Case 5
      ' GREATER OR EQUALS...
      tmp$ = tmp$ + " > = "
      nLen = Len(CndSelList(nCndIdx).szCndValue)
      If nLen > 0 Then
         ' there is a condition value...
         tmp$ = tmp$ + "'" + CndSelList(nCndIdx).szCndValue + "'"
      Else
         ' the condition value is BLANK...
         tmp$ = tmp$ + "' '"
      End If
   Case 6
      ' GREATER THAN...
      tmp$ = tmp$ + " > "
      nLen = Len(CndSelList(nCndIdx).szCndValue)
      If nLen > 0 Then
         ' there is a condition value...
         tmp$ = tmp$ + "'" + CndSelList(nCndIdx).szCndValue + "'"
      Else
         ' the condition value is BLANK...
         tmp$ = tmp$ + "' '"
      End If
   Case 7
      ' NOT LESS THAN...
      tmp$ = tmp$ + "! < "
      nLen = Len(CndSelList(nCndIdx).szCndValue)
```

```
          If nLen > 0 Then
               ' there is a condition value...
               tmp$ = tmp$ + "'" + CndSelList(nCndIdx).szCndValue + "'"
          Else
               ' the condition value is BLANK...
               tmp$ = tmp$ + "' '"
          End If
     Case 8
          ' NOT LESS THAN OR EQUALS...(i.e., GREATER THAN)...
          tmp$ = tmp$ + " > "
          nLen = Len(CndSelList(nCndIdx).szCndValue)
          If nLen > 0 Then
               ' there is a condition value...
               tmp$ = tmp$ + "'" + CndSelList(nCndIdx).szCndValue + "'"
          Else
               ' the condition value is BLANK...
               tmp$ = tmp$ + "' '"
          End If
     Case 9
          ' NOT EQUALS...
          tmp$ = tmp$ + "!= "
          nLen = Len(CndSelList(nCndIdx).szCndValue)
          If nLen > 0 Then
               ' there is a condition value...
               tmp$ = tmp$ + "'" + CndSelList(nCndIdx).szCndValue + "'"
          Else
               ' the condition value is BLANK...
```

```
            tmp$ = tmp$ + "'"
          End If
        Case 10
          ' NOT (GREATER OR EQUALS)…(i.e., LESS THAN)
          tmp$ = tmp$ + " < "
          nLen = Len(CndSelList(nCndIdx).szCndValue)
          If nLen > 0 Then
            ' there is a condition value…
            tmp$ = tmp$ + "'" + CndSelList(nCndIdx).szCndValue + "'"
          Else
            ' the condition value is BLANK…
            tmp$ = tmp$ + "' '"
          End If
        Case 11
          ' NOT GREATER THAN…(i.e., LESS THAN OR EQUALS
          tmp$ = tmp$ + " <= "
          nLen = Len(CndSelList(nCndIdx).szCndValue)
          If nLen > 0 Then
            ' there is a condition value…
            tmp$ = tmp$ + "'" + CndSelList(nCndIdx).szCndValue + "'"
          Else
            ' the condition value is BLANK…
            tmp$ = tmp$ + "' '"
          End If
        Case 12
          ' IS EMPTY…
          tmp$ = tmp$ + "IS NULL"
```

```
        Case 13
            ' IS NOT EMPTY...
            tmp$ = tmp$ + "IS NOT NULL"
    End Select
    If CndSelList(nCndIdx).nConnector = 1 Then
        tmp$ = "And (" + tmp$ + ")"
    Else
        tmp$ = "Or (" + tmp$ + ")"
    End If
    szTempCndStr = tmp$
End Sub
```

Sub RefreshSQLSelList 0

```
SqlFrm.FBSB.Enabled = TRUE
nLBCount = SqlFrm.TblViewCB.ListCount
If nLBCount > 0 Then
    SqlFrm.TblViewCB.ListIndex = 0
    szCurrTblName = LTrim$(RTrim$(SqlFrm.TblViewCB.LIST(0)))
End If
For I = 1 To 5 Step 1
    SqlFrm.TVRC(I).Caption = ""
Next I

SqlFrm.LX.BackColor = CYAN
SqlFrm.LX.ForeColor = BLUE
SqlFrm.RcTitle.BackColor = CYAN
```

```
SqlFrm.RcTitle.ForeColor = BLUE
SqlFrm.TblViewCB.BackColor = WHITE
SqlFrm.TblViewCB.ForeColor = BLUE
SqlFrm.TblViewCB.Enabled = TRUE
SqlFrm.TvRcVSR.Enabled = TRUE
SqlFrm.SlRcVSR.Enabled = TRUE

SqlFrm.TvRcVSR.Min = 1
SqlFrm.TvRcVSR.Max = 1
nResetTvRcVSR = 0
SqlFrm.TvRcVSR.Value = 1
For I = 1 To 5 Step 1
    SqlFrm.SLRC(I).Caption = ""
Next I
SqlFrm.SlRcVSR.Min = 1
SqlFrm.SlRcVSR.Max = 1
nResetSlRcVSR = 0
SqlFrm.SlRcVSR.Value = 1

SqlFrm.ConditionsPB.Enabled = TRUE
'SqlFrm.ConditionsPB.SymBackColor = GRAYGREEN
'SqlFrm.ConditionsPB.FontColor = BLACK
For I = 1 To 5 Step 1
    SqlFrm.SLRC(I).BackColor = WHITE
    SqlFrm.SLRC(I).ForeColor = BLUE
Next I
```

```
For I = 1 To 5 Step 1
    SqlFrm.TVRC(I).BackColor = WHITE
    SqlFrm.TVRC(I).ForeColor = BLUE
Next I

'SqlFrm.CountPB.SymBackColor = LIGHTGRAY
'SqlFrm.CountDistinctPB.SymBackColor = LIGHTGRAY
'SqlFrm.ColTitleIsPB.SymBackColor = LIGHTGRAY
'SqlFrm.RemoveRedRowPB.SymBackColor = LIGHTGRAY
'SqlFrm.CountPB.FontColor = WHITE
'SqlFrm.CountDistinctPB.FontColor = WHITE
'SqlFrm.ColTitleIsPB.FontColor = WHITE
'SqlFrm.RemoveRedRowPB.FontColor = WHITE
SqlFrm.ColTitleIsTxt.BackColor = WHITE
SqlFrm.ColTitleIsTxt.ForeColor = DARKGRAY
SqlFrm.SLRC(1).Caption = " "

End Sub

Sub ResetSqlFrm ()
Screen.MousePointer = 11
SqlFrm.FBSB.Enabled = TRUE
SqlFrm.FBCB.Visible = FALSE
SqlFrm.ConditionsPB.Enabled = TRUE
'SqlFrm.ConditionsPB.SymBackColor = DARKPURPLE
'SqlFrm.ConditionsPB.FontColor = WHITE
```

```
For I = 1 To 5 Step 1
    SqlFrm.SLRC(I).BackColor = WHITE
    SqlFrm.SLRC(I).ForeColor = BLUE
    SqlFrm.SLRC(I).Enabled = FALSE
Next I
For I = 1 To 5 Step 1
    SqlFrm.TVRC(I).BackColor = WHITE
    SqlFrm.TVRC(I).ForeColor = BLUE
    SqlFrm.TVRC(I).Enabled = FALSE
Next I
SqlFrm.LX.BackColor = CYAN
SqlFrm.LX.ForeColor = BLUE
SqlFrm.RcTitle.BackColor = CYAN
SqlFrm.RcTitle.ForeColor = BLUE
SqlFrm.TblViewCB.BackColor = WHITE
SqlFrm.TblViewCB.ForeColor = BLUE
SqlFrm.TblViewCB.Enabled = TRUE
SqlFrm.TvRcVSR.Enabled = FALSE
SqlFrm.SlRcVSR.Enabled = FALSE
' reset colors...
'SqlFrm.CountPB.SymBackColor = LIGHTGRAY
'SqlFrm.CountDistinctPB.SymBackColor = LIGHTGRAY
'SqlFrm.ColTitleIsPB.SymBackColor = LIGHTGRAY
'SqlFrm.RemoveRedRowPB.SymBackColor = LIGHTGRAY
'SqlFrm.CountPB.FontColor = WHITE
'SqlFrm.CountDistinctPB.FontColor = WHITE
'SqlFrm.ColTitleIsPB.FontColor = WHITE
```

```
'SqlFrm.RemoveRedRowPB.FontColor = WHITE
SqlFrm.ColTitleIsTxt.BackColor = WHITE
SqlFrm.ColTitleIsTxt.ForeColor = DARKGRAY
' colors are now reset...
SqlFrm.CountPB.Enabled = FALSE
SqlFrm.CountDistinctPB.Enabled = FALSE
SqlFrm.RemoveRedRowPB.Enabled = FALSE
SqlFrm.ColTitleIsPB.Enabled = FALSE
SqlFrm.ColTitleIsTxt.Enabled = FALSE
SqlFrm.FindSelTxt.Text = " "
SqlFrm.FindSelTxt.Enabled = FALSE

If nSqlFrmReallyVisible > 0 Then
    If SqlFrm.FBSB.Visible = TRUE Then
        If SqlFrm.FindSelTxt.Enabled = TRUE Then
            SqlFrm.FindSelTxt.SetFocus
        Else
            SqlFrm.TblViewCB.SetFocus
        End If
    End If
End If

Screen.MousePointer = 0
End Sub
```

Sub ParseAndLoadSqlAdHocStmt 0

```
ngSqlAdHocSelListCount = 0
ngSqlAdHocCndSelListCount = 0
'
' ─────────────────────────────
' NOTE-> PARSE the FROM clause...
'        ...>fc<...##...##>endfc<...
' NOTE-> there is only ONE item in the FROM clause at this time...
' ─────────────────────────────

nRetVal% = InStr(1, szTokenSqlCmdStr, " >fc <")
If (nRetVal% > 1) Then
    ' found the beginning of the FROM clause...
    nStart% = nRetVal% + 4
    nRetVal% = InStr(nStart%, szTokenSqlCmdStr, "##")
    If (nRetVal% > nStart%) Then
        ' found the end of the FROM clause...so get it...
        nLength% = nRetVal% - nStart%
        szSqlAdHocFromTblView = Mid$(szTokenSqlCmdStr, nStart%, nLength%)
        ' find the MATCH for this TblView and select it...
        ngLoadingViaSqlAdHoc = 1
        nMatchFound% = 0
        nLBCount = SqlFrm.TblViewCB.ListCount
        If (nLBCount > 0) Then
            For I = 0 To nLBCount - 1 Step 1
                nFound% = InStr(1, SqlFrm.TblViewCB.LIST(I), szSqlAdHocFromTblView)
                If (nFound% > 0) Then
                    ' found a MATCH...so SELECT IT...
                    SqlFrm.TblViewCB.ListIndex = I
                    SelectTblViewItem
```

```
            nMatchFound% = 1
            Exit For
        End If
    Next I
Else
    ' ERROR-> TblViewCB is EMPTY...
    nRetVal = MsgBox3004()
    Exit Sub
End If
If (nMatchFound% < 1) Then
    ' ERROR-> NO MATCH FOUND...
    nRetVal = MsgBox3003()
    Exit Sub
End If
Else
    ' ERROR-> NO FROM clause TERMINATOR...
    nRetVal = MsgBox3002()
    Exit Sub
End If
Else
    ' ERROR-> NO FROM clause...
    nRetVal = MsgBox3001()
    Exit Sub
End If
'-------------------------------------------
' NOTE-> PARSE the SELECT clause...
'    ...> sc <...##...##> endsc <...
```

```
nRetVal% = InStr(1, szTokenSqlCmdStr, ">sc<")
If (nRetVal% < 1) Then
    ' ERROR-> NO SELECT clause...
    nRetVal = MsgBox30050()
    Exit Sub
End If
'
' found the beginning of the SELECT clause...
'
nStart% = nRetVal% + 4

nRetVal% = InStr(1, szTokenSqlCmdStr, ">endsc<")
If (nRetVal% < 1) Then
    ' ERROR-> NO SELECT clause TERMINATOR...
    nRetVal = MsgBox30060()
    Exit Sub
End If
'
' found the end of the SELECT clause..
'
nEnd% = nRetVal%

'
' get each SELECT clause item...
'
```

```
nDone% = FALSE
nFoundAtLeastOneSelectItem% = 0
While nDone% = FALSE
    nRetVal% = InStr(nStart%, szTokenSqlCmdStr, "##")
    If ((nRetVal% > nStart%) And (nRetVal% < nEnd%)) Then
        ' found the end of the SELECT clause ITEM...so get it...
        nLength% = nRetVal% - nStart%
        szSqlAdHocSelectItem = Mid$(szTokenSqlCmdStr, nStart%, nLength%)

        '─────────────────────────────
        ' now...set nStart% to the NEXT ITEM...
        '─────────────────────────────
        nStart% = nRetVal% + 2   ' skip over the "##"...
        nCount% = 0
        nCountDistinct% = 0
        nTitle% = 0
        szSqlAdHocSelectItemTitle = ""

        '─────────────────────────────
        ' check for Count(Distinct(...))
        '─────────────────────────────
        nRetVal% = InStr(1, szSqlAdHocSelectItem, "Count(Distinct(")
        If (nRetVal% > 0) Then
            ' found Count(Distinct()...
            nCountDistinct% = nRetVal% + 15   ' offset for Count(Distinct())...
        Else
            '─────────────────────────────
            ' check for Count(...)
            '─────────────────────────────
```

```
nRetVal% = InStr(1, szSqlAdHocSelectItem, "Count(")
If (nRetVal% > 0) Then
    ' found Count(Distinct()...
    nCount% = nRetVal% + 6   ' offset for Count()...
End If
End If
'----------------------------------------
' check for TITLE (i.e., " = ")...
'----------------------------------------
nRetVal% = InStr(1, szSqlAdHocSelectItem, " = ")
If (nRetVal% > 0) Then
    ' found TITLE...
    nTitle% = 1
    nTitleLength% = nRetVal% - 1
    szSqlAdHocSelectItemTitle = Mid$(szSqlAdHocSelectItem, 1, nTitleLength%)
End If
'----------------------------------------
' now...get the COLUMN NAME...
'----------------------------------------
nRetVal% = InStr(1, szSqlAdHocSelectItem, ".")
If (nRetVal% > 0) Then
    ' found COLUMN NAME beginning...
    nColumnStart% = nRetVal% + 1
    If nCountDistinct% > 0 Then
        nColumnLength% = (nLength% - nColumnStart%) - 2      ' ))...
    Else
        If nCount% > 0 Then
```

```
            nColumnLength% = (nLength% - nColumnStart%) - 1 ')...
      Else
            nColumnLength% = (nLength% - nColumnStart%)            ' none...
      End If
   End If
   nColumnLength% = nColumnLength% + 1  ' because length is short by ONE and I am LAZY...
   szSqlAdHocSelectColumn = Mid$(szSqlAdHocSelectItem, nColumnStart%, nColumnLength%)
End If
'_____
' now...find the MATCH for this ITEM and select it...
nMatchFound% = 0
'_____
For I = 1 To 100 Step 1
   If (TblCols(I).szTblColName = "") Then
      Exit For
   End If
   nRetVal% = InStr(1, TblCols(I).szTblColName, szSqlAdHocSelectItemColumn)
   If nRetVal% > 0 Then
      ' FOUND a MATCH...so MARK TblCols(I)...
      nFoundAtLeastOneSelectItem% = 1
      TblCols(I).nData = 1
      nMatchFound% = 1
   End If
'_____
' now....ADD it to SelList()...
'_____
   nAddedItemToSelList% = 0
   For J = 1 To 100 Step 1
```

```
If (SelList(J).nData = 0) Then
    ' this is the FIRST AVAILABLE row...so use it...
    SelList(J).szTblColName = TblCols(I).szTblColName
    SelList(J).szTblName = TblCols(I).szTblName
    SelList(J).szColTitle = szSqlAdHocSelectItemTitle
    SelList(J).nData = I     ' save the TblCol() INDEX...
    If (nCount% > 0) Then
        SelList(J).nCount = 1
    End If
    If (nCountDistinct% > 0) Then
        SelList(J).nCountDistinct = 1
    End If
    SelList(J).nFlag = 0  ' set COLOR to WHITE...
    nAddedItemToSelList% = 1
    If (ngSqlAdHocSelListCount < J) Then
        ngSqlAdHocSelListCount = J
    End If
    Exit For
End If
Next J
If (nAddedItemToSelList% < 1) Then
    ' ERROR-> Unable to ADD item to SelList()...
    nRetVal = MsgBox30070
    Exit Sub
End If
Exit For
End If
```

```
        Next I
        If (nMatchFound% < 1) Then
         ' ERROR-> NO MATCH in TblCols(I)...
            nRetVal = MsgBox3008()
            Exit Sub
          End If
        Else
           nDone% = 1
        End If
    Wend
    If (nFoundAtLeastOneSelectItem% < 1) Then
      ' ERROR-> SELECT clause is EMPTY...
        nRetVal = MsgBox3009()
        Exit Sub
    End If
    ResetTvRcSlRcObjects
'-----------------------------------------

' NOTE-> PARSE the WHERE clause...
'     ...>wc<...##...##>endwc<...
'-----------------------------------------
    nRetVal% = InStr(1, szTokenSqlCmdStr, ">wc<")
    If (nRetVal% < 1) Then
      ' WARNING-> NO WHERE clause...THIS IS NOT AN ERROR...
```

```
    nRetVal = MsgBox3010()
    ngLoadingViaSqlAdHoc = 0          ' WARNING-> for NOW...we are DONE...
    Exit Sub         '                  if add ORDER BY...or COMPUTE...
End If           '                     then GOTO instead of EXIT...

' found the beginning of the WHERE clause...
'-------------------------------------------------

nStart% = nRetVal% + 4

nRetVal% = InStr(1, szTokenSqlCmdStr, " >endwc<")
If (nRetVal% < 1) Then
    ' ERROR-> NO WHERE clause TERMINATOR...this is an ERROR...because found ' >wc<'
    nRetVal = MsgBox3011()
    Exit Sub
End If

' found the end of the WHERE clause..
'-------------------------------------------------

nEnd% = nRetVal%

' get each WHERE clause item...
'-------------------------------------------------

nDone% = FALSE
nFoundAtLeastOneWhereItem% = 0
While nDone% = FALSE
    nRetVal% = InStr(nStart%, szTokenSqlCmdStr, "##")
```

```
If ((nRetVal% > nStart%) And (nRetVal% < nEnd%)) Then
    ' found the end of the WHERE clause ITEM...so get it...
    nLength% = nRetVal% - nStart%
    szSqlAdHocWhereItem = Mid$(szTokenSqlCmdStr, nStart%, nLength%)

    ' now...set nStart% to the NEXT ITEM...

    nStart% = nRetVal% + 2  ' skip over the "##"...
    nLogicalOperator% = 0
    nRelationOperator% = 0
    nValue% = 0
    szSqlAdHocWhereItemValue = ""

    ' check for LOGICAL OPERATOR...
    ' NOTE-> EACH item MUST have a LOGICAL OPERATOR...
    '       this also applies to the FIRST item...

    logical$ = Mid$(szSqlAdHocWhereItem, 1, 4)
    If (logical$ = "And ") Then
        nLogicalOperator% = 1    ' AND ('And')...
    Else
        nLogicalOperator% = 0    ' OR ('Or ')...
    End If

    ' check for VALUE start (i.e., "'")...

    nRetVal% = InStr(1, szSqlAdHocWhereItem, "'")
```

```
If (nRetVal% > 0) Then
    ' found VALUE start...
    nValue% = nRetVal% + 1
    '----------------------------------------
    ' check for VALUE start (i.e., "'")...
    '----------------------------------------
    nRetVal% = InStr(nValue%, szSqlAdHocWhereItem, "'")
    If (nRetVal% > 0) Then
        ' found VALUE end...
        nValueLength% = nRetVal% - nValue%
        szSqlAdHocWhereItemValue = Mid$(szSqlAdHocWhereItem, nValue%, nValueLength%)
    Else
        ' ERROR-> NO TERMINATOR for VALUE subitem...
        nRetVal = MsgBox30140
        Exit Sub
    End If
Else
    ' NOTE-> NOT AN ERROR:  this is a STATEMENT relation...
    '                       rather than a SYMBOL relation...
    '                       (e.g., "tbl.col IS NOT NULL" rather than "tbl.col = 'value'")
    '                  -----STATEMENT-----        -----SYMBOL-----
End If
'----------------------------------------
' now...get the COLUMN NAME start...
'----------------------------------------
nRetVal% = InStr(1, szSqlAdHocWhereItem, ".")
If (nRetVal% > 0) Then
```

```vb
' found COLUMN NAME start...
nColumnStart% = nRetVal% + 1

' now...get the COLUMN NAME end...
' NOTE-> there is a SINGLE SPACE after the COLUMN NAME...
'        so USE it to determine the END...

nRetVal% = InStr(nColumnStart%, szSqlAdHocWhereItem, " ")
If (nRetVal% > 0) Then
    ' found COLUMN NAME end...
    nColumnLength% = nRetVal% - nColumnStart%
Else
    ' ERROR-> NO TERMINATOR for COLUMN NAME subitem...
    nRetVal = MsgBox30150
    Exit Sub
End If
szSqlAdHocWhereItemColumn = Mid$(szSqlAdHocWhereItem, nColumnStart%, nColumnLength%)
Else

' WARNING-> since we are ALLOWING the user to select '*' as a
'           valid COLUMN NAME (even though this is somewhat STUPID)
'           we have to cover this situation...there is an '*'
'           item in CndTblCols()...so that part is already OK...

' THEREFORE-> if we are HERE...then there was NO PERIOD...and that
'             means that there is NO COLUMN NAME in TBL.COL format...
'             so...the ONLY other possibility is that this item
```

```
'           is an '*'...
'-----------------------------------
'
' CAUTION->   it is somewhat possible that the PRESUMPTION that
'              the FIRST '*' is the CORRECT one may be incorrect
'              because an ASTERISK can be a valid VALUE subitem...
' HOWEVER->  since we are controlling the HORIZONTAL and the
'              VERTICAL (i.e., THE OUTER LIMITS)...the PRESUMPTION
'              is CORRECT...(unless we missed something)...
'
'-----------------------------------
'
' GENERAL NOTE:  ABOUT THIS PARSER/UNPARSER...
'   There are several different ways to write parsers and this is
'   one of them.  It is not very mathematical and may not be
'   perfect, but it is also not ABSTRUSE.  It is NOT an LR() Parser
'   or some other BIG PRODUCTION.  Instead, it is a SIMPLE and
'   PRACTICAL Parser.  The COST of SIMPLICITY is FLEXIBILITY, so
'   this is a VERY INFLEXIBLE parser, but IT WORKS.
'   Everything in this parser is EXPLICITLY DEPENDENT on the
'   PRESUMPTION that we CREATED the string that we are parsing.
'   The parser WORKS when the PRESUMPTION is CORRECT because we
'   do NOT allow ourselves to create BAD SQL Select strings...
'   In general, ONLY CREATING GOOD PARSER STRINGS is the KEY to
'   writing SIMPLE UNPARSERS.
'
'-----------------------------------

nRetVal% = InStr(1, szSqlAdHocWhereItem, "*")
If (nRetVal% > 0) Then
    ' found the ASTERISK...
    nColumnStart% = nRetVal%                ' location of FIRST asterisk...
```

```
        nColumnLength% = 1              ' must be ONE...
    Else
        ' ERROR-> NO COLUMN NAME and NO ASTERISK...so NO LEFT SIDE...
        nRetVal = MsgBox3012()
        Exit Sub
    End If
    szSqlAdHocWhereItemColumn = Mid$(szSqlAdHocWhereItem, nColumnStart%, nColumnLength%)
End If
' -----------------------------------------------
' now...find the RELATIONAL OPERATOR for this ITEM and select it...
' NOTE-> nRelationLength% = (nValue% - 2)- nRelationStart%...if (nValue% > 0)
'        nRelationLength% = nLength% - nRelationStart%...if nValue% < 1
'        nRelationStart% = nColumnStart% + nColumnLength% + 1
' -----------------------------------------------
nRelationStart% = nColumnStart% + nColumnLength% + 1
If (nValue% > 0) Then
    nRelationLength% = (nValue% - 2) - nRelationStart%
Else
    nRelationLength% = nLength% - nRelationStart%
End If
szSqlAdHocWhereItemRelation = Mid$(szSqlAdHocWhereItem, nRelationStart%, nRelationLength%)
' -----------------------------------------------
' now...identify the TYPE of the RELATION...
' NOTE-> if nValue% > 0 then the RELATION is a symbol (i.e., '<', '=', etc.)...
'        otherwise...the RELATION is a statement (i.e., 'IS NOT NULL', etc.)...
'        MATCH on SYMBOL or STATEMENT to IDENTIFY the TYPE of RELATION...
' -----------------------------------------------
```

```
'   -> szSqlAdHocWhereItemRelation:   contains the RELATION...
'
'
' nRelationFound% = 0   ' set to 1 when find ANY relation...
'
' check for SYMBOL or STATEMENT...
'
Select Case szSqlAdHocWhereItemRelation
    Case "IS NOT NULL OR IS NULL"
        nRelation% = 1   ' IS ANY VALUE...
        nRelationFound% = 1
    Case "<"
        nRelation% = 2   ' LESS THAN...
        nRelationFound% = 1
    Case "<="
        nRelation% = 3   ' LESS THAN OR EQUAL...
        nRelationFound% = 1
    Case "="
        nRelation% = 4   ' EQUALS...
        nRelationFound% = 1
    Case ">="
        nRelation% = 5   ' GREATER OR EQUALS...
        nRelationFound% = 1
    Case ">"
        nRelation% = 6   ' GREATER THAN...
        nRelationFound% = 1
    Case "!<"
        nRelation% = 7   ' NOT LESS THAN...
```

```
        nRelationFound% = 1
    Case ">"
        nRelation% = 8  ' NOT (LESS THAN OR EQUALS)...(REDUNDANT)
        nRelationFound% = 1
    Case "!="
        nRelation% = 9  ' NOT EQUALS...
        nRelationFound% = 1
    Case "<"
        nRelation% = 10  ' NOT (GREATER OR EQUALS)...(REDUNDANT)
        nRelationFound% = 1
    Case "<="
        nRelation% = 11  ' NOT GREATER THAN...(REDUNDANT)
        nRelationFound% = 1
    Case "IS NULL"
        nRelation% = 12  ' IS EMPTY...
        nRelationFound% = 1
    Case "IS NOT NULL"
        nRelation% = 13  ' IS NOT EMPTY...
        nRelationFound% = 1
    Case Else
        nRelation% = 0  ' NO RELATION...PROBABLY AN ERROR...
        nRelationFound% = 1
End Select
If (nRelationFound% < 1) Then
    ' ERROR-> RELATION OPERATOR NOT FOUND...
    nRetVal = MsgBox3016()
    Exit Sub
```

End If

'-----------------------------------
' now…find the MATCH for this ITEM and select it…
'-----------------------------------
nMatchFound% = 0
For I = 1 To 100 Step 1
    If (CndTblCols(I).szTblColName = "") Then
        Exit For
    End If
    nRetVal% = InStr(1, CndTblCols(I).szTblColName, szSqlAdHocWhereItemColumn)
    If nRetVal% > 0 Then
        ' FOUND a MATCH…so MARK CndTblCols(I)…
        nFoundAtLeastOneWhereItem% = 1
        CndTblCols(I).nData = 1
        nMatchFound% = 1

'-----------------------------------
' now…ADD it to CndSelList()…
            -> szTblColName
            -> szTblName
            -> szColTitle   ' not used…
            -> szCndValue
            -> nData
            -> nConnector
            -> nRelation
            -> nLeftFunction   ' not used…(reserved for complex expressions)
            -> nRightFunction   ' not used…(reserved for complex expressions)
            -> nCount   ' not used…(reserved for complex expressions)

```
'             -> nCountDistinct   ' not used…(reserved for complex expressions)
'             -> nFlag
'-------------
nAddedItemToCndSelList% = 0
For J = 1 To 100 Step 1
    If (CndSelList(J).nData = 0) Then
        ' this is the FIRST AVAILABLE row…so use it…
        CndSelList(J).szTblColName = CndTblCols(I).szTblColName
        CndSelList(J).szTblName = CndTblCols(I).szTblName
        CndSelList(J).szColTitle = ""           ' N/A…
        CndSelList(J).szCndValue = szSqlAdHocWhereItemValue
        CndSelList(J).nData = I                 ' save the CndTblCol() INDEX…
        CndSelList(J).nConnector = nLogicalOperator%
        CndSelList(J).nRelation = nRelation%
        CndSelList(J).nLeftFunction = 0         ' N/A…
        CndSelList(J).nRightFunction = 0        ' N/A…
        CndSelList(J).nCount = 0                ' N/A…
        CndSelList(J).nCountDistinct = 0        ' N/A…
        CndSelList(J).nFlag = 0   ' set COLOR to WHITE…

        nAddedItemToCndSelList% = 1
        If (ngSqlAdHocCndSelListCount < J) Then
            ngSqlAdHocCndSelListCount = J
        End If
        Exit For
    End If
Next J
```

```
            If (nAddedItemToCndSelList% < 1) Then
                ' ERROR-> Unable to ADD item to CndSelList()...
                nRetVal = MsgBox3017()
                Exit Sub
            End If
            Exit For
        End If
    Next I
    If (nMatchFound% < 1) Then
        ' ERROR-> NO MATCH in CndTblCols(I)...
        nRetVal = MsgBox3018()
        Exit Sub
    Else
        nDone% = 1
    End If
Wend
If (nFoundAtLeastOneWhereItem% < 1) Then
    ' ERROR-> WHERE clause is EMPTY...
    nRetVal = MsgBox3019()
    Exit Sub
End If
ResetCndTvRcSlRcObjects
'_____

ngLoadingViaSqlAdHoc = 0
```

End Sub

Function MsgBox3001 () As Integer
Title$ = "SQL Select Parser"
Msg$ = "ERROR: Unable to locate FROM clause..."
DgDef% = MB_OK + MB_ICONSTOP ' Describe dialog.
Response% = MsgBox(Msg$, DgDef%, Title$)   ' Get user response.
MsgBox3001 = TRUE ' return TRUE
End Function

Function MsgBox3002 () As Integer
Title$ = "SQL Select Parser"
Msg$ = "ERROR: Unable to locate FROM clause TERMINATOR..."
DgDef% = MB_OK + MB_ICONSTOP ' Describe dialog.
Response% = MsgBox(Msg$, DgDef%, Title$)   ' Get user response.
MsgBox3002 = TRUE ' return TRUE
End Function

Function MsgBox3003 () As Integer
Title$ = "SQL Select Parser"
Msg$ = "ERROR: MATCH for FROM clause Tbl/View item NOT FOUND..."
DgDef% = MB_OK + MB_ICONSTOP ' Describe dialog.
Response% = MsgBox(Msg$, DgDef%, Title$)   ' Get user response.
MsgBox3003 = TRUE ' return TRUE
End Function

Function MsgBox3004 () As Integer
```
Title$ = "SQL Select Parser"
Msg$ = "ERROR: Tbl/View LIST is EMPTY..."
DgDef% = MB_OK + MB_ICONSTOP ' Describe dialog.
Response% = MsgBox(Msg$, DgDef%, Title$)  ' Get user response.
MsgBox3004 = TRUE ' return TRUE
End Function
```

Sub SelectTblViewItem ()
```
Screen.MousePointer = 11
'─────────────────────────
For I = 1 To 100 Step 1
    TblCols(I).szTblName = ""
    TblCols(I).szTblColName = ""
    TblCols(I).nData = 0
Next I
'─────────────────────────
For I = 1 To 5 Step 1
    SqlFrm.TVRC(I).Caption = " "
    TvRcData(I).szTblColName = ""
    TvRcData(I).szTblName = ""
    TvRcData(I).nData = 0
Next I
SqlFrm.TvRcVSR.Min = 0
SqlFrm.TvRcVSR.Max = 0
```

```
nResetTvRcVSR = 0
SqlFrm.TvRcVSR.Value = 0
nTblIdx = SqlFrm.TblViewCB.ListIndex
szCurrTblName = LTrim$(RTrim$(SqlFrm.TblViewCB.LIST(nTblIdx)))
GetTblViewColumns
If nCurrColCount > 0 Then
    For I = 1 To 5 Step 1
        If I <= nCurrColCount Then
            TvRcData(I).szTblColName = TblCols(I).szTblColName
            TvRcData(I).szTblName = szCurrTblName
            TvRcData(I).nData = I
            SqlFrm.TVRC(I).Caption = TvRcData(I).szTblColName
            SqlFrm.TVRC(I).Enabled = TRUE
        Else
            Exit For
        End If
    Next I
    SqlFrm.TvRcVSR.Min = 1
    SqlFrm.TvRcVSR.Max = nCurrColCount
    SqlFrm.TvRcVSR.Enabled = TRUE
    nResetTvRcVSR = 1
    SqlFrm.TvRcVSR.Value = 1
    nResetTvRcVSR = 1
End If
'SqlFrm.CountPB.SymBackColor = LIGHTGRAY
'SqlFrm.CountDistinctPB.SymBackColor = LIGHTGRAY
'SqlFrm.ColTitlesPB.SymBackColor = LIGHTGRAY
```

```
'SqlFrm.RemoveRedRowPB.SymBackColor = LIGHTGRAY
'SqlFrm.CountPB.FontColor = WHITE
'SqlFrm.CountDistinctPB.FontColor = WHITE
'SqlFrm.ColTitleIsPB.FontColor = WHITE
'SqlFrm.RemoveRedRowPB.FontColor = WHITE
SqlFrm.CountPB.Enabled = FALSE
SqlFrm.CountDistinctPB.Enabled = FALSE
SqlFrm.RemoveRedRowPB.Enabled = FALSE
SqlFrm.ColTitleIsPB.Enabled = FALSE
SqlFrm.ColTitleIsTxt.Enabled = FALSE
SqlFrm.ColTitleIsTxt.Text = ""
SqlFrm.ColTitleIsTxt.BackColor = WHITE
SqlFrm.ColTitleIsTxt.ForeColor = DARKGRAY
'SqlFrm.CountPB.SymBackColor = LIGHTGRAY
'SqlFrm.CountDistinctPB.SymBackColor = LIGHTGRAY
'SqlFrm.ColTitleIsPB.SymBackColor = LIGHTGRAY
'SqlFrm.RemoveRedRowPB.SymBackColor = LIGHTGRAY
'SqlFrm.CountPB.FontColor = WHITE
'SqlFrm.CountDistinctPB.FontColor = WHITE
'SqlFrm.ColTitleIsPB.FontColor = WHITE
'SqlFrm.RemoveRedRowPB.FontColor = WHITE
For I = 1 To 5 Step 1
    SqlFrm.SLRC(I).BackColor = WHITE
    SqlFrm.SLRC(I).ForeColor = BLUE
    SqlFrm.SLRC(I).Caption = ""
    SlRcData(I).szTblColName = ""
    SlRcData(I).szTblName = ""
```

```
    SlRcData(I).szColTitle = ""
    SlRcData(I).nData = 0
    SlRcData(I).nCount = 0
    SlRcData(I).nCountDistinct = 0
    SlRcData(I).nFlag = 0
Next I
SqlFrm.SLRC(1).Caption = ""
nResetSIRcVSR = 0
SqlFrm.SIRcVSR.Min = 0
SqlFrm.SIRcVSR.Max = 0
SqlFrm.SIRcVSR.Value = 0
nResetSIRcVSR = 1   ' WARNING-> MUST do this to enable scrolling…
'SqlFrm.CountPB.SymBackColor = LIGHTGRAY
'SqlFrm.CountDistinctPB.SymBackColor = LIGHTGRAY
'SqlFrm.ColTitleIsPB.SymBackColor = LIGHTGRAY
'SqlFrm.RemoveRedRowPB.SymBackColor = LIGHTGRAY
'SqlFrm.CountPB.FontColor = WHITE
'SqlFrm.CountDistinctPB.FontColor = WHITE
'SqlFrm.ColTitleIsPB.FontColor = WHITE
'SqlFrm.RemoveRedRowPB.FontColor = WHITE
For I = 1 To 100 Step 1
    SelList(I).szTblColName = ""
    SelList(I).szTblName = ""
    SelList(I).szColTitle = ""
    SelList(I).nData = 0
    SelList(I).nCount = 0
    SelList(I).nCountDistinct = 0
```

```
        SelList(I).nFlag = 0
    Next I

    InitNewSQLCndList

    SqlFrm.FindSelTxt.Text = ""
    If nSqlFrmReallyVisible > 0 Then
        If SqlFrm.FBSB.Visible = TRUE Then
            If SqlFrm.FindSelTxt.Enabled = TRUE Then
            Else
                SqlFrm.FindSelTxt.Enabled = TRUE
            End If
            SqlFrm.FindSelTxt.SetFocus
            SqlFrm.ConditionsPB.Enabled = TRUE
            'SqlFrm.ConditionsPB.SymBackColor = DARKPURPLE
            'SqlFrm.ConditionsPB.FontColor = WHITE
        End If
    End If
    Screen.MousePointer = 0
End Sub
```

Function MsgBox3005 () As Integer

```
Title$ = "SQL Select Parser"
Msg$ = "ERROR: NO SELECT clause..."
DgDef% = MB_OK + MB_ICONSTOP ' Describe dialog.
Response% = MsgBox(Msg$, DgDef%, Title$)   ' Get user response.
```

MsgBox3005 = TRUE ' return TRUE
End Function

Function MsgBox3006 () As Integer
Title$ = "SQL Select Parser"
Msg$ = "ERROR: NO SELECT clause TERMINATOR..."
DgDef% = MB_OK + MB_ICONSTOP ' Describe dialog.
Response% = MsgBox(Msg$, DgDef%, Title$)   ' Get user response.
MsgBox3006 = TRUE ' return TRUE
End Function

Function MsgBox3007 () As Integer
Title$ = "SQL Select Parser"
Msg$ = "ERROR: Unable to ADD item to SelList()..."
DgDef% = MB_OK + MB_ICONSTOP ' Describe dialog.
Response% = MsgBox(Msg$, DgDef%, Title$)   ' Get user response.
MsgBox3007 = TRUE ' return TRUE
End Function

Function MsgBox3008 () As Integer
Title$ = "SQL Select Parser"
Msg$ = "ERROR: NO MATCH in TblCols() for SELECT item..."
DgDef% = MB_OK + MB_ICONSTOP ' Describe dialog.
Response% = MsgBox(Msg$, DgDef%, Title$)   ' Get user response.
MsgBox3008 = TRUE ' return TRUE

End Function

Function MsgBox3009 () As Integer
```
Title$ = "SQL Select Parser"
Msg$ = "ERROR: SELECT clause is EMPTY..."
DgDef% = MB_OK + MB_ICONSTOP ' Describe dialog.
Response% = MsgBox(Msg$, DgDef%, Title$)   ' Get user response.
MsgBox3009 = TRUE  ' return TRUE
End Function
```

Sub ResetTvRcSlRcObjects ()
```
nAtLeastOne = 0
'SqlFrm.CountPB.SymBackColor = LIGHTGRAY
'SqlFrm.CountDistinctPB.SymBackColor = LIGHTGRAY
'SqlFrm.ColTitleIsPB.SymBackColor = LIGHTGRAY
'SqlFrm.RemoveRedRowPB.SymBackColor = LIGHTGRAY
'SqlFrm.CountPB.FontColor = WHITE
'SqlFrm.CountDistinctPB.FontColor = WHITE
'SqlFrm.ColTitleIsPB.FontColor = WHITE
'SqlFrm.RemoveRedRowPB.FontColor = WHITE
SqlFrm.CountPB.Enabled = FALSE
SqlFrm.CountDistinctPB.Enabled = FALSE
SqlFrm.RemoveRedRowPB.Enabled = FALSE
SqlFrm.ColTitleIsPB.Enabled = FALSE
SqlFrm.ColTitleIsTxt.Enabled = FALSE
SqlFrm.ColTitleIsTxt.Text = ""
```

```
SqlFrm.ColTitleIsTxt.BackColor = WHITE
'SqlFrm.ColTitleIsTxt.ForeColor = DARKGRAY
'SqlFrm.CountPB.FontColor = WHITE
'SqlFrm.CountDistinctPB.FontColor = WHITE
'SqlFrm.ColTitleIsPB.FontColor = WHITE
'SqlFrm.RemoveRedRowPB.FontColor = WHITE
For J = 1 To 5 Step 1
    If (SelList(J).nData > 0) Then
        nAtLeastOne = 1
        SlRcData(J).szTblColName = SelList(J).szTblColName
        SlRcData(J).szTblName = SelList(J).szTblName
        SlRcData(J).nData = J
        SlRcData(J).szColTitle = SelList(J).szColTitle
        Col$ = LTrim$(RTrim$(SlRcData(J).szColTitle))
        nLength = Len(Col$)
        If nLength > 0 Then
            Title$ = Col$ + " = "
        Else
            Title$ = ""
        End If
        SlRcData(J).nCount = SelList(J).nCount
        SlRcData(J).nCountDistinct = SelList(J).nCountDistinct
        SlRcData(J).nFlag = SelList(J).nFlag
        Select Case SlRcData(J).nFlag
            Case 0
                SqlFrm.SLRC(J).BackColor = WHITE
                SqlFrm.SLRC(J).ForeColor = BLUE
```

```
Case 1
    SqlFrm.SLRC(I).BackColor = BLUE
    SqlFrm.SLRC(J).ForeColor = WHITE
    SqlFrm.CountPB.Enabled = TRUE
    SqlFrm.CountDistinctPB.Enabled = TRUE
    SqlFrm.ColTitleIsPB.Enabled = TRUE
    SqlFrm.ColTitleIsTxt.Enabled = TRUE
    SqlFrm.ColTitleIsTxt.BackColor = BLUE
    SqlFrm.ColTitleIsTxt.ForeColor = WHITE
    SqlFrm.ColTitleIsTxt.Text = SIRcData(J).szColTitle
    SqlFrm.ColTitleIsTxt.SetFocus
    SqlFrm.ColTitleIsTxt.SelStart = 0
    'SqlFrm.CountPB.SymBackColor = BLUE
    'SqlFrm.CountDistinctPB.SymBackColor = BLUE
    'SqlFrm.ColTitleIsPB.SymBackColor = BLUE
Case 2
    SqlFrm.SLRC(I).BackColor = RED
    SqlFrm.SLRC(J).ForeColor = WHITE
    SqlFrm.RemoveRedRowPB.Enabled = TRUE
    'SqlFrm.RemoveRedRowPB.SymBackColor = RED
End Select
Col$ = LTrim$(RTrim$(SIRcData(J).szTblColName))
If Col$ <> "*" Then
    tmp$ = LTrim$(RTrim$(SIRcData(J).szTblName))
    tmp$ = tmp$ + "."
    tmp$ = tmp$ + Col$
Else
```

```
            tmp$ = Col$
          End If
          ' check for COUNT or COUNT DISTINCT...if ON...then add to DISPLAY...
          If SIRcData(J).nCount > 0 Then
            tmp$ = "Count(" + tmp$ + ")"
          Else
            If SIRcData(J).nCountDistinct > 0 Then
              tmp$ = "Count(Distinct(" + tmp$ + "))"
            End If
          End If
          tmp$ = Title$ + tmp$
          SqlFrm.SLRC(J).Caption = LTrim$(RTrim$(tmp$))
          SqlFrm.SLRC(J).Enabled = TRUE
        Else
          SIRcData(J).szTblColName = ""
          SIRcData(J).szTblName = ""
          SIRcData(J).nData = 0
          SIRcData(J).szColTitle = ""
          SIRcData(J).nCount = 0
          SIRcData(J).nCountDistinct = 0
          SIRcData(J).nFlag = 0
          SqlFrm.SLRC(J).Caption = ""
          SqlFrm.SLRC(J).BackColor = WHITE
          SqlFrm.SLRC(J).ForeColor = BLUE
          SqlFrm.SLRC(J).Enabled = FALSE
        End If
      Next J
```

```
nResetSIRcVSR = 0
If nAtLeastOne > 0 Then
    SqlFrm.SIRcVSR.Enabled = TRUE
    SqlFrm.SIRcVSR.Min = 1
    SqlFrm.SIRcVSR.Max = ngSqlAdHocSelListCount
    SqlFrm.SIRcVSR.Value = 1
Else
    ' ERROR-> should NOT occur…is same as:  SIRcVSR.Value = 0
    '         which at this point would cause an error…
End If
nResetSIRcVSR = 1

End Sub
```

Function MsgBox3010 () As Integer

```
Title$ = "SQL Select Parser"
Msg$ = "INFORMATION:  This SQL Statement does NOT have a WHERE clause…"
DgDef% = MB_OK + MB_ICONINFORMATION ' Describe dialog.
Response% = MsgBox(Msg$, DgDef%, Title$)     ' Get user response.
MsgBox3010 = TRUE  ' return TRUE
End Function
```

Function MsgBox3011 () As Integer

```
Title$ = "SQL Select Parser"
Msg$ = "ERROR: NO WHERE clause TERMINATOR…"
DgDef% = MB_OK + MB_ICONSTOP ' Describe dialog.
```

Response% = MsgBox(Msg$, DgDef%, Title$)   ' Get user response.
MsgBox3011 = TRUE ' return TRUE
End Function

Function MsgBox3014 () As Integer
Title$ = "SQL Select Parser"
Msg$ = "ERROR: NO TERMINATOR for WHERE clause VALUE subitem..."
DgDef% = MB_OK + MB_ICONSTOP ' Describe dialog.
Response% = MsgBox(Msg$, DgDef%, Title$)   ' Get user response.
MsgBox3014 = TRUE ' return TRUE
End Function

Function MsgBox3015 () As Integer
Title$ = "SQL Select Parser"
Msg$ = "ERROR: NO TERMINATOR for WHERE clause COLUMN NAME subitem..."
DgDef% = MB_OK + MB_ICONSTOP ' Describe dialog.
Response% = MsgBox(Msg$, DgDef%, Title$)   ' Get user response.
MsgBox3015 = TRUE ' return TRUE
End Function

Function MsgBox3016 () As Integer
Title$ = "SQL Select Parser"
Msg$ = "ERROR: RELATION OPERATOR NOT FOUND in WHERE clause ITEM..."
DgDef% = MB_OK + MB_ICONSTOP ' Describe dialog.
Response% = MsgBox(Msg$, DgDef%, Title$)   ' Get user response.

```
MsgBox3016 = TRUE  ' return TRUE
End Function

Function MsgBox3017 () As Integer
Title$ = "SQL Select Parser"
Msg$ = "ERROR: UNABLE to ADD ITEM to CndSelList()..."
DgDef% = MB_OK + MB_ICONSTOP ' Describe dialog.
Response% = MsgBox(Msg$, DgDef%, Title$)    ' Get user response.
MsgBox3017 = TRUE  ' return TRUE
End Function

Function MsgBox3018 () As Integer
Title$ = "SQL Select Parser"
Msg$ = "ERROR: NO MATCH in CndTblCols() for WHERE item..."
DgDef% = MB_OK + MB_ICONSTOP ' Describe dialog.
Response% = MsgBox(Msg$, DgDef%, Title$)    ' Get user response.
MsgBox3018 = TRUE  ' return TRUE
End Function

Function MsgBox3019 () As Integer
Title$ = "SQL Select Parser"
Msg$ = "ERROR: WHERE clause is EMPTY..."
DgDef% = MB_OK + MB_ICONSTOP ' Describe dialog.
Response% = MsgBox(Msg$, DgDef%, Title$)    ' Get user response.
MsgBox3019 = TRUE  ' return TRUE
```

End Function

Sub ResetCndTvRcSlRcObjects ()
```
nAtLeastOne = 0
SqlFrm.RemoveCndRedRowPB.Enabled = FALSE
'SqlFrm.RemoveCndRedRowPB.SymBackColor = LIGHTGRAY
'SqlFrm.RemoveCndRedRowPB.FontColor = WHITE
SqlFrm.FBXL.Visible = FALSE
'SqlFrm.RelTxtPB.SymBackColor = LIGHTGRAY
'SqlFrm.RelTxtPB.FontColor = WHITE
SqlFrm.RelTxtPB.Enabled = FALSE
SqlFrm.RelTxt.BackColor = LIGHTGRAY
SqlFrm.RelTxt.ForeColor = WHITE
SqlFrm.RelTxt.Text = ""
SqlFrm.RelTxt.Enabled = FALSE
SqlFrm.FBXR.Visible = FALSE
For J = 1 To 5 Step 1
  If (CndSelList(J).nData > 0) Then
    nAtLeastOne = 1
    CndSlRcData(J).szTblColName = CndSelList(J).szTblColName
    CndSlRcData(J).szTblName = CndSelList(J).szTblName
    CndSlRcData(J).szColTitle = CndSelList(J).szColTitle
    CndSlRcData(J).szCndValue = CndSelList(J).szCndValue
    CndSlRcData(J).nData = J
    CndSlRcData(J).nConnector = CndSelList(J).nConnector
    CndSlRcData(J).nRelation = CndSelList(J).nRelation
```

```
CndSIRcData(J).nLeftFunction = CndSelList(J).nLeftFunction
CndSIRcData(J).nRightFunction = CndSelList(J).nRightFunction
CndSIRcData(J).nCount = CndSelList(J).nCount
CndSIRcData(J).nCountDistinct = CndSelList(J).nCountDistinct
CndSIRcData(J).nFlag = CndSelList(J).nFlag

nCndIdx = J
BuildCndString
```

' NOTE-> because this is being done to RESET the display AFTER
'   loading from a FILE...ALL of the ITEMS will be set to
'   UNSELECTED (nFlag = 0)...therefore ONLY Case 0 will be
'   used at this time...however...it may be useful at a later
'   time to be able to restore SELECTED item STATE INFORMATION...
'   so it is easier to leave the currently UNUSED code here...
'   it is NOT much additional code..anyway...

' GENERAL NOTE:

'   There is probably a good bit of REDUNDANT code throughout the
'   SQL Query Tool. Most of it exists because it is expedient. In
'   Windows and Visual Basic it is quicker to REUSE objects when
'   developing. If an object (or procedure) is already coded that
'   performs a particular task AND several other tasks then it is
'   easy to use that object to perform the particular task even when
'   the other tasks it performs are unnecessary (but correct). For
'   example, when the NEW button is selected, the FORM LOAD procedure
'   is performed because ONE thing is does is clear the display. It

- also does more work that is really unnecessary, but does no harm.
- From my perspective, it does no significant harm to clear ALL of the FORM when it is really only necessary to clear a few display objects. If speed becomes an important factor, then it may be productive to step through the code and determine when tasks are being performed redundantly. However, this form is reasonably fast as it is, especially considering the amount of USEFUL work that it does. If it does become necessary to make this form faster, then the way to do it is to divide the larger procedures into small steps, each of which is a procedure.
- This is not very difficult to do, but it requires both time and a rather detailed analysis of the design. My guess is that an improvement in speed of approximately 20 percent can be achieved if this is done. However, the difference between 5 to 10 seconds and 3 to 8 seconds is not tremendously significant. I do not think that the amount of work involved in making this code super efficient is worth the effort, considering that this is not a HIGH VOLUME transaction.

```
Select Case CndSlRcData(J).nFlag
    Case 0
        SqlFrm.CndSLRC(J).BackColor = WHITE
        SqlFrm.CndSLRC(J).ForeColor = BLUE
    Case 1
        SqlFrm.CndSLRC(J).BackColor = BLUE
        SqlFrm.CndSLRC(J).ForeColor = WHITE
        SqlFrm.FBXR.Visible = TRUE
```

```
SqlFrm.RelCB.ListIndex = CndSlRcData(J).nRelation - 1
If (CndSlRcData(J).szCndValue < > "") Then
    SqlFrm.RelTxt.Text = CndSlRcData(J).szCndValue
Else
    SqlFrm.RelTxt.Text = " "
End If
If ((CndSlRcData(J).nRelation > 1) And (CndSlRcData(J).nRelation < 12)) Then
    SqlFrm.RelTxtPB.Enabled = TRUE
    'SqlFrm.RelTxtPB.SymBackColor = BLUE
    'SqlFrm.RelTxtPB.FontColor = WHITE
    SqlFrm.RelTxt.Enabled = TRUE
    SqlFrm.RelTxt.BackColor = BLUE
    SqlFrm.RelTxt.ForeColor = WHITE
    SqlFrm.RelTxt.SetFocus
    SqlFrm.RelTxt.SelStart = 0
End If
Case 2
    SqlFrm.CndSLRC(J).BackColor = RED
    SqlFrm.CndSLRC(J).ForeColor = WHITE
    SqlFrm.RemoveCndRedRowPB.Enabled = TRUE
    'SqlFrm.RemoveCndRedRowPB.SymBackColor = RED
    'SqlFrm.RemoveCndRedRowPB.FontColor = WHITE
Case 3
    SqlFrm.CndSLRC(J).BackColor = YELLOW
    SqlFrm.CndSLRC(J).ForeColor = BLUE
    SqlFrm.FBXL.Visible = TRUE
    If CndSlRcData(J).nConnector = 1 Then
```

```
                SqlFrm.LogCB.ListIndex = 0
            Else
                SqlFrm.LogCB.ListIndex = 1
            End If
        End Select
        SqlFrm.CndSLRC(J).Caption = LTrim$(RTrim$(szTempCndStr))
    Else
        CndSlRcData(J).szTblColName = ""
        CndSlRcData(J).szTblName = ""
        CndSlRcData(J).szColTitle = ""
        CndSlRcData(J).szCndValue = ""
        CndSlRcData(J).nData = 0
        CndSlRcData(J).nConnector = 0
        CndSlRcData(J).nRelation = 0
        CndSlRcData(J).nLeftFunction = 0
        CndSlRcData(J).nRightFunction = 0
        CndSlRcData(J).nCount = 0
        CndSlRcData(J).nCountDistinct = 0
        CndSlRcData(J).nFlag = 0
        SqlFrm.CndSLRC(J).Caption = ""
        SqlFrm.CndSLRC(J).BackColor = WHITE
        SqlFrm.CndSLRC(J).ForeColor = BLUE
    End If
Next J
'------------------------------------------
nResetCndSlRcVSR = 0
If (nAtLeastOne > 0) Then
```

```
        SqlFrm.CndSlRcVSR.Enabled = TRUE
        SqlFrm.CndSlRcVSR.Min = 1
        SqlFrm.CndSlRcVSR.Max = ngSqlAdHocCndSelListCount
        SqlFrm.CndSlRcVSR.Value = 1
    Else
        ' ERROR-> should NOT occur…is same as:  CndSlRcVSR.Value = 0
        '      which at this point would cause an error…
    End If
    nResetCndSlRcVSR = 1
'_____

End Sub

Function MsgBox3012 () As Integer
    Title$ = "SQL Select Parser"
    Msg$ = "ERROR: NO COLUMN NAME and NO ASTERISK in WHERE clause subitem…"
    DgDef% = MB_OK + MB_ICONSTOP  ' Describe dialog.
    Response% = MsgBox(Msg$, DgDef%, Title$)   ' Get user response.
    MsgBox3012 = TRUE  ' return TRUE
End Function

Sub FindCndString ()
    nCnt% = SqlFrm.CndTvRcVSR.Max
    nRowMatchIdx = -1
    For I = 1 To nCnt% Step 1
        szText = LTrim$(RTrim$(CndTblCols(I).szTblColName))
        nRetVal = InStr(1, szText, szTxt)
```

```
        If nRetVal > 0 Then
            nRowMatchIdx = I
            Exit For
        End If
    Next I
End Sub

Sub FindSelString ()
    nCnt% = SqlFrm.TvRcVSR.Max
    nRowMatchIdx = -1
    For I = 1 To nCnt% Step 1
        szText = LTrim$(RTrim$(TblCols(I).szTblColName))
        nRetVal = InStr(1, szText, szTxt)
        If nRetVal > 0 Then
            nRowMatchIdx = I
            Exit For
        End If
    Next I
End Sub

Function MsgBox2001 () As Integer
    If (nNoSelClrMsgs = 1) Then
        Exit Function
    End If

    Title$ = "Important Message"
```

```
Msg$ = "Selecting a NEW item or the SAME item "
Msg$ = Msg$ + "will cause the CONDITION LIST "
Msg$ = Msg$ + "to be RE-INITIALIZED.  If you continue "
Msg$ = Msg$ + "then ALL of the CONDITION LIST ITEMS "
Msg$ = Msg$ + "that you have already selected will "
Msg$ = Msg$ + "disappear.  Do you wish to continue?"
DgDef% = MB_YESNO + MB_ICONSTOP + MB_DEFBUTTON2 ' Describe dialog.

Response% = MsgBox(Msg$, DgDef%, Title$)         ' Get user response.
If Response% = IDYES Then
    MsgBox2001 = TRUE   ' return TRUE
Else
    MsgBox2001 = FALSE  ' return FALSE
End If

End Function

Function MsgBox2002 ()
If (nNoSelClrMsgs = 1) Then
    Exit Function
End If

Title$ = "Important Message"
Msg$ = "Selecting a NEW item or the SAME item "
Msg$ = Msg$ + "will cause the SELECTION LIST and "
Msg$ = Msg$ + "CONDITION LIST to be RE-INITIALIZED. "
```

```
Msg$ = Msg$ + "If you continue then ALL of the "
Msg$ = Msg$ + "SELECTION LIST ITEMS and CONDITION "
Msg$ = Msg$ + "LIST ITEMS that you have already "
Msg$ = Msg$ + "selected will disappear.  Do you wish "
Msg$ = Msg$ + "to continue?"
DgDef% = MB_YESNO + MB_ICONSTOP + MB_DEFBUTTON2  ' Describe dialog.

Response% = MsgBox(Msg$, DgDef%, Title$)    ' Get user response.
If Response% = IDYES Then
    MsgBox2002 = TRUE    ' return TRUE
Else
    MsgBox2002 = FALSE   ' return FALSE
End If

End Function

Function MsgBox2003 ()
Title$ = "Important Message"
Msg$ = "Selecting a NEW SQL QUERY "
Msg$ = Msg$ + "will cause the SELECTION LIST and "
Msg$ = Msg$ + "CONDITION LIST to be RE-INITIALIZED. "
Msg$ = Msg$ + "If you continue then ALL of the "
Msg$ = Msg$ + "SELECTION LIST ITEMS and CONDITION "
Msg$ = Msg$ + "LIST ITEMS that you have already "
Msg$ = Msg$ + "selected will disappear.  Do you wish "
Msg$ = Msg$ + "to continue?"
```

```
DgDef% = MB_YESNO + MB_ICONSTOP + MB_DEFBUTTON2  ' Describe dialog.

Response% = MsgBox(Msg$, DgDef%, Title$)   ' Get user response.
If Response% = IDYES Then
    MsgBox2003 = TRUE   ' return TRUE
Else
    MsgBox2003 = FALSE   ' return FALSE
End If

End Function
```

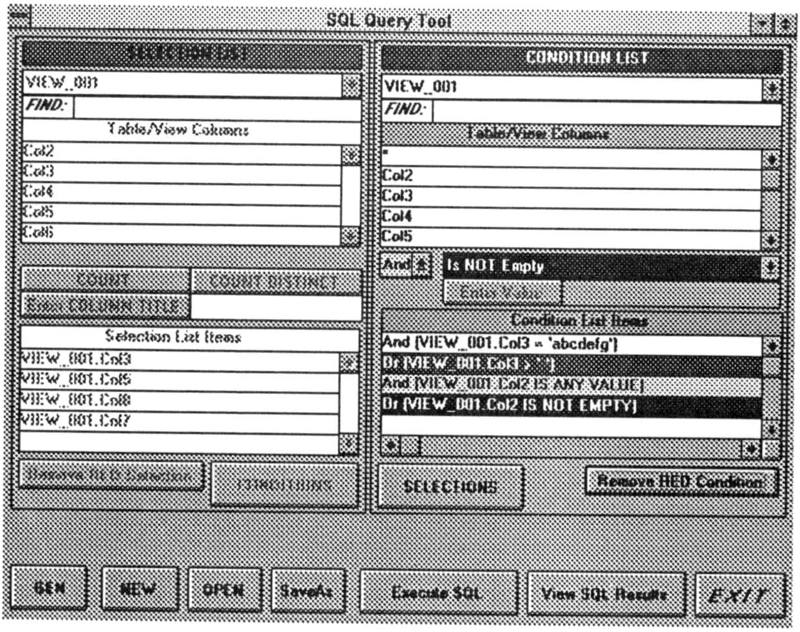
SQL Query Tool
CONDITION LIST
VIEW_001
FIND:
Table/View Columns
Col2
Col3
Col4
Col5
Col6
And
Is NOT Empty
Condition List Items
Selection List Items
VIEW_001.Col3
VIEW_001.Col5
VIEW_001.Col8
VIEW_001.Col7
And (VIEW_001.Col3 = 'abcdefg')
And (VIEW_001.Col2 IS ANY VALUE)
Or (VIEW_001.Col2 IS NOT EMPTY)
SELECTIONS
Remove RED Condition
GEN
NEW
OPEN
SaveAs
Execute SQL
View SQL Results
EXIT

Appendix A: VB Tables and Comments

By my count, Visual Basic has (a) 25 Events, (b) 75 Functions, (c) 30 Methods, (d) 20 Objects, (e) 90 Properties, and (f) 68 Statements. In other words, there are at least 308 things--a good acronym for them is *EFMOPS*--that you need to know about in Visual Basic. You can remember them as *EFMOPS*, but you should assign importance to them in *OEPMFS* order because the most important thing in Visual Basic is the *object*. Next in importance are the *events* that the object recognizes and the *properties* that the object possesses. The *methods* that apply to an object are used to modify its runtime behavior. Finally, the Visual Basic *functions* and *statements* form the basis of the programming language.

If you are not doing any Dynamic Data Exchange, Drag and Drop, or Mouse tasks, you can reasonably ignore nearly all of the Events except two: *Click* and *Change*. Of the 90 Properties available in Visual Basic you will normally use only 20 or so at *run* time. If you use any of the remaining Properties, it will most likely be at *design* time. You will probably use all of the Objects at one time or another. Less than 10 of the Methods are commonly used. The remaining Methods are more *special* purpose than general purpose. You will need to use most of the Functions and Statements but will typically use only half (or fewer) of them frequently.

You can do a lot of work in Visual Basic without having to use more than approximately one third of the 308 total number of Functions, Statements, Methods, Objects, Properties, and Events to do it. You will need to know and understand *all* of them at some point (but not at the beginning). One of the nice things about Visual Basic is that you can begin doing meaningful work almost immediately and then expand your capabilities as you learn more about the language.

Visual Basic is surprisingly complete without *any* of the add-on tool kits. When you include several add-on tool kits in your Visual Basic tool box, you quickly realize Visual Basic is a *very* sophisticated language. As I mentioned earlier, my first impression of Visual Basic was that it was a *toy*. After working with Visual Basic daily for the past ten months, I have realized that Visual Basic is not a toy (except in the sense it really is *fun* to use). Visual Basic is a remarkably powerful, very high level (VHL) Windows GUI programming language.

In the course of writing this book, I have discovered that Visual Basic has depth: it is a multilevel language. A very interesting set of fundamental rules is embedded in Visual Basic. When you reach the point at which the behavior of Visual Basic *smart objects* becomes something you know *unconsciously* (i.e., when you can design Visual Basic forms in your *dreams*), you will find the word *finesse* suddenly springing to the forefront of your *consciousness*. Visual Basic is a complete language. According to my definition, that means you can make Visual Basic do things *recursively* (if you are careful).

I am continually fascinated with languages that can be used to *control* themselves, because that is one of the basic requirements for building *automatic* processors. I am more interested in writing a program that will write a program than in writing a program that performs a specific task more or less automatically. This is because I know that if I have a program that *generates* programs, then I can do more *real* work than if *I* have to generate each program. I have nearly convinced myself that it is possible to design a Visual Basic program that can be used to interactively program other Visual Basic programs.

The general method for doing this is to have a symbolic programming calculator (SPC), similar to the scientific calculator (SC) used in the code sample. The primary difference between the two calculators is that the SPC has a few extra keyboards. One keyboard is used to dynamically define forms--like a recorder of sorts. For example, to design a new form, you press the New Form button on the SPC and a blank form appears. Then you select a Visual Basic smart object and move it to the desired location on the form via movement buttons on the SPC keyboard. When the Visual Basic smart object is in the proper location you define its characteristics and behaviors via other buttons on the SPC. This process is continued until the form is finished, at which time you save it as a *module* (i.e., as a .BAS file) that operates on a single *generic* form.

I think you will agree with me that I can use Visual Basic to *generate* an ASCII text file and that Visual Basic *modules* are ASCII text files (or can be). This is not a trivial process, but it is possible. It is very much like a complex SQL Select Statement Generator, but it is more like a reverse parser in the sense that you are going backwards instead of forwards. In this case, I am using a parser to generate a program. The only thing this program cannot do is *make* the executable file. (I have not found a way to do it as yet.)

Basically, this is the same general method that QuickCaseW uses to generate QuickC For Windows code. The primary difference in the two methods is that I think I can do it all with just an SPC. Furthermore, I think that it can be done entirely symbolically (visually). In other words, the programming is done with *symbols* instead of words. The difficult part is creating the symbols and the set of rules which each symbol *represents*. This is an interesting problem and certainly not a simple one. However, I *see* a solution for it and will leave *learning to see it* as a good mental exercise for you.

If you *think* about the general concept of *symbolic* programming, and if you follow its threads to their logical ends, you will see that there is something of fundamental importance to be observed. Windows is a Graphical User Interface (GUI) environment so it seems very logical (to me) that the most natural way to program in a GUI environment is to program with a GUI programming language. The only problem with this observation is that there are no Windows GUI programming languages. In fact, I do not know of *any* GUI programming languages, Windows or otherwise.

There are quite a few *partial* Windows GUI programming languages (Visual Basic is one of them), but there really are no *full* Windows GUI programming languages. However, the components of a *full* Windows GUI programming language are scattered throughout Windows and Windows applications. I am using Word For Windows Version 2.0 and it is getting very close to what I would call a Windows GUI programming language in the sense that it supports assigning macros to buttons on the toolbar.

I have learned to expect excellence in Word For Windows, and the new version has exceeded my expectations. I continue to believe that the Microsoft applications group should do all of the final interface work for Microsoft products. The only logical way to program in Windows is with a *symbolic* language, and Word For Windows 2.0 can do this to a certain degree. It will even write macros for you via record mode. You can assign macros to buttons when you have the macros. This is a good first step. I have a button on my Word For Windows 2.0 toolbar that builds index entries. I would like to have a macro to build an index for selected groups of words, but have not found one yet.

Please do not misinterpret my statement that there are no GUI programming languages for Windows. It may *appear* to be a foolish statement, but it is not foolish. When I use the term GUI programming language, I am really referring to a *symbolic programming language*. In other words, I am talking about a *language of symbols* that can be used to do programming in Windows. I am talking about a *hieroglyphic* programming language (i.e., a *hieroglyphic Türing machine).* In such a language, there are *no* words--there are only *symbols*. A *symbolic program*, therefore consists of a *set* (or sequence) of *symbols*. Constructing this type of program is done via a *symbolic programming calculator* (SPC). The SPC is a special kind of calculator with buttons that *represent* language *symbols*. Pressing a *symbol* button on the SPC adds the *symbol* to the current program *set*.

The key to developing such a Windows GUI symbolic programming language is designing the fundamental *symbol set*. Using the concept of *result programming* makes the design easier. Most of the major Windows applications are already doing some *result programming* and are using *toolbar symbols* to do it. I think it is just a matter of time before someone invents a complete Windows GUI symbolic programming language. This will not eliminate programming with word languages, but it can certainly relegate word programming to a lower level (much as assembler programming is today). With Visual Basic, several tool kits, and a few DLLs, designing and programming a *symbolic* language is entirely possible and feasible today.

Returning to the topic of the tables in this section, I considered making it a big section on Functions, Statements, Methods, Objects, Properties, and Events but decided the only things that were missing in the **Microsoft Visual Basic** *Language Reference* were a few tables and an index. The Visual Basic documentation is very good. I have nearly *always* been able to find whatever information I needed about the technical aspects of Visual Basic in it. The fact that Visual Basic is well-documented in two, half-inch thick, manuals is a good indication of the work that went into its production.

I always compare language documentation to **The C Programming Language** (Prentice Hall, 1988) by Brian W. Kernigan and Dennis M. Ritchie. If you can fully describe a language as sophisticated as C in less than 300 pages, you have accomplished something significant. The Visual Basic documentation is really two such books. (One is an *introduction* and the other is a *reference.*) You probably have the Visual Basic documentation, but if you do not have a copy of **The C Programming Language** then get one. You will *need* it.

You will also need a copy of the **Microsoft Windows SDK Programmer's Reference Library** (Microsoft Press, 1990). The three books that comprise this library will be useful when you begin to use Windows SDK functions. For Visual Basic programmers, the most important book in this set is the **Microsoft Windows Programmer's Reference** because it contains the technical documentation for all of the Windows SDK functions, subroutines, and messages. Once you have the Visual Basic declarations and definitions for the Windows SDK (available on CompuServe), you can greatly *extend* Visual Basic's capabilities (provided you understand the types of work that Windows SDK functions and subroutines perform.

Programming Windows (Microsoft Press, 1990) by Charles Petzold is another book you really *must* have. Nearly all Windows SDK/C programmers have learned how to program in Windows by studying this book. I have read this book more times than I can count and still continue to discover something new every time I read it. Experienced Windows SDK/C programmers call this book **"Petzold."** If there is any dispute over the correct usage for a particular function, someone will look it up in **"Petzold"** and the information found therein usually ends the dispute.

One of my goals in writing **<u>VB = mc^2: The Art of Visual Basic Programming</u>** was to provide some useful information about Windows application design and programming--using Visual Basic--that was *not* available in other books. When I was first started Windows SDK/C programming, one of the hardest things to learn was how to *design* a Windows application. Therefore, I have included a considerable amount of discussion on designing Windows applications in the book.

I did this because everything in Windows became much easier for me when I learned how to *think* like Windows. I realized, very early in the process, that Windows was a *transaction* environment but did not really understand everything until the *link* between *OOPS* and *transaction* processing became clear. *Objects* are really nothing more than small *transactions*. A Windows application is therefore nothing more than a big *set* of small *transactions*. Visual Basic is really a very high level (VHL), Windows *transaction driver*.

If this book does nothing more than permanently *etch* the fact that Visual Basic is a VHL Windows *transaction driver* into your *mind*, it has served a useful purpose. If you also learned that Visual Basic *smart objects* and *generic forms* are the *unit transactions* (i.e., the *basic components*) which you use to *build* your Windows applications, then all the better!

Visual Basic Events

Name	Page[1]
Change	37
Click	47
DblClick	68
DragDrop	83
DragOver	86
DropDown	93
GotFocus	139
KeyDown	159
KeyPress	161
KeyUp	159
LinkClose	173
LinkError	174
LinkExecute	175
LinkOpen	180
Load[2]	191
LostFocus	198
MouseDown	210
MouseMove	212
MouseUp	210
Paint	234
PathChange	237
PatternChange	239
Resize	259
Timer	316
Unload[3]	324

Notes:

(1) - The *Page* column contains the beginning page number of the documentation for the *event* in the **Microsoft Visual Basic *Language Reference***.

(2) - The *Load* event applies to *forms* and is used to *initialize* and *restore* form-specific data. Since you do not want to have hidden forms, you will nearly always be *loading* forms. Therefore, you should have *both* an *initializing* section and a *restoring* section in your form *Load* event procedures.

(3) - The *Unload* event applies to *forms* and is used (1) to perform any *form-level verification* and *validation* that is necessary *prior* to *exiting* the *form* and (2) to save the *current* data values pertaining to the *form*. The data values *saved* in the form *Unload* event procedure are used to *restore* the *form* to its *prior* state when it is (subsequently) *reloaded*. The *Load* and *Unload* events are *necessary,* and they exist as a *pair*. Coding the *Load* and *Unload* events should be a *mandatory* requirement in your design and programming. The fact that the *Load* and *Unload* events provide a mechanism for *virtually* eliminating *hidden* forms is *not* a coincidence.

Visual Basic Functions [and Statements[1]]

Name	Funct	Stmt[2]	Page[3]
Abs	+		19
Asc	+		25
Atn	+		26
CCur	+		35
CDbl	+		36
Chr$	+		42
CInt	+		43
CLng	+		49
Command$	+		54
Cos	+		58
CSng	+		59
CurDir$	+		61
Date$	+	+	63
DateSerial	+		65
DateValue	+		66
Day	+		67
Dir$	+		78
DoEvents	+		81
Environ$	+		97
EOF	+		98
Err	+	+	100
Erl	+		100
Error$	+	+	102
Exp	+		105
FileAttr	+		107
Fix	+		111
Format$	+		121
FreeFile	+		128
Hex$	+		143

(-more)

Visual Basic Functions [and Statements[1]]
(-continued-)

Name	Funct	Stmt[2]	Page[3]
Hour	+		145
Input$	+		154
InputBox$	+		155
InStr	+		156
Int	+		157
LBound	+		165
LCase$	+		166
Left$	+		168
Len	+	+	169
LoadPicture	+		193
Loc	+		194
LOF	+		196
Log	+		197
LTrim$	+		200
Mid$	+	+	204
Minute	+		207
Month	+		209
MsgBox	+	+	216
Now	+		223
Oct$	+		224
QBColor	+		251
RGB	+		262
Right$	+		263
Rnd	+		265
RTrim$	+		267
Second	+		277
Seek	+	+	278
Sgn	+		288
Shell	+		289

(-more)

Visual Basic Functions [and Statements[1]]
(-continued-)

Name	Funct	Stmt[2]	Page[3]
Sin	+		291
Space$	+		293
Spc	+		294
Sqr	+		295
Str$	+		299
String$	+		300
Tab	+		304
Tan	+		308
Time$	+	+	313
Timer	+		317
TimeSerial	+		318
TimeValue	+		319
UBound	+		321
UCase$	+		322
Val	+		325
Weekday	+		328
Year	+		333

Notes:

(1), (2) - The **Microsoft Visual Basic <u>Language Reference</u>** does not specifically list any Visual Basic *subroutines*. One can therefore speculate there are none. However, there is some basis for presuming that a *statement* (as the term is used in the Visual Basic documentation) is not very different from a subroutine when the *statement* can also be used as a *function*. This occurs a few times, so it is useful to note which functions can also be used as *statements* because this dual usage implies *importance*. However, Visual Basic *does*

455

use many *subroutines*, but they are *event procedures* and do *not* actually exist until you create forms and controls. Some programmers use the terms *function* and *subroutine* interchangeably, but there is a difference (usually) in the two terms: (1) *functions* return value(s), but (2) *subroutines* do *not* return value(s).

(3) - The *Page* column contains the beginning page number of the documentation for the *function* (and *statement*) in the **Microsoft Visual Basic <u>Language Reference</u>** .

Visual Basic Methods

Name	Page[1]
AddItem	21
Circle	44
Clear	46
Cls	51
Drag	82
EndDoc	96
GetData	133
GetFormat	134
GetText	135
Hide	144
Line	172
LinkExecute	176
LinkPoke	181
LinkRequest	182
LinkSend	183
Move	215
NewPage	222
Point	243
Print	246
PrintForm	248
Pset	249
Refresh	255
RemoveItem	257
Scale	269
SetData	285
SetFocus	286
SetText	287
Show	290
TextHeight	310
TextWidth	312

Notes:

(1) - The *Page* column contains the beginning page number of the documentation for the *method* in the **Microsoft Visual Basic *Language Reference***.

Visual Basic Objects

Name	Page[1]
Check Box	40
Clipboard	48
Combo Box	52
Command Button	53
Debug	69
Directory List Box	70
Drive List Box	91
File List Box	106
Form	119
Frame	127
Label	163
List Box	187
Menu	203
Option Button	232
Picture Box	240
Printer	247
Screen	274
Scroll Bars	275
Text Box	309
Timer	315

Notes:

(1) - The *Page* column contains the beginning page number of the documentation for the *object* in the **Microsoft Visual Basic *Language Reference***.

Visual Basic Properties

Name	Page[1]
ActiveControl	20
ActiveForm	20
Alignment	22
Archive	24
AutoRedraw	27
AutoSize	28
BackColor	29
BorderStyle	31
Cancel	33
Caption	34
Checked	41
ControlBox	57
CtlName	60
CurrentX	62
CurrentY	62
Default	75
DragIcon	84
DragMode	85
DrawMode	87
DrawStyle	89
DrawWidth	90
Drive	92
Enabled	94
FileName	108
FillColor	109
FillStyle	110
FontBold	112
FontCount	113
FontItalic	112

(-more)

Visual Basic Properties
(-continued-)

Name	Page[1]
FontName	114
Fonts	115
FontSize	116
FontStrikethru	112
FontTransparent	112
FontUnderline	112
ForeColor	29
FormName	126
hDC	141
Height	142
Hidden	24
hWnd	146
Icon	147
Image	151
Index	152
Interval	158
LargeChange	164
Left	167
LinkItem	177
LinkMode	178
LinkTimeout	184
LinkTopic	185
List	188
ListCount	189
ListIndex	190
Max	201
MaxButton	202
Min	201
MinButton	206

(-more)

Visual Basic Properties
(-continued-)

Name	Page[1]
MousePointer	214
MultiLine	220
Normal	24
Page	233
Parent	235
Path	236
Pattern	238
Picture	242
Pointer	244
ReadOnly	24
ScaleHeight	270
ScaleLeft	272
ScaleMode	273
ScaleTop	272
ScaleWidth	270
ScrollBars	276
SelLength	282
SelStart	282
SelText	282
SmallChange	164
Sorted	292
Style	301
System	24
TabIndex	305
TabStop	306
Tag	307
Text	311
Top	167
Value	326

(-more)

Visual Basic Properties
(-continued-)

Name	Page[1]
Visible	327
Width	142
WindowState	331

Notes:

[1] - The *Page* column contains the beginning page number of the documentation for the *property* in the **Microsoft Visual Basic *Language Reference***.

Visual Basic Statements[1]

Name	Page[2]
AppActivate	23
Beep	30
Call	32
ChDir	38
ChDrive	39
Close	50
Const	55
Date$	64
Declare	70
DefInt	73
DefLng	73
DefSng	73
DefDbl	73
DefCur	73
DefStr	73
Dim	76
Do...Loop	80
End	95
Erase	99
Err	101
Error	103
Exit	104
For...Next	117
Function	129
Get	132
Global	136
GoSub...Return	138
GoTo	140
If...Then...Else	148

(-more)

Visual Basic Statements[1]
(-continued-)

Name	Page[2]
Kill	162
Input #	153
Let	170
LineInput #	171
Load	192
Lock...Unlock	195
LSet	199
Mid$	205
MkDir	208
MsgBox	218
Name	221
On Error	225
On...GoSub	227
On...GoTo	227
Open	228
Option Base	231
Print #	245
Put	250
Randomize	252
ReDim	253
Rem	256
Reset	258
Resume	260
Return	261
RmDir	264
RSet	266
SavePicture	268
Seek	279
Select Case	280

(-more-)

Visual Basic Statements
(-continued-)

Name	Page[2]
SendKeys	283
Sub	302
Static	296
Stop	298
Time$	314
Type	320
Unload	323
While...Wend	329
Width #	330
Write #	332

Notes:

(1) - Some Visual Basic *statements* also have *function* counterparts. The Visual Basic Functions [and Statements] table at the beginning of this section shows these *dual* usage statements and functions.

(2) - The *Page* column contains the beginning page number of the documentation for the *statement* in the **Microsoft Visual Basic *Language Reference***.

Index:

A
address, 93, 141, 142, 145, 146, 150
affect, 51, 110
anchors, 186
ANSI, 141
array, 46, 71, 72, 152 -154, 158, 193 -195, 202
arrays, 158

B
bar, 97, 99, 100 -102, 106, 117
basic, 139, 140, 141, 144 -148, 150 -152, 154 -159
behavior, 5, 6, 17, 19, 40, 41, 43, 44, 59, 75, 76, 79, 93, 112, 117, 139, 174, 176, 186, 190 - 193
box, 40, 41, 45, 67 - 71, 84, 85, 90, 93 -95, 97, 98, 100, 130, 132, 133, 160, 165, 169, 172, 181, 185 - 189, 191 - 194, 199
boxes, 39, 64, 69, 70, 83, 95, 97, 98, 100, 103, 104, 112
button, 6, 7, 11, 14, 40 - 45, 66, 67, 72, 117, 132, 164, 165, 172, 189, 192 -194, 199

C
CDK, 156, 198, 200
character, 141 -144, 148, 150, 151, 153, 154
characteristic, 163
characteristics, 203
check, 39, 95, 173, 192
class, 193
classes, 79
clone, 103, 106 -108
combo, 6, 7, 39, 41, 95, 97, 98, 100, 103, 104, 126, 146, 193, 194
concept, 3, 7, 10, 16, 55, 64, 87, 98, 119, 120, 123, 137, 160, 163, 173, 180, 188, 191, 204
construct, 96, 151, 155

control, 4 - 8, 10, 13, 15, 16, 21, 27, 55 -58, 65 - 72, 77, 81, 93, 112, 120, 124, 125, 127, 128, 130, 132, 134, 156 - 158, 169, 172, 174-176, 189, 193 - 195, 200, 202 -204
controls, 3 - 8, 10, 12, 15, 25, 27, 34, 55, 59, 67 -74, 78, 83, 94, 91, 96, 98, 100 - 102, 104, 111 -113, 122, 124, 125, 127, 131, 134, 135, 156, 157, 159, 169, 189, 192 -194, 201
convert, 122
coupled, 45, 49 - 51, 96, 102, 110, 134
coupling, 50, 51, 75, 96, 104, 112, 134

D

deliver, 127
dependent, 51, 56, 96
design, 55, 56, 62, 72, 75, 78, 91, 92, 94, 95, 98 -106, 108, 109, 111, 117, 121 - 126, 128, 129, 131, 137 -140, 158 - 163, 169, 170, 176, 179, 181, 184, 189, 191, 192, 194, 198, 201 -203
diagram, 13
DLL, 92, 139, 141, 150 -152, 154 -156, 200
domain, 67 - 70, 169

E

edit, 6, 7, 25, 27, 39, 41, 47, 83, 146, 169, 192 -194
effect, 58, 70, 76, 86, 93, 102, 104, 120, 132, 135, 136, 145, 147, 167, 174, 177, 204
embedded, 57, 91, 92, 118, 144, 145, 147, 150
encapsulate, 97, 112
encapsulation, 64, 180
event, 1, 4 - 6, 15, 16, 41 - 47, 50, 57, 66, 71, 72, 79, 81, 87, 94, 97, 108 - 110, 112, 113, 127 -129, 147, 161, 164, 165, 168, 171, 172, 178, 187, 189, 194, 195, 201 -203
events, 55, 56, 65, 70, 79, 80 - 83, 95
expert, 118, 119, 122, 201, 205

F

fixed, 139, 140, 146 -151
flow, 36, 51
flowchart, 13, 55, 129, 136

focus, 82, 83, 101, 102, 123 -133, 135, 136, 169, 171, 172, 175
form, 8, 10 -12, 14, 15, 22, 28, 37, 38, 39, 41, 44, 47, 50, 51, 66, 68, 69, 70 -, 74, 78, 86, 87, 92 - 102, 110 -113, 119, 124, 132, 139, 158, 159, 162, 164, 172, 173, 178, 180, 181, 182, 184, 192 -194, 201 -203
frame, 64, 67 -70, 95, 97, 112, 181
function, 14 -16, 18 - 22, 25, 45, 51, 79, 82, 84, 86 -88, 90, 91, 141, 144 -146, 148 -150, 152 -155, 160, 162, 179 -181, 185 -187, 190, 191, 198, 204

G

generate, 106, 127, 157, 195, 196, 201
generic, 12 -14, 16, 45, 95 - 97, 110 - 112, 120, 122, 124, 137, 138, 152, 153, 179, 180, 181, 184, 192 - 195, 200, 201 - 203
global, 14, 15, 21, 50, 51, 86 -88, 110 -112, 123, 140, 149, 150, 152
graphical, 12, 17, 43, 130, 158, 197, 205

H

heap, 48, 52
hidden, 102, 111
hieroglyphics, 63
Hungarian Notation, 85, 87 - 89
hybrid, 7, 8, 96 - 98, 103, 112
hypertext, 186, 187

I

independent, 14, 16, 28, 29, 56, 58, 96, 110, 120, 125, 137, 167, 178
indeterminate, 151
inherit, 79
instance, 193, 194
invisible, 48, 52, 67, 68, 112, 125, 132, 133, 169, 174, 194

K

kit, 156
kits, 25, 26, 41, 92, 95, 156, 157

L

label, 40, 100, 189, 191, 192, 194
link, 7, 92, 196
linking, 118, 177
list, 6, 12, 13, 39, 40, 41, 45, 51, 57 - 60, 83 - 85, 90, 93 - 95, 97, 98, 126, 132, 133, 138, 160, 162, 169, 185 - 189, 191 - 194
literal, 21, 139, 140, 141, 148, 149, 203
load, 19, 45, 110, 185
local, 23, 47, 48, 52, 86 - 88, 110, 112
loose, 50, 96, 112, 134, 178
loosely, 45, 75, 96, 102, 104, 134

M

machine, 74, 76, 111, 125 - 131, 133, 135, 169, 199
map, 134
match, 42
mechanics, 6, 8
mechanism, 60, 69, 165, 171, 178, 185, 189, 192
memory, 48, 51, 52, 59, 123, 125, 182, 189, 190, 191
message, 17, 51, 71, 81, 82, 126, 127, 135, 171, 172, 174
messages, 5, 7, 13, 24, 73, 81 - 83, 94, 134, 135, 169, 170 - 172, 174, 175
metaphor, 63, 66, 72, 100, 101, 187, 188, 204
method, 56, 83, 84, 90, 138, 147, 158, 162, 167
methods, 55, 79, 84, 91
modal, 39, 125, 201
modeless, 39, 201
modify, 6, 21, 31, 41, 59, 65, 79, 85, 106, 119, 186
module, 15, 47, 86, 87, 94, 97, 109, 110, 112, 202

N

null, 18 - 21, 89, 91 -93, 141 -148, 150, 151, 153 -155

O

object, 19, 41, 42, 55, 56, 58, 67 - 69, 96, 97, 101, 110, 118, 125 -127, 136, 139, 160, 161, 163, 164, 168, 169, 171, 174, 175, 177, 178, 181, 204

objects, 55, 57, 59, 65, 67, 68, 79, 91, 95 -98, 101, 103, 104, 106, 109, 116, 117, 123, 124
OOPS, 181

P

painting, 73
paradox, 122
parameter, 20, 21, 141, 144, 146, 149, 150
pointer, 79, 86, 145, 157
pointers, 139, 157
procedure, 45 -47, 165, 168, 171, 194, 195
properties, 162
property, 42, 67, 71, 100, 131, 132, 158
prototype, 106, 137, 138

Q

queue, 134

R

recursion, 82, 197
recursive, 196
reference, 51, 55, 74, 93, 108, 139, 146, 150, 199
regional, 87, 88, 110 - 112, 140
represent, 61, 72, 203, 204
representation, 136, 168
result, 117, 119 - 122, 125

S

scope, 83, 86, 87, 89, 110, 119, 140
scroll, 6
select, 57, 72, 94, 185, 189
set, 29, 43, 46, 55, 57, 63, 65 - 68, 71, 72, 74, 81 - 83, 87, 90, 98, 100, 106, 118, 129, 132, 134, 136, 139, 141 -144, 155, 156, 159, 160, 162, 175, 185 - 187, 189, 190
smart, 35, 159, 157, 160, 161, 163 - 169, 174 - 181
SQL, 122
standard, 25, 28, 29, 30, 40, 41, 118, 192, 193
state, 40, 42, 48, 169, 170 -172, 174 - 178
statement, 13, 76, 78, 82, 93, 94, 137, 170

string, 86, 88, 89, 90 - 93, 139 - 154, 157
strings, 139 -148, 150, 151, 181
structure, 151 - 155
style, 35, 80
subroutine, 14, 15, 16, 20 -22, 84, 87, 88, 146, 150, 155, 180
symbol, 204
symbolic, 61, 117, 124, 195, 204, 205

T

task, 11, 78, 94, 159, 162, 167, 178, 180
technique, 14, 46, 48, 49, 68, 69, 71, 91, 107, 113, 133, 165, 186
terminator, 142, 143, 153, 154
tight, 50, 96, 104, 112, 134, 191
tightly, 49, 50, 96, 104, 110, 134
tool, 25, 26, 41, 61, 63, 64, 68, 92, 95, 99, 100, 102, 117, 156, 157, 179, 180, 198, 203
toolbox, 4, 8
toolkit, 3
transaction, 4, 5, 41, 43, 56, 91, 92, 138, 157 -159, 167, 168, 170, 177
transform, 119, 134, 177, 191, 192, 201, 204
transformation, 188, 189, 191, 192, 200
transparent, 136
Türing, 76, 177

U

universal, 121, 188

V

value, 2, 25, 67, 71, 72, 80, 94, 95, 100, 131, 132, 140, 143, 145, 146, 158, 162, 172
variable, 14 - 16, 21, 22, 85 - 89, 94, 110, 139, 140, 142, 143, 146 -149, 151, 195, 201
virtual, 97
visible, 49, 50, 52, 58, 67, 68, 80, 102, 111 -113, 125, 133, 162, 169, 172, 174, 201

W

window, 39, 40, 42, 193
WM_KillFocus, 81, 82
WM_SetFocus, 80 - 82

Instructions for Ordering the Companion Disk

The Visual Basic source code for the sample programs in this book is available on a 3.5 inch DS/HD companion disk. Order the companion disk from ETN Corporation.

ETN Corporation
RD4 Box 659
Montoursville, PA 17754-9433
Tel: (717) 435-2202
FAX: (717) 435-2802 (24 hour)

The companion disk is $9.95 (U.S.) plus shipping and handling. PA residents add PA Sales Tax for orders shipped to a PA address.